New Approaches to End-User Training

Saurabh Gupta

New Approaches to End-User Training

Longitudinal Investigation of Collaborative e-learning

VDM Verlag Dr. Müller

Imprint

Bibliographic information by the German National Library: The German National Library lists this publication at the German National Bibliography; detailed bibliographic information is available on the Internet at
http://dnb.d-nb.de.

Any brand names and product names mentioned in this book are subject to trademark, brand or patent protection and are trademarks or registered trademarks of their respective holders. The use of brand names, product names, common names, trade names, product descriptions etc. even without a particular marking in this works is in no way to be construed to mean that such names may be regarded as unrestricted in respect of trademark and brand protection legislation and could thus be used by anyone.

Cover image: www.purestockx.com

Published 2008 Saarbrücken

Publisher:
VDM Verlag Dr. Müller Aktiengesellschaft & Co. KG, Dudweiler Landstr. 125 a,
66123 Saarbrücken, Germany,
Phone +49 681 9100-698, Fax +49 681 9100-988,
Email: info@vdm-verlag.de
Zugl.: Athens, University of Georgia, 2006

Produced in Germany by:
Reha GmbH, Dudweilerstrasse 72, D-66111 Saarbrücken
Schaltungsdienst Lange o.H.G., Zehrensdorfer Str. 11, 12277 Berlin, Germany
Books on Demand GmbH, Gutenbergring 53, 22848 Norderstedt, Germany

Impressum

Bibliografische Information der Deutschen Nationalbibliothek: Die Deutsche Nationalbibliothek verzeichnet diese Publikation in der Deutschen Nationalbibliografie; detaillierte bibliografische Daten sind im Internet über http://dnb.d-nb.de abrufbar.

Alle in diesem Buch genannten Marken und Produktnamen unterliegen warenzeichen-, marken- oder patentrechtlichem Schutz bzw. sind Warenzeichen oder eingetragene Warenzeichen der jeweiligen Inhaber. Die Wiedergabe von Marken, Produktnamen, Gebrauchsnamen, Handelsnamen, Warenbezeichnungen u.s.w. in diesem Werk berechtigt auch ohne besondere Kennzeichnung nicht zu der Annahme, dass solche Namen im Sinne der Warenzeichen- und Markenschutzgesetzgebung als frei zu betrachten wären und daher von jedermann benutzt werden dürften.

Coverbild: www.purestockx.com

Erscheinungsjahr: 2008
Erscheinungsort: Saarbrücken

Verlag: VDM Verlag Dr. Müller Aktiengesellschaft & Co. KG, Dudweiler Landstr. 125 a,
D- 66123 Saarbrücken,
Telefon +49 681 9100-698, Telefax +49 681 9100-988,
Email: info@vdm-verlag.de
Zugl.: Athens, University of Georgia, 2006

Herstellung in Deutschland:
Schaltungsdienst Lange o.H.G., Zehrensdorfer Str. 11, D-12277 Berlin
Books on Demand GmbH, Gutenbergring 53, D-22848 Norderstedt
Reha GmbH, Dudweilerstrasse 72, D-66111 Saarbrücken

ISBN: 978-3-639-00582-0

DEDICATION

In Memory of my Grandfather

To my Parents, Sister and Wife

ACKNOWLEDGEMENTS

I would like to express my deepest gratitude to my chairperson, Dr. Robert P. Bostrom. Bob has been a friend, mentor, colleague, instructor, collaborator, emotional support, and intellectual spark ever since the day I met him as a graduate assistant in the MBA program. His personal support in all aspects of my life has been instrumental in my success. I shall forever be thankful to him for the role he played in putting this dissertation together, both as chair and as the gentleman who opened my eyes to the big picture.

I would also like to express my appreciation to the rest of the members of my committee, who took the time and effort to involve themselves in this project, and provided valuable guidance and insights. I thank Dr. Dale Goodhue, who provided the intellectual stimulation for constant improvement, Dr. Richard Watson, for supporting my research in spite of a very difficult schedule, and Dr. Larry Seligman for providing valuable guidance. A special thanks to Dr. Robert Vandenberg who not only taught me advanced quantitative techniques, but was especially patient with me during the analysis stage.

Justin Cochran and Stacy Campbell, my fellow doctoral students, deserve my thanks for reasons too numerous to list completely. Among the ways in which they helped was by being true friends, by sharing the trials and tribulations associated with completing a dissertation and by assisting me with many of the details of this project. To Justin, I am especially grateful for the outstanding job he did as a facilitator in the experimental sessions.

My gratitude also to Dr. Elena Karahanna, Dr. Mark Huber and Dr. Criag Piercy. Although not on my committee, they were instrumental in the success of this project. I thank Elena for her support in helping me cope with the challenges of the doctoral program. I thank Mark and Craig for accommodating my experiment in their classes. I also wanted to thank Mark for the time spent in the practical assessment of my experiment. The experiment also hinged on the successful participation of the teaching assistants, to all of whom I thank.

I also wish to thank Dr. Vikki Clawson for her supportive and encouraging behavior during this endeavor. Her infectious good nature has been very helpful in getting me through tough times. I also wish to thank Dr. Don Perry for the financial support he provided for the study.

Finally, I wish to thank my wife, Stuti and my parents. Stuti came late into the PhD process but adjusted quickly. She kept my life in order and helped me get up when things became burdensome. My parents provided me with the strength, support, and guidance needed to start towards achieving my goal of scholarship.

TABLE OF CONTENTS

APPENDICES

FIGURES

TABLES

CHAPTER ONE

1. Introduction

Universities and corporate training facilities have been investing in information technologies to improve education and training at an increasing rate during the past decade. Many new companies are emerging to provide tools and services to enable the effective design of IT-based learning solutions. We are seeing similar trends in certain parts of universities and other educational institutions (Financial Times 2005). Although research on technology-mediated learning has increased in recent years, it still lags behind developments in practice. Many predict that the biggest growth in the Internet, and the area that will prove to be one of the biggest agents of change, will be online learning, or e-learning (Bostrom 2003). The boom in the application of technology to education and training underscores a fundamental need to understand how these technologies influences the learning process.

With increasing number of organizations focusing on internal capabilities for success, training is no longer a cost center, but a strategic center. Training is one of the most pervasive methods for enhancing the productivity of individuals and communicating organizations goals to new personnel. Recent meta-analysis (Arthur et al. 2003) shows that the sample weighted effect size of organizational training was 0.60 to 0.63, a medium to large effect (Cohen 1988).

In 2004, U.S. organizations with 100 or more employees budgeted to spend $51.4 billion on formal training (Training magazine 2004). Within this, the use of e-learning technologies for the delivery of training continues to grow rapidly, with 30 percent of the training in 2004 expected through e-learning (Training magazine 2004), with 57.1 percent using asynchronous (self-paced) courseware and 32.4 percent using synchronous virtual classrooms to supplement traditional classroom-based training (Learning Circuits 2004).

Consequently, the revenue from business-focused e-learning software will grow 16.7 percent annually worldwide from 2003 through 2008. This market will more than double in size, to $619.4 million in new license revenue, by 2008 (Gartner 2004a). By year-end 2009, 60 percent of core business processes and software will include an e-learning component (Gartner 2004b). We see similar growth patterns in the U.S. for both K-12 and college Education (Allen et

1

al. 2003). For example, in 2001, over half of all U.S. colleges/universities offered online courses and over half of all U.S. K-12 teachers used the Internet in lessons. Thus, two important trends that can be isolated are 1) there will be growth of e-learning activity and 2) there will be an increased use of non-classroom sites for learning (Roberts 1996).

E-learning research, however, has only recently attracted the attention of Information System (IS) scholars, although the topic has been consistently of interest to Education researchers. In spite of interest, research in this area has been fragmented (Alavi et al. 2001; Bostrom 2003). One of the reasons for this fragmentation is the lack of agreement on definitions and terms, especially e-learning. In this paper, we focus on the definition given by Alavi et al. (2001) – "*Technology-mediated learning/training (or e-learning) is defined as an environment in which the learner's interactions with learning materials, peers, and/or instructor are mediated through advanced information technology.*" This definition puts technology at the center of what is being studied and forces the researcher to investigate issues around understanding the technology and its impact (Zmud 2002).

Although the initial focus of e-learning in Educational literature has been at the individual level in analyzing the impact of technology, a review of Education and IS literature points out that learning strategies are shifting towards a more active and group/team-oriented learning referred to as cooperative or collaborative learning (Alavi et al. 1995; Johnson et al. 1975). It refers to instructional methods that encourage students to work together to accomplish shared goals, beneficial to all. It involves social (interpersonal) processes where participants help each other to understand as well as encourage each other to work hard to promote learning (Johnson et al. 1999).

Collaborative learning (CL) is a versatile procedure and can be used for a variety of purposes, ranging from teaching specific content to ensuring active cognitive processing of information during a lecture or demonstration (Johnson et al. 1992; Johnson et al. 1994). CL procedures have also been found to be more effective than traditional instructional methods in promoting student learning and academic achievement (Johnson et al. 1991b; Johnson et al. 1981; Slavin et al. 1985). In a comparison of CL vis-à-vis traditional classroom learning, researchers found that the collaborative approach increases student involvement with the course (Collier 1980; Cooper et al. 1990) as well as with each other (Cooper et al. 1990), increases the

2

level of critical & active thinking (Bligh 1972; McKeackie 1980), promotes problem-solving skills (Kulik et al. 1979) and increases student satisfaction (Bligh 1972; Kulik et al. 1979). More recent analyses (Lou et al. 1996; Rohrbeck et al. 2003) also support these outcomes.

In spite of the growing importance of e-learning and CL, important research is lacking in collaborative e-learning (CEL). Most of the research in the Education literature has concentrated on face-to-face forms of collaboration or using minimal technology to support it. With advances in information technology, there have been rapid advances in distance learning and virtual team learning. Researchers postulate that collaborative e-learning is likely to become the predominant and effective way of learning and training (Jokela 2003). A greater amount of learning is now done using synchronous or asynchronous technology than ever before and there is an immediate need to understand this phenomenon in detail.

Gartner predicts that knowledge workers' appetite for new tools and capabilities will keep growing, and vendors will keep feeding them with diverse, new technologies to support individual, collaborative and organizational work (Gartner 2004b). End-user training deals with training end-users with these tools (software applications). End-user training expenses can be as high as 20-30% of the overall project budget for a software implementation (Olfman et al. 2000). Within e-learning, end-user training ranked highest in use at 38.4 percent in 2004 (Learning Circuits 2004). In spite of this, much of the research has focused on individual differences and a limited set of learning methods. Limited research exists in the area of end-user training through technology-mediation (Olfman et al. 2000). Thus, we focus on end-user training as our research context.

1.1. Research Questions

Both IS (Olfman et al. 2000) and Education (Johnson et al. 1991b; Lou et al. 2001) research show that much of the past research has suffered from the following shortcomings: restricted the focus on input-output research designs, lack of good grounding in theory and lack of control on the learning contexts. In addition, past research does not address the links between technology characteristics and collaboration variables that might influence the learning process. Finally, most of these studies are cross-sectional in nature, providing limited insight into the learning process. Our focus needs to encompass the learning process to investigate the following

3

research question: *How does information technology and collaboration enhance learning in a given context (students, instructor/mentor, instructional method, environmental factors) over time?* (Alavi et al. 2001; Hannafin et al. 2001; Lytras et al. 2003). Also, there is a need to investigate learning methods that further increase the effectiveness of training. These new methods need to build on our previous understanding in this area.

The theoretical framework presented in chapter 3 (shown here in Figure 1) is used to investigate the learning process involved in collaborative e-learning (CEL). Given the predominant use of IS training using e-learning, the study is placed in the context of end-user training. More specifically, the research questions answered will be:

1. *Are individual learning outcomes improved when vicarious modeling is supplemented by use of the following learning methods alone or in combination?*
   a. *Technology-mediated learning (with enactive learning)*
   b. *Collaboration*
2. *Are the individual learning outcomes improved because of changes in learning methods appropriation over time?*

1.2. Overview of the Conceptual Model

The AST based theoretical model presented in chapter 3 (explicated as a research model in Figure 1) explicitly configures the various elements of a learning/training process. At the heart of any training program is a learning method. Three different components of learning methods are conceptualized i.e. team, technology and technique structures. The model also outlines how different epistemological perspectives and learning goals affect the choice and design of these methods. These design choice alternative have been incorporated into three different learning methods as independent variables. This frame is then used to answer the first research question.

The empirical study draws on social cognitive theory and social development theory for the design of learning methods. Social cognitive theory identifies two kinds of observational learning methods: 1) observation of others actions, referred to as vicarious learning and

4

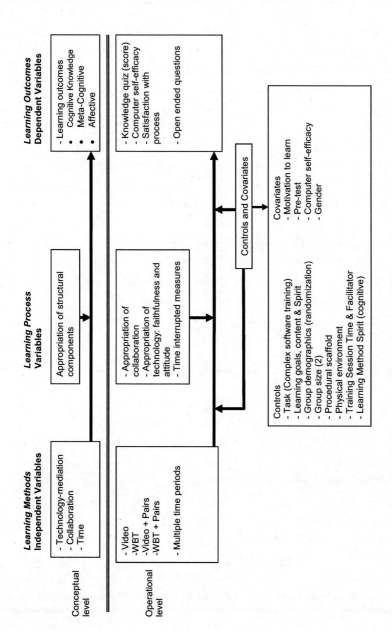

Figure 1: Research Model

5

2) observation of self-actions or enactive learning. Social development theory is used to explain the effectiveness of collaboration. This study investigates the effect of peer collaboration.

The study manipulates three elements of the learning method presented in Figure 1 using four learning methods. The experiment consisted of four experimental treatments. Vicarious modeling is used as a baseline treatment. The rest of the treatments are built on this. Treatment two supplements the baseline treatment with enactive learning in an e-learning environment, while treatment three builds on the baseline treatment by introducing team-based learning. The fourth treatment combines the two enhancements to investigate the combined effectiveness. Finally, time is manipulated by using a longitudinal design. The rest of the elements of the model are controlled using experimental design or using covariates. Learning outcome is measured using multiple constructs and is shown as a dependent variable in Figure 1. Quiz score, self-efficacy and satisfaction are used to measure the learning outcomes.

The learning process is conceptualized as an appropriation of learning method structures. Appropriation measures the faithfulness of use of the learning method by the participants. It is postulated that this mediates the effectives of training methods. The model also outlines the longitudinal process of appropriation, i.e. how appropriation changes over time. This is shown as intermediate variables in Figure 1) This frame is then used to answer research question 2.

1.3. Overview of the Research Methodology

The research methodology is based on a 2 X 2 longitudinal experimental study (research model shown in Figure 1). The study subjects were college level business students taking the Introduction to MIS class. The target system for the study was Microsoft Excel, with the content ranging from introduction to Excel to more complex topics such as graphs, formulas and functions. Only participants with no prior knowledge of the software were considered for the purpose of the study.

Training treatments were conducted across three time periods. An additional initial period was used to measure for covariates and experimental controls (shown in Figure 1), as well as introduce the participants of the experiments to their roles.

Learning outcome and appropriation data was collected at the end of each training phase. The specific hypotheses drawn from the model were tested by analyzing the data using repeated

6

measure MANOVA and structural equation modeling using Latent Growth Modeling and Stacked Group Analysis.

1.4. Importance of the research

Imparting learning has always been an important goal of academic institutes and industry alike. With the expanding role of education and the changing demands of the post–industrialization world, academic institutes are actively looking at improving the learning outcomes of their students. Within the corporate environment, the influence of training on usage of information technology has been widely examined within the IS literature. End-user training, thus, represents a very important area of investment and concern within the corporate environment. It is consequently, very important to understand efficient as well as effective ways of delivering this training/learning.

Two important trends to recognize are: 1) the influence of technology in all scenarios of learning and 2) a move towards a more social or collaborative form of learning/training. The training literature until now has ignored both these trends (Arthur et al. 2003). Both from a theoretical as well as practical point of view, it becomes very important to understand the impact of these two trends, the structures involved in each and the process by which they benefit learning.

From a theoretical point of view, this research integrates two separate streams of literature to present an integrated model for investigation. We use the Educational and IS literatures to understand the underlying constructs in technology-mediated learning and collaboration. The study expands the existing input-output learning model by looking at the process of learning. This study provides the first application of Adaptive Structuration Theory (AST) to the learning context. We believe that AST provides a rich context for studying the impact of learning systems. This study presents the first step towards building a specific model of collaborative e-learning in an end-user training context.

The research investigates the effectiveness of three new enhancements to end-user training: collaboration, e-learning and collaborative e-learning. Current research in end-user training has focused on behavioral/vicarious modeling as a mechanism for effective training. Building on this research, this work contributes to enhancing end-user training in three specific

7

ways. First, this research focuses on the effectiveness of a combination of both the training methods in social cognitive theory, i.e., vicarious and enactive learning. Second, as team-based learning continues to become more important in corporations and academia, this research addresses the effectiveness of collaboration in end-user training. Finally, this study uses an e-learning context, contributing to the understanding of contemporary learning technology.

The study also contributes to enhancing understanding of two statistical techniques, in addition to structural equation modeling (SEM), within the MIS and Education fields, called stacked group and latent growth analysis. Stacked group analysis compares multiple experimental groups with different exogenous variables. Latent growth analysis outlines a longitudinal model of the change in the latent variable over time. Together these techniques can be used to analyze longitudinal experimental studies.

From a practitioner point of view, the focus of training programs is on delivering training rapidly, massively, flexibly and affordably (Masie 2004). The results of this study will provide a richer view for designing training programs using collaboration and e-learning technologies. This is especially important with increasing use of e-learning technologies, as well as the wide variety of technology solutions available. The study also introduces the concept of collaboration or peer learning in end-user training and provides results about its benefits in an end-user training (EUT) context. It provides research evidence for investments in technology-based training programs. Training, in most organizations, is an ongoing activity, and thus, it is important to understand this process over time. Empirical results in this study would help practitioners in developing programs of training from a long-term perspective. Finally, any research effort aimed at providing guidelines for pedagogical purposes will have immediate payoffs especially for proper implementation of technology-mediated and collaborative learning in academic settings.

1.5. Work Overview

The following is the overall chapter outline of the work.

Chapter 2: This chapter presents an integrated view of the previous literature. It draws from Education as well as IS to present the current understanding as well as the gaps in current literature.

8

Chapter 3: To address the gaps highlighted in Chapter 2, this chapter presents a detailed statement of the conceptual research framework, the key variables included in the study, and the propositions that can be drawn from this model.

Chapter 4: This chapter presents the research methodology to test specific hypothesis drawn from the propositions. In addition, results of the pilot studies as well as the data analysis techniques are overviewed

Chapter 5: This chapter presents the hypothesis testing results of the study. An account of the statistical techniques used and the tests of hypothesis undertaken are included.

Chapter 6: This chapter presents significant conclusions to be drawn from the study treatments and findings. Other sections of the chapter include discussions and interpretation of the results and implications of the study to research and practice. Assumptions and limitations of the study are also discussed. The final section includes guidelines for future research in this area.

2. Significant prior research

Research in technology-mediated learning/training (TML), in organizations or business schools, has two strong reference disciplines: IS and Education. Thus, research findings in these areas are relevant to the study of technology-mediated learning. This chapter will provide an integrated view of the relevant research from the two disciplines.

We start by presenting a framework that will help in framing and integrating current literature. This framework is briefly described first. In section 2, we draw upon two social learning theories i.e. social cognitive theory and social development theory, to help understand existing literature in this area. Section 3 discusses the role of technology. In each of the above sections, we also highlight the gaps that exist in the current understanding of the field. After having summarized the literature review and the gaps, the last section presents a case for expanding the existing models of investigation to address the gaps highlighted.

Bostrom et al. (1990) was among the first to propose a framework for investigating end-user training (EUT) training methods. This framework postulated that the target system, training method, and individual differences affect the development of a user's mental model of the target system. Training outcomes, which measure the mental model development, included learning performance and attitudes toward using the target system on the job. Most recently, building on this framework, Sein et al. (1999a) introduced the learning/training strategy model focusing on the broader concept of overall learning strategy, as well as training strategy, of the company.

Neither of these models, however, addresses the contemporary learning/training methods such as e-learning or collaboration explicitly, i.e., the components involved in each method, nor do these model focus on the learning process. In a recent call for research in the area of e-learning, Alavi et al. (2001) presented a framework for e-learning, which is also applicable to EUT. The framework explicitly configures the relationships among technology capabilities, instructional strategy and psychological processes involved in the learning process.

Drawing on the above frameworks, we present an integrated framework for summarizing EUT research in Figure 2. In this model, training methods refers to the method by which

10

participants learn. Technology provides the capabilities for the execution of the instructional strategies. Learning techniques deals with the specific procedures used in training method. Finally, the impact of training is mediated through learning and interaction process to achieve learning outcomes. The learning process is influenced by both, individual differences and support provided. We use this framework to summarize the literature and identify research gaps and directions.

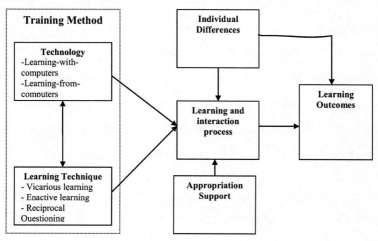

Figure 2: A Framework for Collaborative E-learning Research

In the following sections, we summarize literature in this area from two dominant instructional strategy perspectives in end-user training and collaborative learning: social cognitive theory and social development theory.

2.1. Instructional Strategy: Social Cognitive theory

The most prevalent theory, in both IS and Education fields, to understand participant learning in end-user training is social cognitive theory (Bandura 1977b; Bandura 1986; Bandura 2001). Having its roots in applied psychology, social cognitive theory views people as neither

11

driven by inner forces nor automatically shaped and controlled by external stimuli. In social cognitive theory:

> "Learning is largely an information processing activity in which information about the structure of behavior and about environment events is transformed into symbolic representations that serve as guides for action" (Bandura 1986 pg. 51).

Social cognitive theory subscribes to a model of emergent interactive agency. This theory states that it is not just the exposure to simulation, but agentic action in exploring, manipulating, and influencing the environment that counts (Bandura 2001). Thus, the theory views human functioning in terms of a model of triadic reciprocality in which behavior, cognitive and other personal factors and environmental events all operate as interactive determinants of each other (See Figure 3). The nature of a person is defined within this perspective in terms of a number of basic elements. This theory looks at how these elements influence learning.

According to this theory, learning interventions affect learning outcomes through observations or modeling. Two kinds of observational learning methods have been differentiated in theory: 1) observation of others actions, referred to as vicarious learning and 2) observation of self-actions or enactive learning (Schunk 2004).

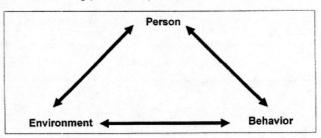

Figure 3: Triadic Reciprocality of Learning

2.1.1. Vicarious Learning

Vicarious learning or behavior-modeling (VM) training emphasizes the importance of observing and modeling the behaviors, attitudes, and emotional reactions of others. Bandura (1977) states: *"Learning would be exceedingly laborious, not to mention hazardous, if people had to rely solely on the effects of their own actions to inform them what to do. Fortunately, most human behavior is learned observationally through modeling: from observing others one forms an idea of how new behaviors are performed, and on later occasions this coded information serves as a guide for action."* (p22). In this method trainees watch someone else perform a targeted behavior and then attempt to reenact it (Yi et al. 2003). People can acquire cognitive skills and new patterns of behavior by observing the actual performances of others and the associated consequences. People form rules of behavior by observing others, and on future occasions are guided by their understanding of these rules.

Table 1: Vicarious Learning Literature in End-User Training

Study	Training intervention	Learning outcomes	Findings
Gist (1988)	VM vs. non-modeling training	Skill: Task performance	VM yielded higher task performance scores for both younger and older trainees
Compeau et al. (1995a)	VM vs. instruction based training	Skill: task performance Affective: Computer self-efficacy (CSE)	Subjects in the VM condition developed higher CSE and performed better than those in the instruction based condition for spreadsheet program, but not for a word processing program
Simon et al. (1996)	Instruction exploration and VM	Cognitive: Comprehension Skill: Task performance Affective: End-user satisfaction	VM outperformed the other two methods in all learning outcome measures

13

Johnson et al. (2000)	Modeling vs. non Modeling	Skill: Task performance Affective: CSE, computer anxiety	Subjects in modeling condition developed higher CSE and performed better than those in non-modeling condition. Computer anxiety was significantly related to CSE and task performance.
Bolt et al. (2001)	VM vs. non-modeling when controlling for complexity	Skill: Task performance Affective: CSE	VM outperformed non-modeling when complexity was high
Yi et al. (2001)	VM with practice vs. VM with retention enhancement vs. VM with retention enhancement and practice	Skill: Task performance Cognitive: Attitude	Subjects in the VM with retention enhancement and practice showed higher levels of learning outcomes when compared to the other groups
Yi et al. (2003)	VM vs. VM with retention enhancement	Skill: Task performance Affective: Self efficacy Cognitive: declarative knowledge	Subjects in the VM with retention enhancement showed higher levels of learning outcomes
Davis et al. (2004)	VM vs. VM with symbolic mental rehearsal (SMR)	Skill: Task performance Cognitive: declarative knowledge	VM with SMR was better than VM alone. Learning outcomes were mediated by the trainees' knowledge structures

Much of the end-user training literature has focused on vicarious modeling as a method of learning. Table 1 summarizes the literature in this area. Vicarious modeling treatment in previous research has been done by using an instructor to demonstrate actions, and is usually packaged in a video. Instructor-based treatment, on the other hand, uses the same content, but without demonstrations of content being taught. A consistent finding is that vicarious modeling yields better training outcomes than other methods such as instructor-based instruction or studying from a manual. Current research has also tested three enhancements to behavioral modeling: practice (Yi et al. 2001), retention enhancement (Yi et al. 2003) and symbolic mental

14

rehearsal (Davis et al. 2004). No significant impact of practice was found, but the latter two enhancements have been shown to further enhance learning outcomes.

Recent conceptual research in Education (Maynard et al. 1997) has started to explore the differences in task complexity on learning outcomes. In IS, post-hoc analysis by Compeau et al. (1995a) provides anecdotal empirical evidence that task complexity is an important construct that affects learning outcomes. This study compared training in Word and Excel and found that vicarious modeling was more effective in case for Excel. Similarly, arguing that learning Excel is a more complex task than Word, Bolt et al. (2001) inferred that behavioral modeling was more effective for complex tasks. This study uses a single context for investigation of various experimental conditions, thus, controlling for target system complexity.

Most of the vicarious modeling studies have followed their treatments with some form of practice through rehearsal. Participants are asked to rehearse what they have just seen without providing practice guidelines or feedback as a part of the learning method. In addition, all of the studies above have been cross-sectional in nature, using small time periods for training. Most learning/training sessions currently in use are longer than this. In fact, contemporary research talks about continuous learning over much longer period (Compeau et al. 1995c). Thus, these studies have limited generalizability in terms of time. Finally, none of these studies have investigated the effectiveness of behavioral modeling in a technology-mediated environment. Technology-mediated environments provide new challenges as well as opportunities for investigation. This study aims to investigate the comparative longitudinal effectiveness of behavioral modeling using a computer-mediated instruction environment.

2.1.2. Enactive Learning

Within the theoretical framework of social cognitive theory, enactive learning is a special case of observational learning. In learning by direct experience, people construct conceptions of behavior by observing the effects of their action.

Most of IS and Education research has focused on the use of rehearsal of modeled behavior, i.e., practicing what the instructor has demonstrated. Participants are asked to rehearse what they have just seen, helping to reinforce the behavior (Yi et al. 2001). Such use of practice derives its roots from operant conditioning theory (Skinner 1953), which says that people learn

15

by doing. Such an approach is primarily tuned towards increasing the efficiency of a particular behavior, rather than increasing the knowledge.

Social cognitive theory, on the other hand, focuses on enactive learning as a mechanism for learning. Learning new software by end-users requires cognition and integration of multiple domains of knowledge attainment (Sein et al. 1999a), rather than focusing on efficiency of operations. Enactive learning involves learning from the consequences of one's actions. Thus, enactive learning includes testing learned mental models in an environment that provides feedback based on action. Research in psychology shows that when informative feedback is eliminated, delayed, or distorted, skills learned deteriorate (Bilodeau 1966; Carroll et al. 1985). Social cognitive theory contends that behavioral consequences, rather than strengthening behavior as postulated in operant theory, serve as sources of information and motivation (Rosenthal et al. 1978). It emphasizes the role of self-modeling in a structured environment, with controls and feedbacks. People's cognitions, rather than consequences, affect learning (Schunk 2004).

Enactive learning is a ubiquitous tutor, however toilsome and costly the lessons learned from experience might be at times. Learning from the outcomes of one's actions has been traditionally portrayed as a mechanistic process in which responses are shaped automatically and unconsciously by their immediate effects. Social cognitive theory views learning through response consequences as essentially a cognitive process relying on the abstractive, reflective, and generative nature of human thought (Bandura 1986). Response outcomes have several functions. First, they impart information on how behavior must be structured to achieve given purposes and point to environmental predictors for likely happenings. Second, contingent outcomes serve as motivators by providing incentives for action. Feedback experiences aid translation of cognition to action (Bandura 1986). Social modeling, when supplemented by enactive learning, is also considered a more effective learning mechanism in most situations (Compeau et al. 1995a).

Learning through enactive learning has received considerable attention over the years outside the end-user training literature (for review see Dekkers et al. (1981)). In this meta-analysis, the author found no significant impact of enactive learning on cognitive ability, though a closer analysis showed that the impact was dependent on the enactive learning characteristics.

16

More recently, however, Skarlicki et al. (1997) found that a training approach that included enactive learning was successful in training organizational citizenship behavior in labor union setting. Similarly, Smith-Jentsch et al. (1996) found that an emphasis on self-modeling and performance feedback was superior to a lecture only or lecture with demonstration format for training assertiveness skills.

Only two studies in EUT literature have studied feedback (Martocchio et al. 1992; Sein et al. 1999b), though not in an enactive learning design. Both have found a positive effect of feedback on learning outcomes. Social cognitive theory postulates that the best training method for a complex task is a combination of vicarious learning and enactive learning (Bandura 1986). In spite of its importance, no research was found that investigated the role of enactive learning alone or in combination with behavioral modeling in an end-user training context. In this study, we use enactive learning as an extension to vicarious learning in an e-learning environment.

2.1.3. Other Antecedents in Social Cognitive Theory

In the social cognitive view, two important antecedents influence learning: forethought capability and symbolizing capability.

Most of an individual's behavior, being purposive, is regulated by forethought. Through the exercise of forethought, people motivate themselves, set goals and plan actions. Perceived self-efficacy and motivation to learn are the two important beliefs that define forethought in a learning context. Perceived self-efficacy is defined as ones' belief about their ability to perform a specific behavior (Bandura 1986). It is concerned not with skills one has but with the judgments of what one can do with whatever skills one possesses. IS literature has distinguished between computer self-efficacy, which deals with a general attitude towards using computers, and specific self-efficacy, which deals with an efficacy towards a performing a specific action using specific application. In both cases, research has found a significant relationship with learning outcome (Compeau et al. 2005; Compeau et al. 1995a; Johnson et al. 2000; Marakas et al. 1998). Social cognitive theory, in its reciprocal nature, argues for self-efficacy as a dependent variable in the training programs as well. In this study, we use the post-training self-efficacy as a dependent variable while pre-training self-efficacy is used as a covariate/control.

Motivation to learn is defined as the direction, intensity and persistence of learning-directed behavior in training contexts (Kanfer 1991). In a meta-analysis of Education literature, Colquitt et al. (2000) found modest correlation between motivation to learn and learning outcomes. This review also suggested that motivation is a multifaceted concept and is composed of intrinsic and extrinsic characteristics. Extrinsic motivation or outcome expectation is a judgment of likely consequences that a behavior will produce desired consequences (Bandura 1986). Intrinsic motivation deals with the participants' affect associated with learning (Schunk 2004). Within the context of social cognitive theory, Yi et al. (2003) examined the intrinsic training motivation and found a positive correlation with outcomes. Their study, though, did not investigate the impact of extrinsic motivators. In this research, both intrinsic and extrinsic motivations are used as statistical controls.

In sum, the causal exogenous effect of self-efficacy and training motivation on learning outcomes are well established in traditional training literature. In a technology driven era, these represent significant challenges and need further investigation (Salas et al. 2001).

An important antecedent to learning effectiveness is the capacity of individuals to use symbols. Through symbols people process and transform transient experiences into internal models that serve as guides for future action. By drawing on their knowledge and symbolizing powers, people can generate innovate courses of action. An advanced cognitive capability coupled with the remarkable flexibility of symbolization enables people to create ideas that transcend their sensory experiences (Bandura 1986). Only one study in end-user training area (Yi et al. 2003) has examined the impact of symbolizing capability. This study found a positive correlation between note-taking and retention, but did not find a direct correlation between observational learning dimensions (attention, retention, production, and motivation) and learning outcomes. In the current study, all participants are given an equal opportunity for note taking. These notes are captured and recorded during the experiment. Analysis of these would reveal more insights into this process, but was not carried out for the purposes of the dissertation.

2.2. *Collaborative Learning*

Complementary to Bandura (1986) work on observational learning is Vygotskiæi et al. (1978) work using social development theory. The major theme of Vygotskiæi's theoretical framework is that social interaction, beyond observational learning, plays a fundamental role in the development of cognition. Vygotskiæi et al. (1978) states: *"Every function in the child's cultural development appears twice: first, on the social level, and later, on the individual level; first, between people (interpsychological) and then inside the child (intrapsychological). This applies equally to voluntary attention, to logical memory, and to the formation of concepts. All the higher functions originate as actual relationships between individuals."* (p57). Vygotskiæi's theory was an attempt to explain consciousness as the end products of socialization. For example, in the learning of language, our first utterances with peers or adults is for the purpose of communication but once mastered they become internalized and allow *"inner speech."*

Vygotskiæi's work provides a general theory of cognitive development. Most of the original work was done in the context of language learning in children (Vygotskiæi et al. 1962), although later applications of the framework have been broader (Wertsch 1985). Forman et al. (1985) extended the framework to collaborative learning. This work is based on the premise that knowledge is socially constructed from cooperative efforts to learn, understand and solve problems. Developmental and Educational psychologists have identified two major categories of peer influence: (a) peers serve as natural teachers and models to simulate cognitive development and (b) peers contribute to task orientation, persistence and motivation to achieve (Rohrbeck et al. 2003).

Benefits of collaborative learning (CL) have been demonstrated in cognitive domains such as mathematics (Webb 1982), science (Okada et al. 1997), problem solving (Chi et al. 1994) and engineering (Dossett et al. 1983). In some studies, peer-to-peer is also conceptualized as the ultimate form of e-learning (Jokela 2003). A meta-analysis of 375 studies of CL in the Education literature, Johnson et al. (1991b) provides evidence to the relative effectiveness of CL in terms of learning achievement, student satisfaction with learning process and outcomes, and quality of interpersonal relationships and emotional climate in the learning environment. Although other meta-analysis have also shown a positive influence of grouping, the average effect size has varied: Lou et al. (1996) and Slavin (1987) reported an average effect size of +0.32, Kulik et al. (1987a) reported +0.17, Kulik et al. (1991) reported +0.25 and Rohrbeck et al. (2003) reported +0.33. Four main reasons have been suggested for the high variability in the results of using collaboration: 1) variance in group size, 2) variance in support, 3) variance in

19

the psychological learning process involved and 4) variance in the length of time the group is together. We examine each one of them further below.

First, meta-analysis in Education show that effects of social context on individual achievement were significantly more positive when students worked in pairs than when they worked in groups of three to five. All group size conditions were significantly positive compared to students learning alone (Lou et al. 2001). In addition, group size is significantly related to learning outcomes, i.e. showing higher learning outcomes for smaller group sizes (Lou et al. 2001; Lou et al. 1996) with dyads showing the greatest benefit. In this study, we use dyads to maximize the impact of collaboration.

Secondly, studies in Education also suggest that the peer interaction process itself must be guided and monitored with various scaffolding strategies (Ge et al. 2003). Johnson et al. (2003) summarizes the various scaffolding strategies that can be used to enhance group collaboration. In IS, initial studies comparing dyads in programming to solo programmers (Cockburn et al. 2001; Williams et al. 2003) supports that pair programming produces a higher quality code in about half the time. Rules governing pair programming provide a mechanism for structured scaffolding and organized interaction between peers. These rules are also finding their way into training/learning in the form of pair learning (Williams et al. 2002). However, Ryan et al. (2000) used similar rules to govern learning of a complex data modeling skill in a group environment and found no significant differences. Only one study (Davis et al. 2004) used paired learning in end-user training, also found no significant effects. Their study though, did not provide for scaffolding structures for interaction or control for the level of interaction. This study extends Davis et al.'s study via using a guided collaboration method as well as measuring the level of interaction.

A third reason for the high variation in collaboration studies is the lack of understanding of the learning process involved (See Figure 2). It has been suggested that collaborative groups perform better than competing groups (Johnson et al. 1975; Lou et al. 1996). In a recent review of collaboration techniques Johnson et al. (2003) found that, the effectiveness of the learning outcome were strongly dependent on the technique used. Thus, the benefit of a collaborative learning is strongly dependent on the intrinsic characteristics of the team. As conceptualized later, these characteristics are a result of the participants in the team interacting with the elements

20

of the collaborative technique as well as themselves. For example, education studies point (e.g. Dyer 1993) that positive interdependence is a key characteristic in teams that influence learning outcomes. In IS, Ryan et al. (2000) implemented positive interdependence as well as rules of conduct as a part of the technique, but did not look at its impact on the learning process. Only one study (Davis et al. 2004) that we know of has investigated a combination of behavioral modeling and peer collaboration, finding no significant effects. This study did not investigate underlying team characteristics. Thus, the results of the study can be explained by the possible lack of certain group characteristics. The current study not only uses pairs, but also investigates the team characteristics involved in collaboration. Results from the study would help explain the social learning process involved during the learning process.

A fourth possible reason suggested for the variance in the research is the cross-sectional nature of most studies. Studies have suggested that collaborative learning is more likely to produce positive effects in longer studies than shorter ones (Davis et al. 2004; Slavin 1983). One possible explanation is that increased time spent learning together influences the team characteristics to be in line with the collaborative technique. This study investigates learning over three periods in order to explain the effect of time on individual learning within a collaborative learning environment.

In summary, previous research both in Education and IS, have provided inconsistent results on the effects of collaborative learning. These inconsistent results primarily stem from insufficient attention to the structures underlying the learning method, lack of understanding of structures, lack of understanding the learning process involved in collaboration and the cross-sectional nature of the investigations. This study, thus, extends previous work by investigating the effectiveness of structured paired training while also measuring for the level of appropriation of collaborative structures over time.

2.3. *Role of Technology in Learning*

Computer technology has been widely used in Educational literature. Large meta-analysis on the effectiveness of computers in groups in Education have shown that, in the majority of experiments, the use of technology has improved the learning outcomes (for review see Lou et al. (2001)) However, these meta-analysis do not distinguish between the pedagogical uses of technology.

Instructional use of computer technology is now distinguished as learning-from-computers and learning-with-computers (Jonassen et al. 2001; Salomon et al. 1991). Learning-from-computers occurs when the computer is the medium of instruction (e.g. computer-based training) whereas learning-with-computers occurs when computer technology is used as a tool to support teaching and learning (e.g. use of website by instructor, collaborative technology). Meta-analysis in Education have shown that learning-with-computers leads to higher achievement (Kulik 1994; Kulik et al. 1987b). For a recent review of computer supported collaborative learning literature in higher Education see Strijbos et al. (2004). Thus, supplementing existing pedagogical methods with computer support does have a positive effect on learning outcome.

On the other hand, research comparing effectiveness of learning-from-computers to standard methods of instruction has provided inconclusive results in both Education and IS literature (Kovalchick et al. 2004). A summary of the research and gaps is presented below. More research is needed focusing on the use of computer technology as a source of learning. In this study, we focus on learning-from-computers.

2.3.1. Learning-From-Computers: Computer-Based Training

Learning-from-computers occurs through computer-based training (CBT). Limited research in end-user training using CBT provides inconclusive understanding of the impact of learning-from-computers. Table 2 provides a summary of the technology-mediated end-user training literature. A major problem with these studies is that CBT tools used are not grounded in theory or research. Gist et al. (1989) used computer technology to provide examples and programmed instructions without showing demonstration. Drawing from inference, other studies have used CBT tools for vicarious modeling method. Investigating such use, Bowman et al. (1995) found no significant difference when comparing classroom to computer-based training. Bohlen et al. (1997) found that computer-based training is either more effective or had no positive effect depending on individual differences. Inconclusive results were also found in a more recent study done by Desai (2000). His study found a significant impact for Microsoft Excel training but not significant for Microsoft Word training. Overall, these results are not

22

surprising because of four possible reasons: 1) lack of use of CBT's grounded in theory, 2) insufficient attention to the influence of the target system, 3) insufficient attention to the learning process involved and 4) lack of distinction between the effect of collaboration and technology used.

First, most of these studies used computer technology to deliver information. In a typical use of computer technology, the student sits in front of the computer, which presents information on the screen. The student reacts to the information presented by working with the mouse and/or keyboard. The student has control over the pace and sequence of instruction (Kovalchick et al. 2004). When used as a basic mechanism to deliver information, a lecture method might be a superior mechanism in transmitting information.

Table 2: Technology-Mediated End-User Training

Study	Training intervention	Learning outcomes	Findings
Gist et al. (1989)	VM vs. computer aided instruction	Skill: Task performance Affective: CSE	BM yielded higher CSE and task performance scores
Bowman et al. (1995)	CBT vs. lecture based instruction	Skill: Task performance Affective: Satisfaction	No significant difference
Bohlen et al. (1997)	CBT vs. lecture based instruction	Skill: Task performance, efficiency Affective: Satisfaction	Difference mediated by individual difference
Desai (2000)	Vicarious modeling CBT vs. lecture based instruction	Skill: Task performance	Positive effect for Excel. No effect for Word.
Zhang et al. (2004)	Virtual mentoring though a multi-based system	Skill: Test grade	e-learning can be at least as effective as conventional classroom learning under certain situations

CBT's currently in use by most organizations have grown beyond the means of basic information delivery media. Drawing from social cognitive theory, concepts of vicarious modeling and enactive learning can be programmed into computers. Thus, they not only present information, but also enable the trainee to enact the information provided in a controlled micro-simulated environment. A process model of the system is constructed incorporating the major factors and their interrelationships how the system works. This is then used to present demonstrations of reality enabling vicarious learning. This simulated environment also allows individuals to interact with the model, providing sensory and verbal feedback about actions, enabling self-reflective behavioral modeling i.e. enactive learning. Current studies have not only ignored the role of enactive learning, especially in an e-learning environment, but also have not operationalized both learning components of observational learning together. This study investigates the effectiveness of CBT that has both vicarious and enactive learning components built into it.

Empirical validation of CBT environments often presents problems that are not easily solvable (Lehman 1977). Unless there is a good fit between CBT environment and real environment, the theory cannot be validated (Bandura 1986). If computers are to serve as reliable tools for understanding complex systems, simulated outcomes should match real-world occurrences under comparable conditions (Taylor 1978). This is very difficult for social systems, but relatively simpler for end-user applications. The technology components of the social system in end-user training are based on objective programming theory, which specifies the variables and the processes relevant to the application. This unique capability of end-user applications to be programmed into a micro-simulated environment, faithfully represents how real world events would operate based on user interactions. This study made sure that the WBCT chosen faithfully implements the target software environment.

The second reason deals with target system characteristics. Studies in Education have used a variety of tasks in different situations to analyze the impact of collaboration. Task activity structures have been acknowledged to have an impact on learning outcomes, but no broad guideline exists to classify tasks (Vedder et al. 2003). Social cognitive theory postulates a positive relationship between the level of cognitive complexity of the task and the impact of observational learning. Within EUT literature, Desai et al. (1999) also provides prima-facie evidence in this regard. Post-hoc analysis revealed that students found Excel to be more complex than Word. In this study, we control for this by using Excel as the target system.

24

Social cognitive theory further states that the incremental impact of enactive learning will be higher for complex tasks. As technology becomes more complex, higher level of cognitive knowledge need to be achieved to develop accurate mental models (Coulson 2002). Contemporary CBT have the potential to develop students knowledge to higher levels (Gredler 2001), by providing an environment for observational learning though a combination of enactive and vicarious learning. No research to date has investigated the impact of CBT's on these knowledge levels in complex task context. This study addresses this research gap.

Next, most learning tasks studied in IS and Education are short (1-2 hour sessions). The studies are thus, cross-sectional in nature, either using a single snapshot or using repeated measures. These studies have also just focused on the basics of the target system. This provides an incomplete picture of end-user training as the influence of training methods on learning outcomes might be different for complex components of the target system. In addition, learning or training activities in an organization are continuous operations, and thus, there is a dire need to study the process of learning longitudinally. This study uses time as an independent variable helping the field understand the longitudinal evolution of the learning process. The study also includes more complex components of the target system as a part of the training context.

The third reason for inconclusive pattern of results is the lack of measurement of learning process involved. For example, attitude towards CBT was listed as a major cause for concern in Desai (2000), but was not measured. The effect of technology and instructional strategy are mediated through the learning process, and thus, it becomes imperative to study the process. No research to date has investigated the impact of the psychological learning process of contemporary CBT's on learning outcomes. This study investigates the learning process by looking at the technical structures as well as the spirit of learning method (Poole et al. 1990). Spirit is the general intent with regard to values and goals underlying a given set of structural features.

Fourth, studies in Education as well as IS do not differentiate between the benefits derived due to collaboration and the benefit of using technology (Gupta et al. 2004; Lehtinen et al. 2003), restricting internal validity about the advantages of using technology. This study uses a fully factored experiment with an ability to differentiate the effect of technology and collaboration. Such an experiment will help clarify the impact of technology as well as collaboration in an end-user training context.

Finally, studies in IS also suffer from poor research design, not controlling for external influences on learning outcomes (e.g. Desai et al. (1999)). This study focuses on a CBT grounded in theory, more specifically social cognitive theory, while analyzing the learning process and outcomes over time in a well-controlled experimental environment.

2.4. Other End-User Training Literature

Most other research on EUT focuses on the relationships between training methods and individual differences and how these variables influence training outcomes. This research (summarized in Olfman et al. (2000)) has shown that individual differences or diversity among users, such as learning style, may affect a user's learning about end-user application packages. Individual difference variables measure learner characteristics, including learner aptitudes, cognitive styles and information processing capabilities. There are many components to the individual difference construct, including the difference between traits (long lasting characteristics) and states (characteristics related to the current context); most research in EUT has been related to traits (for examples of studies see Martocchio et al. (1997), Sein et al. (1989) and Sein et al. (1993)). This diversity can directly influence the formation of mental models or indirectly affect via aptitude-treatment interactions.

In this study, we control for these individual differences though randomization and using them as statistical covariates.

2.5. Summary: Process Lens

Table 3 summarizes the gaps and problems in the current understanding in literature, and how this study addresses these issues. Each of these concerns was discussed in depth in the previous sections and is summarized here for the reader.

This chapter brought together literature from two different disciplines highlighting a need for a theoretical model for understanding issues involved in individual and collaborative e-learning in an end-user training context. Not only is there a need to expand the research from

26

learning into technology-mediated end-user training, but also to present a model for investigation of the components involved in this context.

Table 3: Summary of the Concerns in Literature

Concerns in literature	Focus of current research
Focus only on one component of social cognitive theory: vicarious learning	Study focuses on operationalization of both components of social cognitive theory: vicarious and enactive learning
Limited focus on technology-mediated learning.	This study uses contemporary web-based training software that implements both vicarious learning and enactive learning
Studies are input-output in nature and do not focus on the learning process	This study focuses on the learning process and its impact on learning outcomes
Only one study used collaborative learning in EUT – no significant impact	This study uses paired peers to investigate the effectiveness of collaboration
Studies do not distinguish the incremental benefit of collaboration	Experimental treatments in this study help us explicitly tease out the impact of collaboration vs. computer-technology
Inconsistent results when studying collaboration	Study focuses on the development of collaboration to get a richer view
Limited studies using technology and learning theories in end-user training	Study uses end-user training as a context
No studies in EUT doing a longitudinal investigation of the learning process	Study uses time-intercepted design to analyze the impact of time.

More recently, Education literature has expanded to view IS from an emergent perspective, investigating the impact of technology on outcomes as mediated through participants actions (Jonassen et al. 2001). This has focused research on the role of people (focusing on social communication situation, message exchange, cognitive load and participation of the learners) (Hron et al. 2003), ignoring the role of IS.

Given the complexity and the breath of issues, neither of the lenses discussed previously i.e., input-output lens (Alavi et al. 2001) or emergent lens (Jonassen et al. 2001), seem to be adequate to address the concerns highlighting in Table 3. In her research, Orlikowski (1992) documents the need to view IS from a duality perspective, highlighting the reciprocal relationship between technology and people. This reciprocal nature of this relationship is also consistent with social cognitive theory. Using the duality perspective, we articulate a theoretical model for further analysis into collaborative e-learning area. The framework elaborates the structures involved due to a given learning strategy, their appropriation, as well as their impact on learning outcomes. The focus of the model is on 1) learning methods, 2) understanding the appropriation involved in the learning process, and 3) their effect on the learning outcomes. Finally, the model should be able to be applied in both cross-section research as well as longitudinal research.

3. Conceptual Model

In this chapter, we develop a theoretical model focusing on the learning process involved in collaborative e-learning. The motivation for theoretical models stems from two interrelated sources a) inconsistent results across studies and b) an assumption that theory-based research will advance the area rapidly.

The main thrust of prior research has been to try and establish the effectiveness of computer support to individuals as well as groups. As summarized in the Chapter 2, studies have found mixed results. These inconsistencies in results are at least partly due to the lack of comprehensive theoretical models incorporating major constructs. These studies also suffer from differences in contexts, the task assigned to participants, and the measures used to establish effectiveness. The result is an accumulation of data that fails to provide a cogent picture of the phenomena associated with e-learning (Moore 2002).

Given the limitations and the lack of research in this area, a theoretical model to guide research in this area is needed. The model needs to focus on both on the inputs as well as on the learning process. This chapter articulates such a theory driven model.

Daft (1985) argues that theory provides the story that gives meaning to data. Popper (1968) says *"Theories are nets cast to catch what we call 'the world': to rationalize, to explain, and to master it"*. Theories provide the communality necessary amongst researchers to build a clear and rapid understanding of any area. The area of e-learning is no exception. To ground e-learning research and practice, designs must be based in defensible theoretical frameworks that can be both articulated clearly and differentiated from other perspectives. We need to understand the nature of e-learning approaches, the activities enabled, the underlying goals and perspectives of developers, and the extent to which the approaches have yielded or are likely to yield productive outcomes (Hannafin et al. 2004).

The model articulated below is based on Adaptive Structuration Theory (AST) (DeSanctis et al. 1994; Poole et al. 2003). It provides the mechanism for grounding and integrating e-learning research and practice. Although the model is applicable to both individual and collaborative e-learning settings, the focus of the current chapter will be on collaborative settings.

The chapter is organized as follows: Section 3.1 provides an overview of AST and its benefits. The section after that outlines a detailed theoretical model used to study collaborative e-learning. Propositions are drawn in light of the current study. The final section summarizes this model.

3.1. Theoretical Lens: Adaptive Structuration Theory (AST)

Integrating the framework presented in Alavi et al. (2001), Fjermestad et al. (2005) and Sasidharan et al. (2006) with Adaptive Structuration Theory (AST) (DeSanctis et al. 1994), we create a theoretical model for explaining and investigating collaborative e-learning. AST provides a lens for looking at the learning process embedded within a learning task. AST is an ideal framework for studying the underlying phenomena of e-learning because of its global perspective, focus on both the process and structures, and focus on the actor.

First, AST has a global perspective on interaction between human teams and technology. Many of the more predictive and narrow but relevant theories can be integrated into AST. For example, task and technology are viewed as inputs to learning process in AST, enabling the investigation of the interactions between various learning method components using task-technology fit theories. Theories from Educational Psychology, such as social cognitive theory and social development theory, can also be integrated into this framework. AST also takes a socio-technical perspective (Bostrom et al. 1977a; Bostrom et al. 1977b), encompassing the entire system under investigation. It deals with all the four elements of a socio-technical system i.e. the people, their relationships, the technologies they use as well as the tasks they do. As a result, using AST to build the theoretical framework enables a broad exploration of e-learning.

The ultimate outcome of this line of research is to facilitate the development of specific research models and research programs for different learning contexts. Such a model would embed other relevant theories within the global perspective of AST framework. Examples of the development of such specific models, using AST, focusing on a specific technology and/or task domain already exist in the literature. In a technology context, DeSanctis et al. (1994) developed a model for group support systems (GSS) which has focused primarily on decision making tasks

30

and Jankowski et al. (2001) developed a model for geographic information systems (GIS) focusing primarily on information disbursement and decision making. Sarason (1995) focused on organizational transformation and strategic management and Roberts et al. (1985) focused on accounting practices in an organizational context. The model's applicability can subsequently be extended to multiple levels, from micro to institutional (Poole et al. 2003).

Second, an AST view focuses on both the learning process and method. AST describes learning in terms of appropriation, the process by which people use a specific e-learning technology in a given context and time, and how such use influences later patterns of behavior (DeSanctis et al. 1994). Rather than the traditional deterministic perspective that focuses on technology, AST is an action-oriented, social view. It makes human agents part of the system itself, and thus, it can account for the interplay between people and technology (Fulk 1993). This lens takes into account the reciprocal causation between technology and people, where technology design not only affects individual use, but individuals' use also affects how the technology's design is perceived (Orlikowski 1992). The concept of reciprocal causation is central to most Education theories like social cognitive theory. AST views the learning process as an appropriation of learning methods, while also allowing the researcher or instructional designer to focus on the functional aspects of learning method.

Third, a major strength of AST is that one can emphasize either actors' influence on process or process's influence on actors (Poole et al. 2003). In either case, the actor is a critical focus. In learning, the key actor is the learner. Thus, AST provides good lens for focusing in the learner's actions and outcomes.

3.2. *Theoretical Model of Collaborative e-Learning*

Poole et al. (2003) identify seven requirements for applying AST effectively. These seven requirements guided the development of the proposed model, shown in Figure 4. In this section, we will overview the model and then the subsequent sections will discuss each component in depth.

The design of a learning program is driven by the learning goals and epistemological perspective. Much of the literature has failed to focus adequately on these. Learning goals focus on the desired knowledge to be attained (Kang et al. 2003; Sein et al. 1999a). Epistemology

31

establishes overarching beliefs and values about the nature of this knowledge and about what it means to "*know*" something (Hannafin et al. 2004). Naturally, the belief about the nature of knowledge and knowledge itself, reflected in the learning goals, are interrelated. The learning goals and epistemological perspective chosen influence the design of the learning method as shown in Figure 4.

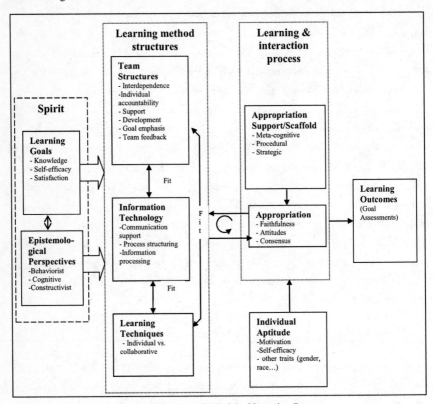

Figure 4: Conceptual Model of Learning Process

At the heart of the learning process is the learning method composed of structures participants use to achieve the learning goals. Structures are formal and informal procedures, techniques, skills, rules and technologies, embedded in elements of learning method. In a

32

collaborative e-learning environment, the learning method is conceptualize in terms of three sets of structures: teams or the social setup of the team (Johnson et al. 1999); information technology or the array of possible use of technology in interpersonal interaction and cognition (DeSanctis et al. 1994); and learning technique or the specific procedures to attain learning goals (Schunk 2004).

DeSanctis et al. (1994) stated that technology structures can be described in three ways: their features, dimensions and spirit. We argue that this structural perspective can also be used to describe team and learning technique structures. Structural features are the specific types of capabilities, rules and resources offered by or associated with a technology, learning technique or team. For example, features of a typical instant messaging system might include two way text and audio communication, share whiteboard, and file transfer capabilities. Features govern how information is accessed, processed, shared and managed by learners.

Because of the many possible combinations of features associated with the implementation of technology, techniques, or team structures, researchers have utilized structural dimensions to differentiate structures instead of features. A dimension describes some aspect or characteristic of structure. For example, Silver (1991) used the dimension of restrictiveness to differentiate between decision support systems. The restrictiveness dimension would be applicable to most technology and technique structures. The more restrictive a structure, the more limited the set of actions the learner can take; the less restrictive structure provides more options to the learner.

Finally, learning methods can be described in terms of their spirit. The *'spirit'* is the general intent in terms of values and goals underlying the choice or design of structures and features by the instructional designers or instructors. Spirit is the *"official line"* which the learning method presents to participants regarding how to act, interpret the features and fill in gaps in procedure which are not explicitly specified (DeSanctis et al. 1994). In a learning/training context, the spirit of a learning method would be described in terms of the learning goals and epistemological perspective of the designer/trainer as shown in Figure 4.

Together, the spirit, features and dimensions of a structure form its structural potential, which participants can draw upon to generate particular patterns of interaction and learning (DeSanctis et al. 1994). These patterns guide coordination among people and provide procedures

33

for accomplishing learning goals. In this sense, the structural potential influences the social aspects of learning process (Dennis et al. 2001).

The model highlights the fact that learning outcomes are governed by a fit between the structures within a learning method: team, technology, and learning techniques (see Figure 4). The model also argues that these fits are a necessary but not sufficient condition to improve performance. Without proper appropriation of these structures, learning outcomes are less likely to improve even if fit exists (Dennis et al. 2001).

Appropriation is a social process where participants learn and adapt the structures based on their interpretation of the spirit (Poole et al. 2003). These structures are produced and reproduced through interactions with learners. The learning process, thus, represents a process of reciprocal causation (represented with dual arrows and ⊊ symbol in Figure 4), where the appropriation at any time influences structures, which in turn influences appropriation in the next cycle. When well designed and relevant structures are successfully appropriated (i.e. used in the spirit they were designed to be used), they should lead to contribute to higher learning outcomes. An unfaithful or ironic appropriation of well-designed and relevant structures, on the other hand, might result in lower learning outcomes.

As shown in Figure 4, appropriation may be supported by providing help, through facilitation or other forms of support or scaffolds (Hannafin et al. 2004). Scaffolds can be used to enhance understanding of the content or the process of appropriating the learning method structures. Individual aptitude can also affect the level of appropriation. For example, a greater level of motivation to learn leads to higher effort to understand the spirit of the learning method, leading to a greater faithful appropriation.

Learning outcomes are the evidence of learning goal attainment. These are measured though various forms of assessment such as quizzes, surveys etc.

Next, we provide a detailed description of the components of the model.

3.2.1. Learning Goals

Learning goals of a collaborative e-learning task are multi-pronged. Training not only seeks accomplishment of a task, but its primary goal is the development of individual models of learning as well as to provide a good learning experience for future learning

34

Knowledge represents an understanding of the principles by which a system can be applied to a business task (Garud 1997). Individual's learning outcomes includes conceptual knowledge about the business domain of the task, the process of doing the learning task, and how the knowledge gained can be applied to specific business need. Two types of knowledge have been identified in training literature i.e. declarative and procedural (Anderson 1982). Declarative knowledge, or know-what knowledge, is factual knowledge that describes physical features and relationships between the components. Procedural knowledge, also called know-how knowledge, describes the order of operations to apply and when to apply a certain procedure. These two knowledge types have been the focus of previous research in IS and are used as for assessment in the current study as well.

An objective of a learning program is also to enhance learner satisfaction. This is especially important for encouraging future participation in learning programs. Satisfaction has been a widely used parameter to evaluate the effectiveness of learning environments both in academic (Alavi 1994; Alavi et al. 1995) and business settings (Wolfram 1994). Thus, satisfaction from process is considered as a very important learning goal and is assessed in this study.

Another important outcome of the training is perceived self-efficacy of the individual in using the technology. Bandura (1977a) conceptualized it as the most important factor affecting subsequent behavioral change. Within IS, perceived self-efficacy has been found to be an important factor influencing technology adoption (Fenech 1998; Venkatesh et al. 2000). Thus, perceived self-efficacy not only acts a covariate as described in Section 2.1.3, but is also acts as a dependent variable. Marcolin et al. (2000) confirmed that self-efficacy and knowledge are different constructs, using a multi-trait multi-method analysis, wherein both declarative knowledge and self-efficacy were measures with both multiple-choice tests and questionnaire-based self-reports. Please see Compeau et al. (2005) for a review of self-efficacy research and a summary of research issues. Self-efficacy is also assessed in this study.

3.2.2. Epistemological Perspectives

Epistemology establishes overarching beliefs about the nature of knowledge and about what it means to "*know*" something (Hannafin et al. 2004). It provides a normative frame with

35

regard to behaviors that are appropriate in a given context. It also helps learners understand and interpret the underlying assumptions as well as roles/duties of the learner. Thus, an epistemological perspective provides a design template for creating process and content structures embedded in the learning method.

Many different epistemological perspectives have been explored in the literature (Leidner et al. 1995). Many of these schools of thought overlap, and thus, cannot be independently isolated. For example, social cultural perspective incorporating cultural uniqueness can be incorporated in all of the other perspectives. Early efforts to come up with a global comprehensive epistemological perspective were unsuccessful and abandoned (Mowrer et al. 2000). Thus, we classify epistemological perspectives into three fundamental schools of thought: behaviorist, cognitivism and constructivism (Leidner et al. 1995; Mowrer et al. 2000; Reeves et al. 1997) which represents a comprehensive as well as mutually exclusive framework. Table 4 summarizes the main components of each of these perspectives.

Table 4: Epistemological Perspectives

Epistemological perspectives	Assumption about the state of knowledge	Learning outcomes focus on	Learning happens by	Sample learning technique
Behaviorist/ Instructivist	Objective	Conditioning learner behavior	Response to stimulus	Direct instruction
Cognitiveist (Social)	Objective within context	The learner's thought process	Acquiring and reorganizing the cognitive structures	Behavioral modeling
Constructivism (Social)	Constructed reality	The learner's ability to construct reality	Learning is a function of one's prior beliefs and experiences	Unguided case study

The behaviorist or instructional design is based on the presumption that human behavior is predictable. Under this theory, learning occurs when new behaviors or changes in behaviors are acquired as the result of an individual's response to stimuli. Thus, the end goal is defined upfront, and each step necessary to achieve the goal is given to the team (Burton et al. 2001). For

36

example, direct instruction, which is the most popular form of learning technique, is based on this perspective.

The cognitiveist perspective states that learning is a process that is dictated by the participant's cognitive structures, and how the information is presented to the student. Under this theory, learning is a change in the knowledge stored in the memory by modifying mental representations. Thus, tasks under this theory have a predefined goal along with information necessary to reach the goal, but the process of cognition of the information is left to the learners (Winn et al. 2001). Learning methods based on cognitive perspective often include behavioral modeling.

Constructivist theory says that individuals construct knowledge by working to solve realistic problems. Under this theory, learning is the process where individuals construct new ideas or concepts based on prior knowledge and/or experience. Constructivists believe that the environment needs to be highly adaptive to the participant. A constructivist designer might provide all the information necessary for learning, but will allow the student to learn the materials and information that is most comfortable to the student to arrive at his/her own conclusion. Learners are presented with an idea about the solution, and the tools necessary are provided, but the learners are left on their own to figure out the exact solution, and thus, the process required to reach it (Duffy et al. 2001). An example of a learning technique based on this approach might be an unguided case study.

Each of the above epistemological perspectives can use e-learning and collaborative learning. For example, cognitiveist epistemological perspective can be implemented in a social context by setting up teams and allowing them to interact.

As outlined above, the epistemological perspectives and learning goals guide the choice of learning methods, their features and structures (see Figure 4). This study focuses on the cognitivist perspective. We use social cognitive theory (SCT) for designing the training. Participants in the study go though the demonstrations and enactive learning with pre-defined learning goals. It is then supplemented by using the collaborative environment from a social development theory standpoint, i.e. , the social aspect of cognitivist perspective.

37

3.2.3. Learning Method

A learning method is a combination of structures that guide individuals to achieve the learning outcomes. Structures are the specific types of rules and resources offered by the learning method elements (DeSanctis et al. 1994). We argued earlier that the AST structural perspective is applicable to learning methods. In this section, we focus our discussion on the features and dimensions of the learning method structures.

A feature of a learning method represents the class of tools used for learning. Much research has been done by focusing on these features (e.g. Hashaim et al. (1991)). However, these features can be implemented in a variety of ways in different situations, impacting the learning outcome. For example, Desiraju et al. (2001) shows the difference between two implementations of a learning technique i.e. McAleer Interactive Case Analysis (MICA) and Harvard case methods. Thus, given the variety of techniques as well as variety of implementations, such focus suffers from a plethora of inconsistent and non-generlizable research.

These issues highlight the need for focus on structural dimensions. Structural dimensions describe some aspect or characteristic of the learning method, i.e., the bundled set of features implemented in a particular context. These dimensions reflect the richness of the features or structures associated with that dimension. Consulting manuals, reviewing the statements of designers, educators, or noting the comments of participants, can accomplish scaling of these dimensions. For example, based on a review of techniques, Desiraju et al. (2001) found that MICA scored high on the feedback dimension, affecting learning outcomes. A focus on dimensions helps us not only in enhancing our understanding the spirit and methods, but also in investigating the comparative effectiveness between methods.

In a collaborative e-learning environment three structural sets exists within learning methods: teams or the social setup of the team, information technology or the array of possible uses of technology in interpersonal interaction and cognition, and learning technique or the specific procedures to attain learning goals. Below we examine each of these in terms of the structural dimensions, before briefly highlighting the need for a consistent spirit and discussing the learning process.

Since the focus of the study is in the use of social cognitive theory (SCT) and social development theory (SDT), the discussions below dominantly reflect the view embedded in these theories, though the general model is also applicable to other perspectives.

3.2.3.1. Information Technology Structures

The role of information technology in end-user training research has been summarized in Section 2.3. This research focused on the pedagogical use of technology. As stated earlier, rather than focusing on this, the focus should shift to structural dimensions. Researchers have identified several dimensions of technology. Based on a review of the literature, we have identified several dimensions. Some of the dimensions are relative restrictiveness (Silver 1991), level of sophistication (DeSanctis et al. 1987), degree of structure, control, synchronicity (Poole et al. 1990), comprehensiveness (Cats-Baril et al. 1987), self-directivity / learner control, flexibility, just-in-time knowledge, personalization (Zhang et al. 2004), interactivity or feedback (Piccoli et al. 2001), richness (Webster et al. 1997) and telepresence (Papa et al. 1998). This however, does not represent an exhaustive list of dimensions and research exploring new dimensions is needed. These structural dimensions can be applied to both learning-from-computer and learning-with-computer use.

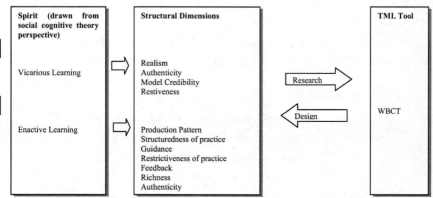

Figure 5: Relationship between Theory, Structural Dimensions and E-learning

39

This study is based on an SCT perspective in a learning-from-technology environment. Figure 5 summarizes the relationship between the SCT perspective, structural dimensions and the e-learning tool. The two techniques for delivering knowledge are vicarious modeling and enactive learning. Vicarious modeling is usually done in the form of demonstrations of actions. Structural dimensions of realism (showing the realism of action & consequence) and restrictiveness (keeping learner focus on a restrictive set of functionality) emerge out of this learning technique. Enactive learning relies on self-modeling. Dimensions of interactivity with technology, realism of reactions and quality of feedback & guidance were used to implement enactive learning. There are also technology specific dimensions like smaller task focus and learner control that have been identified in the figure that emerge out of e-learning literature.

The structural view on these techniques can be applied from both a design and a research perspective. In a design perspective, the focus should be on building the outlined structural dimensions into the learning system. In a research perspective, the focus should be on taking an existing tool and dimentionalizing it. Scaling of these dimensions can be accomplished by consulting manuals, reviewing the statements of designers, educators, or noting the comments of participants (DeSanctis and Poole 1994). This study uses the later perspective of taking an existing tool and dimentionalizing it. Research drawing from each the perspectives is expected to feed the other.

The advantage of web-based computer-based training (WCBT), such as used in this study, is the ability to integrate the various structural dimensions to work together to support the accomplishment of learning task. Based on an assessment of the e-learning technology used in the current research, five important structural dimensions that influence learning are isolated (see Figure 5).

The first structural dimension deals with the smaller task focus. E-learning technologies have the ability to build control over the entire learning process. These tools are able to provide substantially smaller learning objects combining vicarious and enactive learning to make an entire course when compared to non-WBCT environments.

Next, information technology can provide dimension of relative restrictiveness (Silver 1991) when compared to real world. Enactive learning is done in a simulated environment. Within such an environment, actions that the user can take are limited to focus the users' action on specific area of learning. This prevents participants from wandering into other features of the software, or even getting lost into new capabilities not yet taught. For example, when focusing on how to enter data in Excel, WBCT restricts the possible interactions of other menu options, homing participants focus on entering data correctly. This is impossible to do in a non-WCBT, where fully functional applications are used.

The third structural dimension is learner-controlled activity (Zhang et al. 2004). In an e-learning environment, a learner has greater control over the learning environment compared to traditional methods. This is usually in the form of the pace of learning. For example, in the current study, students can choose their own pace of going through specific concepts of the training program.

The fourth structural dimension of WBCT environment deals with the richness of feedback (Cats-Baril et al. 1987) and learning guidance (Silver 1991). According to Bandura (1986), the quality of feedback is an essential component that affects learning outcomes. Research in psychology shows that when informative feedback is eliminated, delayed, or distorted, learning outcomes of a learning process are negatively affected (Bilodeau 1966; Carroll et al. 1985). The simulated environment that participants work in during enactive learning, not only provides instant feedback based on learners' action, but also provides contextualized feedback for each user. This not only increases the speed and focus of feedback, but also allows us to push feedback to the learner (guidance), rather than waiting for the learner to request for it as is the case in non-WBCT learning.

The fifth structural dimension dealing with feedback and realism is system interactivity (Zhang et al. 2004). Feedback based on user action is also dependent on the extent of realism that can be built into the simulated learning environment. This has been identified as a very important factor influencing training within social cognitive theory (Bandura 1986). In programming end-user application simulated environments, where responses by the applications to user actions are well documented and predictable, these can be easily built into the instruction technology. This increases the ability of the user to get a realistic experience of his/her actions, and thus reflect on the consequences similar to the real world.

In summary, in a learning-from-computer use, the learning technique is incorporated into the information technology integrating these two structural sets (see Figure 4). Thus, similar to

41

design theorists (Hevner et al. 2004; Reeves et al. 2005), we content that it is not the technology, but the structural dimensions of the learning technique embedded in the technology that determine its effectiveness. Not only do information technology structures implement (sometimes with greater richness) the dimensions of the learning technique, it also enables certain new dimensions to be implemented. The focus on dimensions will also help us explain the inconstancies in previous research, which has focused primarily on technology features.

P1: *E-learning with higher perceived levels of critical structural dimensions will positively affect learning outcomes.*

3.2.3.2. Team Structures

Teams provide an environment where participants gain social understanding through observation and reflection on the learning process as a whole. As summarized in section 2.2, team interaction is postulated to have a direct impact on the learning outcomes.

Researchers investigating team learning have focused on various collaboration techniques (see Johnson et al. (2003) for review of some techniques) derived from the spirit of the above theories. However, as pointed out earlier, various methods of collaboration exist, as well as implementation differences the result in widely different effect sizes in different meta-analyses (Rohrbeck et al. 2003).

Drawing on team research in Education (Johnson et al. 1999) and management (Franklin et al. 1976), six important structural dimensions of teams that influence learning are identified: positive interdependence, individual accountability, support, development, goal emphasis and team feedback. These dimensions are summarized in Table 5.

The first two dimensions, i.e. interdependence and individual accountability, are usually part of the initial learning method design. Positive interdependence is the perception that participants are linked in a way that some benefit is accrued to the collaborating individual. Structures used to implement this dimension are role or reward interdependence, resource scarcity, and shared goals. Role interdependence is structured by assigning each student a role. Reward interdependence is structured by providing a reward for successful individual performance of all participants. Resource interdependence is created by giving each member a scarce resource for problem solving. Finally, goal interdependence is structured by providing the

42

team with a mutually shared team goal (Johnson et al. 1991a). This study uses role, reward, and goal interdependence to operationalize this dimension. Role interdependence is implemented by following the guidelines of reciprocal interdependence, while reward interdependence is implemented by having a common reward for performance. Goal interdependence is operationalized by providing dyads shared overall goals for trying and specific shared goals for learning technique used.

Table 5: Team Dimensions

Team Dimensions	Definition	Example of Structures
Positive Interdependence	Individual within the teams are linked in a way so that some benefit is accrued to the collaborative individual	Role, resource, reward or goal interdependence
Individual accountability	Individual accountability exist when the performance of each individual participant can be assessed and feedback seen by the team as well as the individual.	Using an average score to reflect the score of each individual in the team, random selection of individual outcome to represent the team outcome
Support	Supportive interaction exists when participants more readily offer the help that fellow team members can use, or provide information that may be useful in understanding a concept.	Shared goals, rewards
Development	A developed team exists when interactions among participants promote an effective working team.	Ground rules (e.g. conflict management), roles, shared goals
Goal Emphasis	Goal emphasis exists when participant behavior is directly related to the task and its accomplishment	Goal setting procedures, Tracking the extent of achievement of goal
Team feedback	Team feedback exists when participants discuss how well they are achieving their goals and maintaining effective working relationships.	Team performance assessments in weekly meetings, online discussion forum

Individual accountability exists when the performance of each individual student can be assessed and feedback seen by the team as well as the individual. It is important that team

43

members know (a) who needs more assistance and (b) they cannot *'hitch-hike'* on the work of others. Common ways of implementing this dimension include giving an individual test to each student and randomly selecting one student's work to represent the efforts of the entire team. In this study, individual accountability is operationalized by linking the reward to the cumulative performance of the team.

The rest of the dimensions are usually associated with the internal norms of the team. The support dimension exists when members behaviors enhances mutual feelings of being important persons. Since individuals are working together in learning tasks, they have many opportunities to supplement each others learning efforts. When team norms favor support, individuals more readily offer the help that fellow team members can use, or provide information that may be useful in understanding a concept. This study draws these dimensions from a collaborative technique called reciprocal questioning (King 1992). This technique outlines rules of interaction, support, feedback and goal emphasis.

The team development dimension deals with the cooperative working relationships (Chidambaram et al. 1996; Chidambaram et al. 1997). Structures implementing this dimension, e.g. conventions and rules of behavior, sets out processes by which social learning happen though the formation of values and convergent expectations. A higher level of team development not only lowers the costs of communication, but establishes explicit and tacit rules of coordination and influence the direction of search and learning (Kogut et al. 1996). Collaboration methods that feature skill development in the areas of leadership, decision-making, trust-building, communication and conflict-management enhance the richness of the above dimensions. In this study, initial team development is done by introducing participants and allowing them to develop a relationship (in a controlled environment) before the training.

Goal emphasis directly relates to the task and its accomplishment. At the higher levels of this structural dimension, it stimulates an enthusiasm among participants for setting and achieving goals contributing to high quality learning (Franklin et al. 1976). Structures that promote this dimension include goal setting procedures and tracking the learning goal achieved by the team. In this study, participants were given behavior and question guidelines to facilitate goal emphasis.

Team feedback exists when team members discuss how well they are achieving their goals and maintaining effective working relationships. The individual who experiences the eagerness of other members to do well will be challenged and encouraged by this enthusiasm and also take pride in a job well done (Franklin et al. 1976). Performance appraisal and feedback are among the structures that are commonly used to implement this dimension. As participants interacted in this study, they provided each other feedback based on the reciprocal questioning technique.

In summary, team-based learning methods are rooted in the social interaction aspect of epistemological perspective. Drawing from the arguments presented above, for individuals to benefit from team-based learning, team interactions need to facilitate the existence of the team structures outlined above. Various collaboration methods focus on different dimensions and different levels of richness of these dimensions. However, as argued above, the greater the richness of the team dimensions, the greater the learning outcomes. A recent meta-analysis comparing collaboration learning methods provides evidence in this area and suggests that collaboration methods richer in these team dimensions showed the largest effect size on learning outcomes (Johnson et al. 2003). Since in this study, we have focused on all the dimensions, we postulate a positive effect. Thus,

P2: *Individuals in learning teams with higher perceived levels of team structural dimensions will have higher learning outcomes.*

3.2.3.3. Learning Technique Structures

Learning techniques are specific procedures/structures to attain learning goals (Weinstein et al. 1986). These techniques draw upon the same dimensions discussed above.

In this study, we draw from social cognitive theory for designing learning techniques. Behavioral modeling was used as a baseline treatment, with other techniques building on it. In case of e-learning, self-modeling is also used. In this case, the structures of enactive learning are incorporated in the technology. Similarly, in case of techniques drawn from social development theory i.e. reciprocal questioning, the structures are incorporated in the discussion on team structures.

45

In effect, learning techniques also act as the treatment variables. It is also important to note that some of the dimensions of learning technique overlap with the other technology and collaboration in their respective treatments. Other dimensions that might exist (like complexity) are controlled for by providing all participants with similar learning process.

3.3. Relationship between Structures

Research evidence suggests that some combination of learning method structures provides a consistent and present a clear sprit, whereas others do not. For effective learning to occur, learning method structures need to reflect a consistent spirit across all structures. A consistent spirit exists when individuals are able to interact with the structures in a definite direction. Thus, the three categories of structures - collaboration, learning technique and information technology structures - all have to support (or fit) each other to form a learning method that can enhance learning. Consistent with IS literature (Zigurs et al. 1998), fit is conceptualized as a profile matching between the various learning method dimensions. A decomposition of this three way fit results in three two-way fits i.e. information technology & collaboration fit, information technology & learning technique fit, and collaboration & learning technique fit. An incoherent spirit (mis-fit) would be expected to exert weaker influence on member behavior. An incoherent spirit might also send contradictory signals, making use of the learning method more difficult (Poole et al. 1992).

The focus in this research is on the process of appropriation of the structures, thus, the learning methods were structured for good fit.

3.4. Learning and Interaction Process

The core of the learning process deals with the participants interacting with the learning method, instructor and other participants to achieve the learning goals. The investigation of this process is missing from IS as well as Education literatures. We argue that it is important to investigate this process, and that it mediates the impact of learning methods discussed above (see Figure 4). The focus on the learning process will also help us explain the inconsistencies in earlier research (Cohen 1994).

46

Structures in a learning method together represent the structural potential available to the individual. As shown in Figure 4, the structural potential guides the interaction with the learning method, instructor and other participants. They provide support for coordination among people and procedures for accomplishing the learning goals. In this sense, these structures influence the social aspects of learning process. However, the users base this interaction on the interpretation of the spirit. Like all perceptions, this varies between users.

Appropriation is the process by which the participants use, adapt and reproduce structures (Poole et al. 2003). The degree to which participants interact in a manner consistent with the spirit of the learning method is captured by the faithful-ironic distinction (Poole et al. 1990).

Assuming that the learning method has a coherent spirit, a faithful appropriation occurs when participants interaction is consistent with the spirit (Poole et al. 1992). Faithfulness is not necessarily concerned with the precise duplication of the procedures provided; rather, it is concerned with whether the structures are used in a manner consistent with the overall goals and epistemological perspectives. A unique or innovative use of the structures by the participant may well be faithful appropriation as long as the use is consistent with the spirit that the learning method intended to promote (Chin et al. 1997). For example, in DeSanctis et al. (2003) participants in a collaborative e-learning environment achieved higher levels of learning outcomes by successfully appropriating the structures involved in electronic discussion board and development of group norms.

Ironic appropriation occurs when the participants' interactions violate the spirit of the structure with or without abandoning the underlying learning method (Poole et al. 1990). This introduces internal contradictions into the structures governing interaction. Over time, these contradictions will cause tensions in interactions that might lead to lower effectiveness of the structures. Contradictions must be addressed, detracting the participant(s) from the learning focus, leading to lowering of learning outcomes. A recent study by Alavi et al. (2002) highlights this issue where participants with sophisticated systems had lower learning outcomes because of lack of faithful appropriation of technology. This led to a shifting of focus towards technology understanding, detracting the team from the learning focus.

When analyzing technology appropriation, Poole et al. (1989a) suggests three dimensions that affect how faithfully a structure is appropriated: faithfulness, attitudes and level of

47

consensus. That is, learning technology structures will only have its intended effect if its design principles are kept intact (faithfulness), if members do not react negatively to it (attitudes), and if members agree substantially over how structure is used (consensus). Learning technique appropriation can be measured similarly.

Collaborative structures appropriation, however, deals with the perceptions of rules and norms within the team. Since these perceptions can be directly measured, researchers have focused on these. For example, Slavin (1989) found that students learned significantly more in teams which perceived high interdependence and individual accountability. Thus, the perceived richness on each of the structural dimensions suggests how faithfully collaboration structures are appropriated (Gupta 2006). This study developed a scale for measuring the faithfulness of appropriation of collaboration structures.

Thus, the structures of the learning method provide a structural potential that participants draw on to interact. Assuming that the learning methods are well designed and represent a coherent spirit, and faithfully appropriated, interactions as driven by the sprit are likely to emerge. These positively influence learning outcomes. Drawing on AST, we postulate that the effects of the learning method would be dependent on the extent of appropriation of the structures. Thus, we state

P3: *Assuming that the learning method represents a coherent spirit, faithfulness of appropriation of information technology, collaboration and learning technique structures will have a positive impact with learning outcomes.*

Structures of learning method are constituted recursively as participants regularly interact with them and thus, shape the set of rules and resources that serve to shape their interaction (Orlikowski 2000) (represented by G in Figure 4) The idea of structure being continuously produced and reproduced through action also leads to another significant aspect of structuration, that of routinisation. Giddens argues that routine is '*integral to the continuity of personality of the agent ... and to the institution of the society*' (Giddens 1984).

Limited empirical research exists using AST longitudinally (Jones 1999). However, the process of appropriation over time can be characterized by two kinds of dynamics. First, there is a continuous production and reproduction of structures as they are employed, resulting in higher levels of appropriation. In particular, individuals acquire ontological security through their

48

engagement in predictable routines and encounters (Jones 1999). For example, Bhattacherjee et al. (2004) also showed that attitudes and beliefs about technology change over time. However, at certain junctures major shifts in the learning process can also occur resulting in new structures-in-use. Participants might drop structures that do not work, or come up with new structures based on experience. Poole et al. (1992) identify nine such structural moves. In either case, these emergent structures (Orlikowski 2000) will thus continue to influence the changes in learning. Thus, we hypothesize,

P4: *Increase in faithfulness of appropriation of information technology, collaboration and learning technique structures will positively influence changes in learning outcomes over time.*

Appropriation of learning method structures is often supported or scaffolded. AST literature has ignored this. However, appropriation support or scaffolding can influence the faithfulness of appropriation. A scaffold provides initial assistance to support learning that gradually faded as learners become more independent, confident and competent. Education researchers postulate e-moderating (a mechanism of providing scaffold using information technology) as a key component of e-learning (Salmon 2003). Three forms of process scaffolds have been identified in IS and Education: meta-cognitive, procedural and strategic (Grise et al. 1999; Hannafin et al. 2004).

Meta-cognitive scaffolds support individual reflection on learning, such as soliciting estimates of current understanding or cuing participants to identify prior related experiences they can reference. Mao et al. (2005) provides some evidence of impact of such support on appropriation by looking at how online wizards enhance the learning process. Procedural scaffolding helps participants make navigation decisions, such as how to utilize available resources and tools. Ge et al. (2003) found that procedural scaffolding enhanced team collaboration in a team-learning environment. Empirical studies in GSS (Jessup et al. 1993; Kelly et al. 1997/98; Wheeler et al. 1996) also support this assertion. Strategic or chauffeured scaffolds support participants in anticipating their interactions, such as analyzing, planning and making tactical decisions. No research that we know exists investigating this scaffold.

49

The application of any of these scaffolds acts to facilitate the learning process via increasing the faithfulness appropriation of the structures involved. In this study, scaffolding is a control variable and was restricted to process scaffolding.

3.5. Summary

The declining cost and continued convergence of computing and communication technologies as well as the prevalence of the Internet is making collaborative e-learning an increasingly viable Educational alternative. Furthermore, an increase in the requirements for continuous learning and growth in the number of adult, part-time students is creating a *"demand-pull"* for going beyond the traditional classroom.

This section brings together literature from two different disciplines to present a theoretical model for understanding issues involved in collaborative e-learning. We articulate a theoretical lens for further analysis into collaborative e-learning area. The focus of the model is on understanding the appropriation process and its consequences. The chapter presents testable propositions for empirical validation of the model.

In the next Chapter, we present a multi-period quasi-experiment for testing the validation of the model in an end-user training context.

CHAPTER FOUR

4. Research Methodology

This study provides a rigorous exploration of learning methods using a longitudinal laboratory experiment. Experiments offer several advantages for the study of appropriation. First, they have a high internal validity because an experiment allows for a direct comparison of the effects of diverse IT structures on social interactions and they control factors that might offer competing explanations for the role of IT in social processes, thereby leading to *"clearer"* analysis. Through the use of experimental controls, it is possible to access the impacts on learning without the confounding factors present in real settings. Secondly, the external validity is higher than case studies or observational studies because they consider more replications of the phenomenon under study (Poole et al. 2003).

In this study, to further increase the external validity of the experimental treatments, every attempt was made to make them consistent with how they would be applied in the field. Finally, experiments provide richer environments for study where constructs can be clearly defined. The importance of experiments in studying this phenomena is also highlighted by Poole et al. (2003) when he states *"For IS researchers, experimental studies are vital to a vibrant research agenda if the structuration power of technology is ever to be understood"*.

This chapter presents the research methodology used. The following section overviews the experimental design, task, treatments, variables involved and sample and subjects. Following that, we described the experimental procedure, experimental roles and data collection methods. We also describe the specific hypotheses drawn from the conceptual model for this experimental setting and the data analysis strategy for each hypothesis. We summarize the pilot studies done and conclude with the summary of the chapter.

4.1. Experiment Design

This study aimed to provide a rigorous exploration of training methods using an interrupted multi-period quasi-experiment (Cook et al. 1979). It involved the study of three independent variables (time, technology-mediation & collaboration).

51

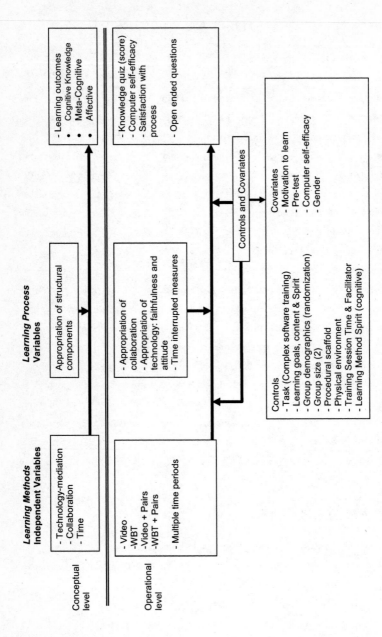

Figure 6: Independent, Intermediate and Dependent Variables involved in the Study

Figure 4 provides an overview of the variables involved in the experimental setting. The variables are broadly categorized into independent, intermediate, controls, covariates and dependent variables. This section describes these variables, the research design, research setting, task and session procedures, sample and subjects and data analysis method.

The experiment manipulates three elements of the learning method presented in Figure 4: collaboration using paired peer training, training methods using vicarious modeling and Web-based CBT including enactive learning and time by using a longitudinal design. Learning and interaction process is mapped to the appropriation of structural elements while learning outcomes are measured using quiz scores, satisfaction and self-efficacy. The rest of the elements of the model are controlled using experimental design or using covariates.

Quasi-experiment compares the dependent variable across multiple non-equivalent groups. The groups are designed to be equal though randomization, except for the treatment. An important condition to making causal statement for difference in dependent variables based on treatments is the pre-specification of the causal model. In a sense, quasi-experiments require making explicit the irrelevant causal forces hidden within the *ceteris paribus* of random assignment (Cook et al. 1979). The sampling procedure describes the randomization condition; where as the causal assertions are drawn from the model presented in Chapter 3.

Time as an independent variable, the longitudinal aspect of the experiment, is analyzed by using a multi-period design. The variables are measured at three well-defined and equally spaced points during the training process (shown in Figure 9).

		Technology-Mediated training methods	
		Vicarious modeling + Practice	**WBCT grounded in vicarious modeling & enactive learning**
Collaboration	No	*LM1:* Participants going through vicarious /modeling via video followed by practice (Baseline)	*LM2:* Participants using elementK (e-learning treatment)
	Yes	*LM3:* Participants in pairs going through vicarious modeling via video followed by practice (Collaboration treatment)	*LM4:* Participants in pairs using elementK (Combined treatment)

Figure 7: Experimental Treatments

Considering this, other independent treatments are done by a fully factored 2 X 2 design for technology-mediated and collaboration treatments (see Figure 7). These treatments are explained in the section 4.3 below.

4.2. Target System

The target system to be learned is contemporary application package. The situation emulates introduction of an application package in an organization and subsequent end-user training. The application selected for training is Microsoft Excel 2003. Microsoft Excel is undoubtedly the most used application package in the industry besides word processing. It is an application package with manageable complexity representing software currently introduced in most organizations. Given the complexity, the training is designed to be done in three logically separate sessions, each building on the previous one. Finally, the application software can be learned within the time frame of an experimental setting. Microsoft Excel has also been used in previous studies in end-user training, making the results of this study more comparable to the existing literature.

4.3. Treatments

The experiment design has four treatments, summarized in Figure 7, varying across the two dimensions: technology-mediated and collaborative learning methods. For each treatment group, a complementary group without the treatment exits.

4.3.1. Technology-Mediated Learning Methods

All learning methods use vicarious modeling as a pedagogical technique. Participants in the control group (LM1) used technology-driven video demonstrations for vicarious modeling followed by unstructured practice, replicating previous studies. Though not a web-based technique, video demonstrations are used in many contemporary learning methods.

Learning method in the second group (LM2) was implemented using contemporary web-based computer-based training delivery system (WBCT), elementK (version as of January 2005). Universities and organizations alike are currently using elementK to train their trainees. It has various training modules, which can be accessed by participants. Participants access these on their terminals as the content is displayed to them. elementK offers training grounded in social cognitive theory. The technology-mediated method had the ability to provide quick feedback in a simulated environment as well as packaging enactive and vicarious learning in a small, integrative learning object, operationalizing the structure described in Section 3.2.3.1. Using Macromedia Flash technology, elementK presents demonstrations to activate vicarious modeling, similar to baseline treatment. It also has hands-on interactive training which simulates the actual application, thus, operationalizing enactive learning. The learning is also supplemented by the use of a structured lab session with detailed steps and feedback, intended at further operationalizing enactive learning.

4.3.2. Collaborative Learning method

In the collaboration treatment, participants were trained in pairs. Drawing from studies in Education, a group size of two has led to the best outcomes (Lou et al. 2001). Therefore, this study uses dyads. Participants were randomly paired with another participant for the rest of the experiment. Each of the above learning methods are supplemented with collaboration (LM3, LM4).

All the collaboration structures within this method, except interdependence and individual accountability, are operationalized by providing participants with collaborative guidelines shown in Appendix D. Interdependence and individual accountability is operationalized by providing groups with a monetary incentive based on aggregate pair performance.

A technique adapted from the concept of self-questioning called reciprocal questioning was used to structure interaction. Participants ask each other self-generated questions about the learning material (Webb et al. 1996). Answering each other's questions is likely to encourage participants to recognize their own misconceptions and gaps in understanding. Since its development by King (1990) and King (1992), this technique has been extensively used in Education literature (Rohrbeck et al. 2003). This technique further encourages the team structures.

4.4. Intermediate Variables

Apart from looking at the impact of various treatments on learning outcomes, the research interest is also in understanding the learning process. Thus, we have three intermediate variables measuring appropriation (faithfulness of WBCT use, attitude towards WBCT use and faithfulness of collaboration) and four dependent variables measuring learning outcomes (Knowledge, Satisfaction, Specific self-efficacy and Computer self-efficacy), three times during the training session.

The intermediate variables measure the faithfulness of appropriation of technology-mediation and collaboration structures. Appropriation, in both cases, is expected to show a positive change over a period. In addition, in spite of groups being in the same treatment, variation is expected within each treatment as different participants will appropriate at different levels.

Extent of appropriation for technology-mediation is measured at individual level, and thus, has two dimensions: faithfulness and attitude. Faithfulness is measured by using items from Chin et al. (1997). Attitude has been conceptualized as level of comfort participants feel with the use of the structure and the degree of respect they have about learning from that structure (Poole et al. 1989b; Poole et al. 1990). These are measured using items developed by Sambamurthy (1989). The final measure of appropriation, consensus, measures the agreement about how to use a software when multiple options and multiple people are present. In the current study (in the collaboration treatment: LM4), the use of e-learning software as well as lab exercise is constrained though the use of guidelines and supervision. Thus, participants did not have any alternative forms of using technology. Consequently, consensus is not measured.

Faithfulness, consensus, and attitude towards each of team structures cannot be measured independently because each influences the other. Instead, a perceived measure on the appropriation of team structures is measured using a scale developed by the researcher as outlined in section 3.2.3.2. Since no measures for the underlying dimensions existed, items were developed using items from team development literature (Franklin et al. 1976). These items measure the richness of team dimensions that exist within the dyad. Items were piloted to a sample of 65 EMBA students and were found to have good internal consistency (inter-item correlation for the items was greater than 0.80 on average). See Appendix J for details.

Items for the above measures are shown in Appendix F[1].

4.5. Covariates

Empirical research in psychology and IS has also shown that individual differences, predominantly motivation to learn and self-efficacy, also affect training outcomes beyond the effects of cognitive ability. To control for these individual differences, participants were randomly assigned to treatment groups. Additionally, these variables were measured and, if necessary, used as statistical covariates. This ensured statistical equivalence among different groups in terms of individual differences.

Motivation theories often distinguish between two broad classes of motivation to perform an activity: extrinsic motivation and intrinsic motivation. Prior research assessing the influence of motivation on computer technology acceptance has measured extrinsic motivation as perceived usefulness and intrinsic motivation as perceived enjoyment (Davis et al. 1992). Perceived usefulness refers to an individual's expectation that computer usage will result in enhanced job performance/productivity (Davis 1989; Davis et al. 1992) and is measured using a four-item scale (Davis et al. 1989).

Similarly, intrinsic motivation has been measured in a variety of ways including individual's perceived enjoyment. Specific to computer technology, enjoyment has been defined as the extent to which using a computer is perceived to be enjoyable distinct from any performance outcomes that might be obtained (Davis et al. 1992; Wicker et al. 1992) and is measured using a three-item scale adapted from Davis et al. (1992). These items were used to measure motivation-to-learn and are shown in Appendix E.

Self-efficacy, defined as the beliefs of one's ability to perform a particular behavior (Bandura 1986), has been examined in the IS literature. Pre-training self-efficacy has been

---

[1] Appendix provides the reliability measures (where applicable) of previous studies and how the constructs were scored for data analysis

shown to be positively related to improvements in training performance (Gist 1986; Gist et al. 1989; Johnson et al. 2000). As shown in Figure 8, IS research has developed measures for two types of self-efficacy. The first measure, developed by Compeau et al. (1995b), measures the general computer self-efficacy for an unknown task. The second measure, developed by Marakas et al. (1999), measures the self-efficacy of using a specific application (in this case Excel) for a set of well-defined tasks. A third measure, developed by Hollenbeck et al. (1987) (used in IS by Martocchio (1994)), measures perceptions of task-specific ability. In the current study, the focus is on self-efficacy of Excel technology, but at both levels of task specificity. Thus, for the general task level, a modified version of Compeau et al. (1995b) measure as well as Hollenbeck et al. (1987), where the technology is specified, is used. Marakas et al.'s (1999) scale is also used to measure specific self-efficacy, modified based on the training provided. The items for the measure are shown in Appendix E.

The extent of initial knowledge on Excel is also likely to influence learning. Results of the pretest conducted (described in section 4.8) were used for selecting the sample for the study. The test was developed to be representative of the post-test quizzes, by randomly selecting procedural and declarative questions.

Technology specificity		Task Specificity	
		General	**Specific**
	General	Compeau et al. (1995b)	No studies.
	Specific	Modified Compeau et al. (1995b) & Hollenbeck et al. (1987)	(Marakas et al. 1999)

Figure 8: Self-efficacy Conceptualizations

Training sessions were structured to measure 75 minutes each. Participants were monitored and were instructed to stick to time limits for various segments. As expected and experienced during the pilot, participants had sufficient time to go through the experimental procedure in 75 minutes.

58

4.6. Dependent variable

Dependent variables or training outcomes includes the level of skill/cognitive (quiz score), satisfaction and affective (self-efficacy). For the participants, learning a complex application package through training is focused on increasing two kinds of knowledge (Anderson 1982; Sein et al. 1999a): procedural and declarative. A process similar to one used by Coulson (2002) and other EUT researchers was used to asses this knowledge. Procedural knowledge, or knowledge about how to do things, is measured though a test of six multiple-choice questions. Declarative knowledge, or factual knowledge that describes the physical features and the relationship between components of the system, is also measured though a test of nine multiple-choice questions. The author, based on existing guidelines in the research, developed the quizzes.

Satisfaction from the learning process is also component of the learning outcomes. A five item scale from Green et al. (1980) was used to measure the satisfaction of the individual with the process. Since the interest is in understanding and explaining the changes in learning over time, learning outcomes are measured three times during the training session. This measurement is done in conjunction with the measurement of intermediate variables. Items for the above measures are shown in Appendix F.

Computer self-efficacy, as a dependent variable, is measured using the same scale as discussed in Section 4.5.

4.7. Sample and Subjects

The sample for the experiment was students in the introductory MIS course for undergraduates from the University of Georgia. Similar to Johnson et al. (2000), all prospective participants were asked to answer a pretest. This pretest was drawn from all three training quizzes. Though all participants went though the training process, only participants with scores less than 35% were included in data analysis.

Individual differences have been shown to have a significant influence on learning/training outcomes (Bostrom et al. 1990). A quasi-experiment controls for non-treatment differences through random assignment. Students, thus, were randomly assigned to various treatments. To further control for individual differences, other critical variables were used as

59

statistical controls during data analysis. Within collaborative treatments, participants were randomly assigned to their pairs. To control for the non-existence of zero-history dyads, the extent of existing relationship between the participants, if any, was measured (Appendix E).

A sample size analysis using the technique suggested in MacCallum et al. (1996) was conducted to identify a sufficient power to achieve an acceptable Type II error level. Degree of freedom for multiple scenarios was conducted using the procedure suggested by Rigdon (1994) as well as dummy models in LISREL. This analysis yielded a minimum sample size of 52 for medium power of 0.5 ($\alpha = 0.05$) for each treatment. For hypothesis testing in a controlled environment, medium power is deemed acceptable. Fan (2003) also shows that for latent growth modeling analysis, small sample sizes are adequate for detecting medium group differences.

4.7.1. Participant Incentive

To participate in the research study and to provide motivation for appropriate participation, participants were given the following incentives: learning Microsoft Excel and Excel project credit in their final grade. Consistent with human subject's requirements, students were given an option to opt out of participation in the study.

Participants were offered Excel training using methodology used in organizations, thus, providing them with an opportunity to experiance how organizations work. The incentive included learning Excel. They were also given Excel course credit for participating in the experiment. Given the logitudinal nature of the experiment, this was necessary to ensure participation through out the study.

Monetary incentives[2] to the top three performing pariticpants or groups within each treatment were also offered. Awards were given to the top three performers in the individual treatments and top three dyads in collaboration treatments (1st - $30.00, 2nd - $20.00 and 3rd - $15.00). A total of 12 prizes were awarded. This was done to ensure motivation for appropriate pariticipation during the experiment.

---

[2] Monetary incentives were sponsored by the Executive MBA department at the Terry College of Business, University of Georgia

4.8. Experimental Procedure

All participants, either in pairs or alone (depending on the treatment), went through a comprehensive Excel 2003 training. The training was divided into three sessions of 75 minutes each. Figure 9 shows the experimental procedure for the four treatments. The physical setting for all treatments was restricted to two commonly used labs designed for software training. Appendix B describes the details of each training session. Procedures are overviewed in this section. The content is same across all treatments, but different for three training sessions.

Treatments	Microsoft Excel 2003 End-User Training							
VM + Practice	Pre-test	Introduction	Working with existing workbooks	Observation 1	Analyzing and managing data	Observation 2	Writing formulas	Observation 3
WBCT								
VM + Pairs								
WBCT + Pairs								
	{Time 0}		{Time 1 – 75 min}		{Time 2 – 75 min}		{Time 3 – 75 min}	

Figure 9: Experimental Procedure

Broadly, the participants go though an initial introduction session followed by three training sessions as shown in Figure 9. The introduction session outlines the roles and responsibilities of the participants and is used to collect pre-training data. The rest of the sessions include the actual training session and collection of post-training data. Each is discussed below. Before participating in the experiment, participants were required to sign a consent form as shown in Appendix F.

4.8.1. Experiment Process

The key activities in the introduction phase include pre-test, pre-training questionnaire administration, introduction to the experiment as well as setting the agenda for the rest of the experimental activities. This provides an opportunity for the subjects to concretely relate to the learning task. To control for individual differences in self-efficacy and motivation to learn, the introduction included a questionnaire capturing these constructs.

61

A fifteen question pre-test (Appendix A), representative of the entire training, was initially administered to the participants. Only participants performing below 35% in this pre-test were subsequently used in data analysis. This is a process that has been used in the previous EUT research (Yi et al. (2003) use 40%), and has yielded successful results.

Pre-training questionnaire was used to capture their initial self-efficacy and motivation to learn at the beginning of each session. This questionnaire is shown in Appendix E.

For collaboration treatments (LM3 & LM4), participants were assigned to pairs (dyads). The selection of a group size of two was influenced by studies in Education and pair programming, which provided evidence for the effectiveness of dyads. Within each section of the experiment, the instructor, using a random number generator in Excel, randomly assigned participants to a pair. In case participants were not present in the introduction session or decided not to participate, pairs were randomly formed in the lab session. In sections with odd number of students, three participants were assigned to one group. This group was eliminated in data analysis.

During the introduction session, participants were introduced to their pairs. They were also allowed to converse with each other for 5 minutes. Pairs were also introduced to initial collaboration structures by taking then through the guidelines listed in their workbooks (Appendix D). The focus here was to make sure that they understand their roles as dyads. These pairs were fixed for the rest of the experimental session.

The introduction phase was followed three training phases. Each of the phases involved training on Excel, with the content of time 2 and time 3 building on the previous one. The first phase trained participants on *working with existing workbooks*. The second phase, building on the first one, trained participants on *analyzing and managing data* in Excel while the third phase, building on the second one, trained participants on *writing formulas* in Excel. The learning method for the participants depended on their treatment condition. Each training phase was followed by observation phase for data collection. These are both described below.

4.8.2. Training

All participants were provided with a workbook, which contained space for notes, elementK guide (for the WBCT treatments), space to write questions (for collaboration

62

treatments) and a checklist of topics covered. Workbooks for the first session of each of the four treatments are attached in Appendix D. The workbooks for the rest of the sessions were similar and are available upon request from the author. Since the lab exercise changes for the WBCT treatments, they have been highlighted in the workbook in Appendix D.

The experimental design had four treatments (LM1-4), each providing a different combination of treatments. Participants were randomly assigned to any of these treatments. All participants were be encouraged to take notes, which is considered as a form of symbolic retention enhancement (Yi et al. 2001). Participants were asked to submit a copy of their notes at the end of each session for each treatment. Analysis of these notes provided a further insight into the process and impact of symbolic retention, though this analysis was not considered for the purpose of this dissertation.

Within each treatment appropriation support was also provided, but limited to helping participants in groups understand the WBCT or collaboration guidelines. Appropriation supported was primarily focused on understanding the experimental procedure and any technical questions relating to the WBCT. No support was given for queries regarding Excel learning content. Each treatment is described below.

The first treatment emulates a traditional classroom or training session. Participants were instructed in a training room though a behavioral modeling supported video demonstration. Following the session, participants were given time for practice. No guidelines were given for the practice. This session served as the baseline for the rest of the treatments.

The second treatment operationalizes behavioral modeling as well as enactive learning though technology-mediation. This treatment uses elementK for training. After training, instead of practice, participants were given structured lab sessions and feedback in the form of correct answers that further operationalized enactive learning. A comparison with the second treatment would help isolate the increment benefit of enactive learning in a technology-mediation.

The other two treatments replicate the earlier two treatments while adding paired learning. In the third treatment, video demonstration was followed by a period where dyads would follow the process of reciprocal questioning. The details of the technique are descriebd in their workbook in Appendix D. Following this, the dyads in the third treatment worked together in the practice session using guidelines of reciprocal questioning techniques presented in the workbook.

In the fourth treatment, participants of the dyads went through elementK independently. Following this, participants went though the process of reciprocal questioning. Finally, dyads worked together to finish a structured lab. In this, after discussing the steps, one person acts as the driver and the second person acts as the checker. A comparison of these treatments with their counterpart gives an idea of the incremental benefit of paired learning.

The design also ensured minimum overlap and interaction between experimental treatments of collaboration and WBCT.

4.8.3. Observation

During the post-training stage, participants were required to fill a questionnaire on their experience of the training and take a test to measure their learning and fill a questionnaire to measure their self-efficacy measures. The questionnaire also had measures for intermediate variables needed for the study (post-training questionnaire is shown in Appendix F). These measures are explained above. The test has measures for the dependent variables described earlier (Appendix G).

Multiple objective measurements are also included to check for treatment manipulation. First, the participants had to return the workbook provided to them. This workbook contained a checklist of topics covered, which the participants had to check as they went through the workbook. It also contained space to write questions during the collaboration treatments. The participants were also asked to note time spent on each activity set. Finally, e-learning participants were asked to submit the results their lab exercise. The experimenter collected these items.

4.9. Experimental roles

4.9.1. Instructor

An instructor was involved in creating the video for the vicarious learning treatments. This instructor had been training students in computer software for six years. The instructor was also the designated instructor for the class from which the students were sampled. The instructor was provided, by the researcher, with a detailed script that was used to create the video (Appendix B).

4.9.2. Experimenter

One person besides the researcher was used during the study in the role of the experimenter. He was a doctoral student in the Management Information Systems program. He volunteered to participate. Each experimenter ran a group of participants through the experimental treatments. Experimenters were assigned based on convenience, with the researcher handling most of the sessions. The second experimenter was taken through a training session to ensure 1) their competence in using the technology, 2) clarity of scripts and 3) a basic consistency in approach.

Their primary experimenter role involved carrying out procedures in all the treatments, across all periods and administering the surveys. A detailed script was used to perform these duties (Appendix C). In addition, experimenters were responsible for recording time. One or two teaching assistants assisted the experimenters during the sessions. Their actions were at the discretion of the experimenters. The teaching assistants assisted in handing out and collecting workbooks and headphones.

Another responsibility of the experimenter was to keep a journal of observations of the performance during the experimental sessions. This journal provided an independent source of information for understanding the study results and assessing the training program. However, qualitative analysis of these journals was not formally undertaken as a part of this dissertation.

Experimenters, in their restricted capacity, also acted as facilitators in case of a query by a participant. Such appropriation support was restricted only to helping participants troubleshoot the WBCT and collaboration guidelines involved. Experimenters recorded such support in their journal when it occurred. As expected, this was not substantial.

4.10. Data Collection

Three forms of data collection were used in the study. First, participants were requested to return the filled workbooks. These contained data regarding the topics covered by the participants, collaboration questions, time spent and the outcome of the lab exercise.

Second, participants were asked to complete a questionnaire. All questionnaire data was collected using a web-based survey. All participants had access to the internet, and used it for all university activities, ranging from registration, to grade check and housing. Research done comparing various methods of data collection shows that there is no significant difference between the factors among methods, thus reducing the risk of method bias (Cobanoglu et al. 2001). Researchers have also suggest the use of web-based data collection for two reasons. First, when all participants have access to the internet, not only does this method reduce cost, it also increases response rates of valid data points. Secondly, since web-based surveys code the data automatically, eliminating the hand-coding, it saves coding errors and the researchers time and resources (Cobanoglu et al. 2001; Klassen et al. 2001). Web-based survey was done using well-established industry recognized software (www.zoomerang.com).

Third, participants were asked some open-ended questions. This provided valuable qualitative insight into the learning process. A detailed analysis of this data was not included as a part of the dissertation but is used to help explain the results.

4.11. Hypothesis testing

Hypothesis testing in a quasi-experiment involves a prior statement of the causal statement followed by data analysis. Below we state the hypothesis and the proposed data analysis method.

4.11.1. Hypotheses

The hypotheses listed below are based on the theoretical development in Chapter 3. All of these were tested after controlling for covariates described above.

The WBCT used in this experiment is based on a social cognitive theory. In Section 3.2.3.1. five structural dimensions of such systems that enhance learning are described: smaller task focus, restiveness, learner-centered activity, feedback & learning guidance and interactivity. Drawing on the arguments presented in that section, we state:

H1 (for each learning outcome): *Individuals in WBCT treatments will perform better on learning outcomes when compared to non-WBCT treatments. (LM2 would do better than LM1, LM3 will do better than LM4: See Figure 7).*

Paired teams create an environment where participants gain social understanding through observation and reflection. They bring in their own understanding and exchange it with their pair. They also share experiences with each other and enhance motivation. Finally, pairs are also able to assist each other in case of queries. Thus, and drawing the from literature summarized in section 2.2 and social development theory, we state

H2 (for each learning outcome): *Individuals in paired treatments will perform better on learning outcomes when compared to non-paired treatments. (LM3, LM4 will do better than LM1, LM2: See Figure 7)*

In the treatment combining e-learning and collaboration, participants independently went though WBCT training followed by interaction based on reciprocal questioning technique. The treatment was designed such that combination of the structural dimensions provided a consistent spirit of learning. Drawing on the theoretical foundations argued earlier, we expect that each treatment will continue to have their independent effect on learning outcomes. Thus, we state

H3 (for each learning outcome): *Individuals in combined treatment will perform better on learning outcomes when compared to other treatments. (LM4 will do better than LM1, LM2, LM3: See Figure 7)*

According to AST, the impact of the above structures is mediated through the level of appropriation of these structures. The extent of appropriation is determined by measuring the faithfulness and attitude towards WBCT use of technology treatments and using team dimensions measured in paired treatments. Thus, drawing on the conceptual model, the effects of

67

the above mentioned treatments would be dependent on the faithfulness of appropriation of the structures. Thus, we state

> **H4 (for each learning outcome)**: *Faithfulness of appropriation of structures in learning methods will have a positive correlation with learning outcomes: a) technology-mediation, b) collaboration.*

The idea of structure being continuously produced and reproduced through action also leads to another significant aspect of structuration, that of routinisation. As limited empirical research exists using AST longitudinally, anecdotal evidence from group development literature (Chidambaram et al. 1996; Chidambaram et al. 1997) is used for deductions. Based on this literature as the learning process moves forward in time, the level of appropriation for the above structures will change. Since the level of appropriation of the WBCT and collaboration structures defines the structural potential for learning outcomes, changes in this will induce changes in learning outcomes achieved over time. Thus, we hypothesize,

> **H5 (for each learning outcome)**: *Rate of change in appropriation of structures in learning methods over time will have a positive correlation with the rate of change in learning outcomes over time: a) technology-mediation, b) collaboration.*

4.11.2. Data analysis

The treatment effects of the three independent variables (H1 to H3) can be assessed by performing a multivariate repeated measure analysis of variance (MANOVA) analysis on the means of the learning outcomes. Rao (1952) first introduced multivariate repeated measures analysis of variance. Since then, this analysis has found extensive usage. Among the most extensive reviews of this technique appears to be that of Lovie (1981). MANOVA is a statistical inference procedure used to assess statistical differences between groups (treatments). In MANOVA, the null hypothesis tested is the equality of vectors of means on multiple dependent variables across groups. The unique aspect of MANOVA is that the variate optimally combines the multiple dependent measures into a single value that maximizes the differences across groups (Hair 1998). Repeated measures are used when repeated observations are taken of the same subject. Analysis of variance (ANOVA) is carried out to see effects on each of the dependent variables. The purpose of analysis of variance is to test the significant difference between means. If statistically significant differences in means are found, the treatment effect can be concluded.

The proposed method of statistical analysis for hypothesis H4 and H5 is structural equation modeling (SEM). This study collects data across four similar groups across three time periods. Thus, the interest is not only in the treatment effect of the variables, but also in the changes in the dependent and independent variables across time, and how these changes correlate.

There are two prominent reasons why this method is used. First, SEM uses regression for explanation of variation in dependent variables to know how well the predictors explain the criterion variable and which specific predictors is most important in predicting. Second, in most behavioral science research, predictors are not completely orthogonal. Further, given the physiological nature of end-user training research variables, such an assumption would be incorrect. SEM techniques allow for the correlations between the predictor variables, addressing this issue (Maruyama 1997). Two important extensions to this technique will be used: stacked group analysis and latent growth modeling.

Stacked models have been used relatively infrequently in psychological research, especially MIS experimental research. Stacked models are models with multiple groups, but with subsequent groups being a subset of the fully identified or incomplete information group. For example, there may be an extra characteristic or question asked to some respondents or, as in this case, there are experimental subjects that are compared to control subsets. If there are several additional indicator variables available in one of the groups, these can be utilized in a stacked group model (Hayduk 1996; Maruyama 1997). Hayduk (1996) identifies four benefits of using stacked groups: 1) identifying under-identified models, 2) controlling for unmeasured variables, 3) testing the sufficiency of known mechanisms and 4) integrating model segments from diverse data sets. In this analysis, we use stacked groups to compare across different experimental treatments. The complete information treatment (LM4) will be stacked with incomplete information treatments (LM3, LM2) and the control group (LM1).

Latent growth modeling (LGM) is a statistical technique with the ability to analyze a longitudinally measured variable by analyzing its constant and the growth effect (Lance et al. 2000). In this study, the constant shows the initial faithfulness of appropriation, while the growth

69

shows the change in faithfulness between two periods. Duncan (1999) summarizes four shortcomings in the traditional approaches to studying change that are overcome by the LGM. First, traditional approaches assume means to be zero. However, in models depicting change, sample means carry useful statistical information needed to estimate both inter- and intra-individual differences in change. Second, traditional approaches fail to provide adequate generalizations to more than two points in time. This also constrains the growth curves to linear models. Third, by controlling initial levels (including autoregressive effect), traditional models eliminates all predictors except those that predict changes in rank order of observations over time. This is a disadvantage when studying monotonically stable phenomenon (Meredith et al. 1990) where the rank order is same although significant change at individual and group level is occurring. Finally, when "*cause*" is the issue, it is questionable whether autoregressive effect is true casual effect.

The two extensions of SEM are applied simultaneously. A statistically significant path coefficient will show that a relationship exists, as predicted by the hypothesis.

4.12. *Pilot Studies*

An initial pilot study was carried out with three objectives 1) test the technology, 2) test the procedure and 3) provide content validity of the questionnaires. This study was done with business undergraduate students in the Introduction to MIS (Honors section). The study was done for a single session. Since these people already knew basic Excel, content related to creating a workspace and data consolidation in Excel was used in treatments. LM2 and LM4 treatments were focused on in this study. Given the limited sample size, statistical results could not be computed. The results of the pilot study confirmed the use of technology and procedure. Based on the feedback from the study, instruments and procedures were tweaked. The study did not find a difference in the learning outcomes for collaborative and individual treatments. Upon analysis, it was found that the collaborative treatments did not appropriate the collaborative structures faithfully. Based on this result, reciprocal questioning as a technique was added to directly influence the underlying collaborative structures.

An additional pilot study, testing all the treatments and updated instruments was also conducted. The results were used to further fine-tune the instruments and procedures, as needed.

70

This pilot study was carried out using business undergraduate student from Introduction to MIS (Honors section) before they were exposed to Excel. No significance test was done due to the small sample size.

4.13. Summary

This chapter discussed the research methodology used in the present study. The research design was controlled laboratory experiments, utilizing a two-factor design including the dichotomous independent variables of e-learning and collaboration. E-learning was conducted using WBCT tool called elementK. Collaboration was operationalized by putting students in pairs. Hypothesis were constructed for testing regarding the treatment effects, process effects and longitudinal effects on individual learning outcomes.

Microsoft Excel 2003 was selected as the end-user application to be learned. Business undergraduate students in the Introduction to MIS class were selected as participants to the experiment. Data analysis strategy for each the hypothesis was also described in this chapter. The chapter concluded with a discussion of the pilot study used to validate the instruments and procedures as well as to provide an initial assessment of hypothesis.

5. Analysis of Results

This chapter presents analytical procedures and findings for the study. The chapter is organized around the steps in the analysis process. Broadly, two analysis techniques were used for data analysis.

The first section presents data describing the experimental session and subjects. Methods of filtering data are also presented. Special attention was given to uncovering factors which were not randomly distributed among treatments. Microsoft Excel 2003 SP 2 was primarily used for data analyses.

The second section presents a test of the primary assumptions for the analysis. This section presents results of factor and reliability analysis. The dependent variables involved in the primary analysis were also checked to assess potential violations of analysis of variance model assumptions.

The third section describes a brief overview of the first statistical technique used, i.e., repeated measures multivariate analysis of variance. It also describes the tests of assumptions, information on covariates, manipulation check followed by the multivariate and univariate tests.

Section four presents details on hypothesis testing of the hypothesis H1-H3. This is done using pair wise comparison of means estimated after the effects of covariates. This section also presents tests for hypothesis H1-H3. SPSS 12.2 was used for data analyses reported in second, third and fourth sections.

Section five presents the second statistical analysis i.e. structural equation modeling (SEM) using stacked models in a latent growth model. The section also covers the literature leading to the development of the SEM model.

Section six describes the results of the SEM analysis and hypothesis testing for H4 and H5. The analysis combines the above findings to provide a holistic analysis. LISREL 8.72 was used for data analysis reported in section five and six.

Section seven highlights some post-hoc analysis carried out by the author. The post-hoc analysis covered analyses not covered in the hypothesis testing.

The last section briefly summarizes the entire set of findings.

5.1. Experimental Sample and Subjects

This section reviews data describing subjects and sessions. Distributions of key variables were tested for successful randomization across experimental treatments.

5.1.1. Sample Frame and Sample

The sample frame for the experiment were students from the Introduction to Management Information Systems (MIST 2090) spring 2005. The sample frame had 701 students. To be used as a part of the sample for the experiment, students also had to participate in all four experimental sessions. Overall, 597 students attended all four sessions.

In the case of paired treatments, only pairs who attended all four sessions were considered for further analysis. Similar to Johnson et al. (2000), all students were asked to answer a pretest. This pretest contained questions equally spread across the entire contents of the training session. Only participants with less than 35% marks were included for further sampling. The final sample size for subsequent analysis consisted of 432 (~61% of sample frame) students.

5.1.2. Session Descriptive Data

The experiment was conduced in four sessions using four treatment conditions. The first treatment condition (LM1) used a vicarious learning method followed by practice, second treatment (LM2) used web-based computer training method, third treatment (LM3) replicated the first treatment and introduced paired collaboration and the fourth treatment (LM4) replicated the second treatment and introduced paired collaboration to train participants in Microsoft Excel 2003. Table **6** summarizes the data by experimental treatment.

Biographical data: - In all, 435 students who participated fitted the screening criteria (113 students in LM1, 117 in LM2, 85 in LM3 and 120 in LM4). LM3 saw a significant difference in sample size because one of the experimental sessions was conduced late in day and showed significant attrition. The cumulative mean GPA was 3.25 with 60.5 percent females. Most of the students were business majors. A one-way ANOVA and CHI-square confirmed that

73

Table 6: Subject Biographical Data by Treatment

Attribute	VM+Practice (LM1)	WBCT (LM2)	VM+Pairs (LM3)	WBCT+Pairs (LM4)	Overall
Sample size	113	117	85	120	435
BIOGRAPHICAL DATA					
CGPA	3.2	3.26	3.22	3.33	3.25
Gender (%)					
Males	72.6*	56.4	61.2	51.7	60.5*
Females	27.4	43.6	38.8	48.3	39.5
MAJOR (%)					
Accounting	6.19	12.82	10.59	11.67	10.32
Economics	4.42	5.13	3.53	0.83	3.48
Finance	10.62	11.11	9.41	16.67	11.95
Int' Business	6.19	8.55	4.71	7.50	6.74
Management	10.62	11.97	7.06	8.33	9.49
MIS	0.88	0.85	3.53	1.67	1.73
Marketing	13.27	11.11	9.41	21.67	13.87
Real Estate	11.50	8.55	10.59	6.67	9.33
Risk Management	2.65	0.85	1.18	2.50	1.80
Other	33.63	29.06	40.00	22.50	31.30
INDIVIDUAL DIFFERENCES – Aggregates of items					
Outcome expectations	12.17	11.99	12.29	12.33	12.19
Intrinsic motivation	13.57	13.2	13.2	13.9	13.49
Quiz Totals	3.06	2.78	2.73	2.58	2.79
Self-efficacy (Excel)	2.50	2.55	2.40	2.08	2.38
Computer self efficacy	52.96	52.76	51.69	56.04	53.51*
Specific self-efficacy	17.13	18.20	15.86	15.32	16.82
* $p < .05$					

the randomization procedure provided an even distribution of the subjects except for gender differences. LM1 showed a significantly larger number of female participation. Since there exists some empirical evidence regarding the effect of gender on the learning process (Busch 1996), it was included in the analysis as a covariate.

Individual differences:- As a part of the pre-test, students were asked to respond to individual differences questions relating to outcome expectations, intrinsic motivation, self-efficacy, specific self-efficacy and computer self-efficacy. The indicators of these constructs were aggregated to calculate the construct score (see Appendix E). One-way ANOVA tests found no significant differences for the construct means scores at $p<0.05$, except for computer self-efficacy.

Participants who indicated a prior knowledge of Excel were asked to take a quiz on Excel as indicated earlier. A one way ANOVA on quiz totals also resulted in no significant differences between groups.

For paired treatments (LM3 & LM4), participants were also asked the extent to which they know their pair. Of the 205 individuals, over 92% did not know each other at all. In LM4, 3.5% participants knew each other for 48 months or more, with the rest being below 6 months. These did not affect the learning outcomes and were kept in the analyzed data set. No significant differences were found in the individual differences between LM3 and LM4.

In summary, the sample for the study consisted of 435 participants assigned to the four treatments. Random assignment was successful, with two exceptions. First, LM1 had a significantly greater representation of females, and second LM4 participants, on average, had a higher computer self-efficacy. In subsequent analysis, gender was included as a covariate, while Compeau's computer self-efficacy was dropped from the analysis (for a note on the computer self-efficacy measure, please see Section 0).

5.2. Measurement

This section describes the adjustments made to data as well as issues of reliability and validity as they arose during the analysis.

5.2.1. Data Coding

The constructs used to measure learning outcomes were self-efficacy, computer self-efficacy (Excel), specific self-efficacy, satisfaction and quiz score. Three adjustments were made to the data to prepare it for further analysis.

First, items 3, 4 and 5 in self-efficacy were reversed to show a higher value for higher self-efficacy. Second, specific self-efficacy is calculated as a change in the specific self-efficacy score from the initial level.

The third adjustment related to quiz scores. The focus of the research is to keep grade constant while varying learning method (Gates 2005). However, learning, unlike other topics, cannot be repeated. Learning in a specific topic builds on previous classes and gets increasingly difficult. This is also reflected in quiz scores, i.e., the quiz scores are a combination of difficulty of the content and the content learned. We, thus, used the level of perceived difficulty to adjust the quiz scores. Variants of this technique are used in standardized test like GRE and GMAT (http://www.ets.org). In this specific case, we used the individual's perception of difficulty for the 2nd and 3rd session (measured using a 4-item instrument in Appendix F) as compared to the 1st session and multiplied the quiz sores with these perceptions. On an average, the second quiz score was multiplied by 1.49 and the third by 1.51. All calculations were done at the individual level of analysis. This ensured that all the new quiz scores were evaluated at the same difficulty level and the quiz results were not biased for different content.

Finally, it is important to note that satisfaction construct continues to be negatively measured, i.e., higher mean score represents a lower satisfaction for satisfaction construct.

5.2.2. Construct Validity

Construct validity is defined broadly as the extent to which an operationalization measures the concept it is supposed to measure (Cook et al. 1979). A review of literature in this area for instrument development by Goodhue (1998) suggests using the framework proposed by Bagozzi et al. (1982). He suggests that its six concerns highlighted by Bagozzi are a superset containing all other author's concerns. These are 1) theoretical meaningfulness of constructs 2) observational meaningfulness of concepts 3) discriminant validity 4) convergent validity 5)

Table 7: Rotated Factor Matrix for Dependent Variables

Rotated Factor Matrix

Item	Time A				Time B				Time C				Time D			
	CSE	IM	OE	Self-efficacy	CSE	Difficulty	Satisfaction	Self-efficacy	CSE	Difficulty	Satisfaction	Self-efficacy	CSE	Difficulty	Satisfaction	Self-efficacy
SE 2(Reversed)	-0.055	0.001	-0.077	0.892	0.144	0.009	-0.042	0.760	0.079	-0.059	-0.113	0.844	0.138	-0.065	-0.087	0.831
SE 4(Reversed)	-0.098	0.063	-0.095	0.597	0.103	0.012	0.025	0.827	0.078	-0.028	-0.085	0.814	0.197	-0.021	-0.093	0.898
SE 5(Reversed)	-0.055	-0.200	-0.083	0.582	0.065	-0.006	0.049	0.589	0.107	-0.051	0.001	0.472	0.045	-0.080	0.035	0.559
CSE 3	0.574	-0.107	-0.015	0.171	0.626	-0.220	0.069	0.153	0.687	-0.057	-0.104	0.160	0.722	-0.102	-0.068	0.140
CSE 4	0.741	0.053	-0.028	-0.077	0.750	-0.127	-0.099	0.116	0.798	-0.171	-0.144	0.093	0.820	-0.120	-0.129	0.132
CSE 5	0.600	0.085	-0.030	-0.141	0.814	0.011	-0.049	-0.017	0.797	-0.046	-0.059	0.009	0.823	-0.100	-0.150	0.044
CSE 6	0.665	0.109	0.211	-0.159	0.804	-0.054	-0.044	0.118	0.813	-0.129	-0.070	0.069	0.855	-0.096	-0.111	0.121
CSE 7	0.753	0.103	-0.016	0.047	0.752	-0.072	0.050	0.097	0.750	-0.095	-0.085	0.090	0.762	-0.099	-0.144	0.117
CSE 8	0.573	-0.047	-0.054	-0.076	0.705	-0.139	-0.031	0.088	0.710	-0.084	-0.036	0.117	0.709	-0.147	-0.077	0.078
CSE 9	0.530	0.120	0.198	-0.187	0.751	-0.143	-0.124	0.072	0.768	-0.120	-0.047	-0.008	0.775	-0.154	-0.156	0.006
CSE 10	0.702	0.024	0.138	-0.041	0.733	-0.161	-0.057	0.072	0.745	-0.142	-0.178	0.079	0.767	-0.131	-0.197	0.060
Satis 1	n/a	n/a	n/a	n/a	-0.057	0.013	0.777	0.030	-0.122	0.038	0.887	-0.054	-0.190	0.017	0.828	-0.072
Satis 2	n/a	n/a	n/a	n/a	-0.095	0.135	0.784	0.095	-0.172	0.158	0.767	-0.021	-0.172	0.087	0.743	0.020
Satis 4	n/a	n/a	n/a	n/a	-0.005	-0.041	0.718	-0.063	-0.106	0.118	0.756	-0.124	-0.201	0.037	0.814	-0.069
Difficult 1	n/a	n/a	n/a	n/a	-0.152	0.925	0.042	0.012	-0.190	0.894	0.126	-0.038	-0.182	0.886	0.086	-0.082
Difficult 2	n/a	n/a	n/a	n/a	-0.158	0.866	0.018	-0.001	-0.180	0.859	0.088	-0.036	-0.159	0.884	0.032	-0.038
Difficult 3	n/a	n/a	n/a	n/a	-0.132	0.873	-0.009	0.041	-0.103	0.859	0.051	-0.079	-0.135	0.854	-0.019	-0.077
Difficult 4	n/a	n/a	n/a	n/a	-0.192	0.891	0.079	-0.041	-0.117	0.919	0.126	-0.064	-0.166	0.916	0.093	-0.056
OE 2	0.056	0.214	0.968	-0.116	n/a	n/a	n/a	n/a	n/a	n/a	n/a	n/a	n/a	n/a	n/a	n/a
OE 4	0.078	0.337	0.716	-0.216	n/a	n/a	n/a	n/a	n/a	n/a	n/a	n/a	n/a	n/a	n/a	n/a
IM 1	0.066	0.866	0.146	-0.009	n/a	n/a	n/a	n/a	n/a	n/a	n/a	n/a	n/a	n/a	n/a	n/a
IM 2	0.039	0.817	0.156	-0.094	n/a	n/a	n/a	n/a	n/a	n/a	n/a	n/a	n/a	n/a	n/a	n/a
IM 3	0.069	0.876	0.175	-0.026	n/a	n/a	n/a	n/a	n/a	n/a	n/a	n/a	n/a	n/a	n/a	n/a

Note: SE=Self efficacy, CSE= Computer self-efficacy, Satis = Satisfaction, Difficul = perceived difficulty, OE=Outcome expectation,

IM=Intrinsic motivation

Factors calculated based on Eigen value cutoff of 1

77

internal consistency and 6) nomologicial validity. Since this study uses existing measures rather than scale development (except for team dimensions), this section focuses on the dicriminant validity, convergent validity and internal consistency with necessary digressions (Boudreau et al. 2001). For details on the theoretical development of appropriation of team dimensions scale please refer to Appendix J.

5.2.2.1. Discriminant and Convergent validity

Discriminant validity is concerned with the extent to which participants respond similarly to different constructs. This is usually demonstrated using an exploratory factor analysis (EFA). Convergent validity is the degree to which multiple attempts to measure the same concepts are in agreement (Bagozzi et al. 1991). It can be assessed by inspecting the estimates of item variance, i.e., is there agreement among the measures of the same trait. This is usually assessed by looking at the factor loading of the measures (Bagozzi et al. 1991). Thus, discriminant and convergent validity was assessed by verifying item factor loading with the factor it is measuring is maximally different from other constructs and maximally similar to the construct it is measuring.

Table **7** shows the factor matrix using maximum likelihood with varimax rotation for dependent variables and covariates for all pretest (time A) and the post training observations (time B-D). Due to inconsistent loadings across constructs, the following items were dropped because of low validity – self-efficacy 2, self-efficacy 3, computer self-efficacy 1, computer self-efficacy 2, satisfaction 3, outcome expectation 1 and outcome expectation 3. Except for CSE items, all of the items were reversed with respect to others and such items have been known to have convergence issues (see appendix F for items of the constructs).

Table **8** shows a similar matrix for intermediate variables. These constructs measure appropriations of the experimental treatments. Appropriation is viewed at as a manipulation check for the first half of the analysis and then as exogenous variables in the structural equation modeling section. Faithfulness, respect and comfort deal with appropriation of WBCT, while collaboration items dealt with appropriation of collaboration structures. Two important points need to be highlighted here. First, the variables *"respect of WBCT"* and *"comfort with WBCT"* did not load as separate constructs. This is not surprising as they are both attitudinal constructs and was conceptualized as such in chapter 3. Thus, they were combined into one construct – attitude towards using WBCT (Poole et al. 1989a). Second, rspt1, rspt2 and comf2 items did not show high convergence and were dropped from subsequent analysis.

Table 8: Rotated Factor Matrix for Intermediate Variables

	Time B			Time C			Time D		
For LM2 and LM4									
Factor	Attitude	Faith	Collab	Attitude	Faith	Collab	Attitude	Faith	Collab
Faith 1	-0.10	0.77	n/a	-0.21	0.78	n/a	-0.15	0.68	n/a
Faith 2	-0.13	0.63	n/a	-0.18	0.58	n/a	-0.17	0.64	n/a
Faith 3	-0.16	0.71	n/a	-0.17	0.83	n/a	-0.14	0.72	n/a
Faith 4	-0.17	0.67	n/a	-0.08	0.67	n/a	-0.15	0.69	n/a
Rspt 2	0.51	-0.24	n/a	0.58	-0.25	n/a	0.65	-0.23	n/a
Rspt 3	-0.68	0.16	n/a	-0.74	0.17	n/a	-0.72	0.34	n/a
Comf 1	0.80	-0.10	n/a	0.83	-0.08	n/a	0.86	0.03	n/a
Comf 3	0.88	-0.01	n/a	0.92	-0.09	n/a	0.91	-0.04	n/a
For LM3 and LM4									
Collab 1	n/a	n/a	0.57	n/a	n/a	0.66	n/a	n/a	0.70
Collab 2	n/a	n/a	0.57	n/a	n/a	0.77	n/a	n/a	0.78
Collab 3	n/a	n/a	0.81	n/a	n/a	0.83	n/a	n/a	0.88
Collab 4	n/a	n/a	0.82	n/a	n/a	0.87	n/a	n/a	0.88
Collab 5	n/a	n/a	0.68	n/a	n/a	0.80	n/a	n/a	0.91
Collab 6	n/a	n/a	0.86	n/a	n/a	0.88	n/a	n/a	0.86

Faith=Faithfulness of use of WBCT, Rspt=Respect of WBCT, comf=Comfort with WBCT, collab=Collaboration

Based on an examination of the factor matrix's for dependent and intermediate variables, the items used in the analysis load dominantly on the construct they are representing and show low levels of cross loadings. Thus, it can be concluded that sufficient discriminent and convergent validity was achieved.

5.2.2.2. Internal Consistency or Reliability

Table 9: Construct Reliability across Time

Construct	Time A	Time B	Time C	Time D
Extrinsic Motivation	0.852	NA	NA	NA
Intrinsic Motivation	0.890	NA	NA	NA
CSE	0.872	0.911	0.921	0.934
Self-efficacy	0.714	0.773	0.756	0.815
Satisfaction	NA	0.796	0.86	0.859
Difficulty	NA	0.946	0.946	0.946
Faithfulness	NA	0.801	0.818	0.798
Attitude	NA	0.808	0.853	0.866
Collaboration	NA	0.865	0.914	0.933

Reliability concerns the extent to which measurements are repeatable (Nunnally et al. 1975), or have a relatively high component of true score and relatively low component of random error (Carmines et al. 1979). Table 7 and Table 8 show the extent to which the same measure is repeatable, i.e., the items load on the same construct at Time B, Time C and Time D. Reliability, as measured by of a multi-item measures, is often estimated by Chronbach's alpha. Table 9 shows the alpha values for the constructs used in this study across time. These values are consistently >.70, showing good reliability of the constructs.

5.2.3. A Note on Excel Self-efficacy Measure

This study used three measures of excel self-efficacy, two focusing on the general level of efficacy in Excel and one focusing on the specific self-efficacy of the various concepts in Excel. The first measure derives from the measure developed by Compeau et al. (1995b). Two basic concerns exists in the measurement of self-efficacy using this measure as highlighted by Compeau et al. (2005).

First, some recent studies suggest the evidence of multidimensionality in this measure. Gundlach et al. (2000) argued this because the measure reflects *"human-assisted"* and *"individual"* self-efficacy measure. Based on the items of the survey, a second factor dealing with the self-efficacy of getting assistance from the source is included in the measure. This becomes extremely critical in training and learning scenarios.

Second, a comparison of results from Compeau et al. (1995a) and Marcolin et al. (2000) measurement using this scale do not show changes in the means of self-efficacy over time, nor did they converge to one specific level. In both these studies, the post-training CSE was not significantly different from pre-training. This is especially true for a student population (Compeau et al. 2005), as is the case in the current study. These results are also confirmed by the current study, where Compeau's general CSE measure did not show a significant change over time or difference between groups.

Confronted with these two issues, Compeau's general CSE measure was dropped from subsequent analysis. This was possible because of the presence of a complementary validated general self-efficacy measure (derived from Hollenbeck et al. (1987)). This measure has been extensively used in psychology literature.

Specific self-efficacy measure also is designed on the same guidelines and thus, suffers from similar issues. Among the other big concerns with that measure is that it treats various activities in Excel with the same weighted difficulty. However, in this work, we continue to use specific self-efficacy as an exploratory construct to understand its behavior. Though results of the same are reported, conclusions are not drawn in depth based on this measure.

5.3. *Statistical Analysis 1: Repeated Measures MANOVA*

The first statistical technique used to test hypothesis H1-H3 is multivariate repeated measures analysis of variance (MANOVA). MANOVA has a rich tradition of use in experimental research to compare multivatriate data across groups. The outputs shown below are derived from SPSS GLM (multivariate option) analysis.

It was determined prior to data collection that the criterion for rejecting the null form of the hypothesis would be set at an alpha level of 0.05. The reason for 0.05 level was to follow the convention used in behavioral research in general and in information systems research in particular. Hypothesis which met this criterion were described as supported.

5.3.1. Test of Assumptions

Hair (1998) outlines three assumptions that underlie the appropriate use of repeated measures MANOVA. These assumptions include independence of samples, multivariate normality and equality of variance/covariance matrix across treatments.

Independent random samples: Like all statistical analysis, it is assumed that the subjects are randomly distributed. This means that the various replications of the sample are independent. This was accomplished by randomly assigning treatment to subjects. Care was taken to broadly have equal number of participants per experimental treatment.

Multivariate Normality: The assumption of multivariate normality means that not only must the variables individually be normally distributed, but that their conjoint distributions must also be normal. Although this is a necessary assumption, it has been demonstrated that the multivariate analysis of variance is robust with respect to this assumption (Neter et al. 1985). That is, even if this assumption is not satisfied, the Type 1 error rate is not materially affected (Gardner 2001). However, to check for normality, Levene's test for equality of error variance was carried out (see Table **10**). Except for satisfaction measure in the second training period, no substantial deviations were observed. Thus, it was felt that the condition was satisfactorily met.

81

Equality of covariance/variance matrix: This assumption of MANOVA is the equivalence of covariance matrixes across groups. Though it is desirable to have this test, a violation of this test does not significantly affect the results, especially when the sample sizes are approximately equal (Hair 1998; Neter et al. 1985). However, Box test for testing this assumption was carried out and differences were found to be significant. The equality of covariance/variance matrix condition was not satisfied. However, since research shows that this is not a mandatory condition for MANOVA, especially when treatment sizes are almost same, we did not investigate it further at this time.

Table 10: Levene's Test of Equality of Error Variances

	F	*df1*	*df2*	*Sig.*
ΔB_SSE	.682	3	431	.564
ΔC_SSE	.292	3	431	.831
ΔD_SSE	.504	3	431	.680
B_SE	.489	3	431	.690
C_SE	.361	3	431	.781
D_SE	.837	3	431	.474
B_TOTAL	1.334	3	431	.263
C_TOTAL	.767	3	431	.513
D_TOTAL	.878	3	431	.452
B_SATIS	2.577	3	431	.053
C_SATIS	4.538	3	431	.004
D_SATIS	1.455	3	431	.226

The prefix A, B, C, D represent the time periods. SSE= specific self-efficacy, SE = self-efficacy, Total = quiz score, Satis = Satisfaction
Tests the null hypothesis that the error variance of the dependent variable is equal across groups. Design: Intercept+A_IM+GENDER+A_SE+A_OE+Group

Table 11: Box's Test of Equality of Covariance Matrices

Box's M	337.407
F	1.370
df1	234
df2	345916.777
Sig.	.000

Tests the null hypothesis that the observed covariance matrices of the dependent variables are equal across groups. Design: Intercept+A_IM+GENDER+A_SE+A_OE+Group

5.3.2. Covariates

The earlier analysis of group randomization showed that gender was significantly different between treatment groups. In addition, initial levels of motivation and self-efficacy have been shown to be important covariates in Compeau et al. (1995a) and Yi et al. (2001). These were measured in the pretest and used as covariates in subsequent analysis.

5.3.3. Manipulation Check

Apart from observations by the experimental facilitators for manipulation and other observational checks described earlier, students were also asked to fill in a survey regarding their appropriation of technology and/or collaboration on a scaled on 1-7 (strongly disagree – strongly agree). Across the respective treatments, participants showed high faithfulness (average score per item 6.2) and good collaboration (average score per item 4.7). The appropriation results suggest that the students, on average, performed the tasks as laid out by the experimenter. Thus, it was concluded that experimental manipulations of getting good appropriation of structures was successful.

Students were also asked to self-assess their use of elementK and collaboration time with their partner outside the experiment sessions. All students (except 4) included in the analysis followed the guidelines and did not use elementK or collaborate outside the class. These four did not show significant difference with respect to other participants.

5.3.4. Multivariate and Univariate Tests

Given that learning outcomes were at the individual level, individual level data was used for this analysis. Dependent variables included in learning outcomes were specific self-efficacy, self-efficacy, quiz score and satisfaction. We choose Pallai's trace as the F-statistic because it is the most robust against any violations of assumptions (Gardner 2001), though other statistic are also significant.

5.3.4.1. Covariate Analysis

Repeated measure multivariate covariate analysis of variance was carried out next. Table 12 summarizes the overall results of the multivariate tests. Overall, all covariates had significant effect on the learning outcomes – intrinsic motivation (Pallai's trace $(4,424)$ =

0.043, p<.001); Gender (Pallai's trace $(4,424)$ = .023, p<.040); self-efficacy (Pallai's trace $(4,424)$ = .676, p<.0001) and initial extrinsic motivation (Pallai's trace $(4,424)$ = .056, p<.0001). After taking into account the effect of these covariates, treatment impact continued to be statistically significant (Pallai's trace $(12,1278)$ = 0.154, p<.0001).

Table 12: Overall Multivariate Tests

	Statistic	Value	F	Hypothesis df	Error df	Sig.	Partial Eta Squared
A_IM	Pillai's Trace	.043	4.814	4.000	424.00	**.001***	.043
GENDER	Pillai's Trace	.023	2.527	4.000	424.00	**.040***	.023
A_SE	Pillai's Trace	.676	221.042	4.000	424.00	**.000***	.676
A_OE	Pillai's Trace	.056	6.310	4.000	424.00	**.000***	.056
Group	Pillai's Trace	.154	5.767	12.000	1278.00	**.000***	.051

* p< 0.05
A_IM= Initial intrinsic motivation, A_SE= Initial self-efficacy, A_OE=Initial extrinsic motivation
Each row F tests the multivariate effect of GROUP(1-LM1,2-LM2,3-LM3,4-LM4). These tests are based on the linearly independent pairwise comparisons among the estimated marginal means.

Table 13: Univariate Tests

Source	Measure	Type III Sum of Squares	df	Mean Square	F	Sig.	Partial Eta Squared
A_IM	sse	328.096	1	328.096	.708	.401	.002
	se	8.727	1	8.727	.466	.495	.001
	score	40.840	1	40.840	3.825	.051	.009
	satis	302.674	1	302.674	17.535	**.000***	.039
GENDR	sse	449.517	1	449.517	.970	.325	.002
	se	1.594	1	1.594	.085	.771	.000
	score	18.431	1	18.431	1.726	.190	.004
	satis	87.908	1	87.908	5.093	**.025***	.012
A_SE	sse	333739.52	1	333739.521	720.053	**.000***	.628
	se	169.556	1	169.556	9.061	**.003***	.021
	score	7.719	1	7.719	.723	.396	.002
	satis	.023	1	.023	.001	.971	.000
A_OE	sse	1045.760	1	1045.760	2.256	.134	.005
	se	152.873	1	152.873	8.170	**.004***	.019
	score	22.997	1	22.997	2.154	.143	.005
	satis	204.963	1	204.963	11.875	**.001***	.027
Group	sse	3647.008	3	1215.669	2.623	**.050***	.018
	se	431.662	3	143.887	7.689	**.000***	.051
	score	302.247	3	100.749	9.436	**.000***	.062
	satis	411.635	3	137.212	7.949	**.000***	.053

* p< 0.05
Source: A_IM= Initial intrinsic motivation, A_SE= Initial self-efficacy, A_OE=Initial
extrinsic motivation, Group=Treatment. Measure: SSE = Specific self-efficacy, SE = Self-
efficacy, score = quiz score, satis = Satisfaction. Each F tests the multivariate effect of
GROUP(1-LM1,2-LM2,3-LM3,4-LM4). These tests are based on the linearly independent
pairwise comparisons among the estimated marginal means.

Univariate covariate analysis of variance for each of the dependent variables was subsequently carried out. Table 13 summarizes the results. All four dependent variables comprised in learning outcomes - specific self-efficacy, self-efficacy, quiz score and satisfaction - showed a significant difference between treatments.

The results also showed that intrinsic motivation had a significant impact on quiz score and satisfaction outcomes. Gender also played a significant part in satisfaction, such that females gave a higher satisfaction score as compared to males. As expected, initial self-efficacy had a strong effect on specific self-efficacy and self-efficacy, while extrinsic motivation had a statistically significant effect on self-efficacy and satisfaction. Thus, the analysis of variance tests showed that there was a statistical difference between the learning outcomes of different treatments. The univariate tests also confirmed that in spite of the statistically significant effects of the covariates on different learning outcomes, treatments effects continued to remain significant after taking into account the effects of the covariates. Next, detailed tests of each hypothesis were carried out.

5.4. Hypothesis Testing (H1-H3)

Tests of means can be performed following a significant F-ratio for treatments. In this section, we first briefly describe the data on the learning outcome constructs across the three treatments. A graph showing the movement of the mean of the construct is presented, followed by an estimated overall mean (mean of means) for each treatment. Each of the four constructs is detailed individually – specific self-efficacy, self-efficacy, quiz score followed by satisfaction from the learning process.

The graph in Figure 10 shows changes in specific self-efficacy mean values over the three treatment periods. The graph shows the highest specific self-efficacy for paired collaboration and WBCT treatment, and the lowest for the control group. Table 14 shows the estimated means across time after controlling for covariates. The highest change in specific self-efficacy is shown in combined treatment (LM4: 44.186)), followed by dyad (LM3: 43.095), WBCT (LM2:42.671) with the lowest in control (LM1: 39.715) treatments.

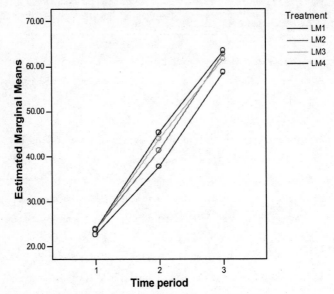

Treatments: LM1 = Control, LM2=WBCT, LM3=dyads, LM4=Combined

Figure 10: Specific Self-Efficacy over Time

Table 14: Mean Estimates of Specific Self-Efficacy

| Measure | Treatments (LMx) x= | Mean of Means | Std. Error | 95% Confidence Interval | |
				Lower Bound	Upper Bound
Specific self-efficacy	1	39.715	1.179	37.397	42.032
	2	42.671	1.153	40.405	44.938
	3	43.095	1.351	40.439	45.751
	4	44.186	1.143	41.939	46.432

Treatments: LM1 = Control, LM2=WBCT, LM3=dyads, LM4=Combined

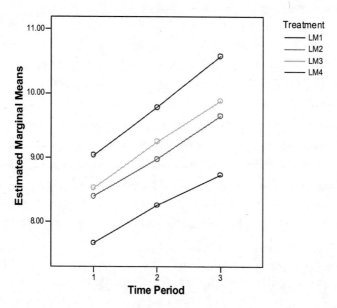

Treatments: LM1 = Control, LM2=WBCT, LM3=dyads, LM4=Combined

Figure 11: Self-efficacy over Time

Table 15: Mean Estimates of Self-Efficacy

Measure	Treatments (LM-x)	Mean of means	Std. Error	95% Confidence Interval	
				Lower Bound	Upper Bound
Self-efficacy	1	8.220	.237	7.754	8.686
	2	9.007	.232	8.551	9.462
	3	9.218	.272	8.685	9.752
	4	9.798	.230	9.347	10.250

Treatments: LM1 = Control, LM2=WBCT, LM3=dyads, LM4=Combined

Figure 11 shows self-efficacy mean values over the three treatment periods. The graph shows the highest specific self-efficacy for paired collaboration and WBCT treatment, and the lowest for the control group. Table 15 shows the estimated means across time after controlling for covariates. The highest in estimated mean of self-efficacy is shown in combined treatment (LM4: 9.798), followed by dyad (LM3: 9.218), WBCT (LM2: 9.007) with the lowest in control (LM1: 8.220) treatments.

The graph in Figure 12 shows quiz scores over the three treatment periods. The graph shows that individuals in the WBCT treatments shows a higher than the non-WBCT treatments. In addition, paired collaboration treatment without WBCT shows the highest slope. Table 16 shows the estimated means across time after controlling for covariates. The highest in estimated mean of quiz score is shown in WBCT (LM2: 11.687), followed by combined (LM4: 11.546), dyad (LM3: 10.887) with the lowest in control (LM1: 9.798) treatments.

Figure 13 shows satisfaction construct mean values over the three treatment periods. The graph shows that individuals in the WBCT treatments shows a higher than the non-WBCT treatments. The third period also shows a drop off for the non-WBCT treatments, with a rise for WBCT treatments. Table 17 shows the estimated means across time after controlling for covariates. The highest level of mean satisfaction combined (LM4: 7.212), followed by dyad (LM3: 7.286), control (LM1: 8.269) with the lowest in WBCT (LM2: 8.458) treatments.

This section provided an overview of the dependent variables across different groups across time. Visual inspection of the graphs shows that broadly the hypothesis held with the combined treatment doing favorably in each case. However, based on the mean estimates in the above tables in this section, below we present the pairwise test of univariate mean differences using the Tukey HSD comparison for the hypothesis stated in Section 4.11.1.

A summary of pair wise comparison for the WBCT vs. non-WBCT is shown is Table 18, dyads vs. non-dyads is shown in Table 19 and the combined treatment vs. the rest is shown in Table 20. Significant differences are discussed below.

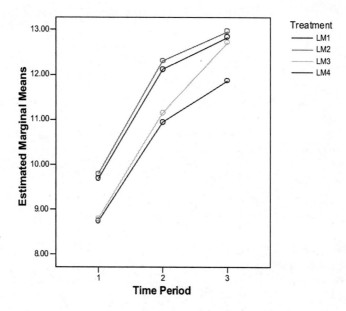

Treatments: LM1 = Control, LM2=WBCT, LM3=dyads, LM4=Combined

Figure 12: Quiz Score over Time

Table 16: Mean Estimates of Quiz Score

Measure	Treatments (LM-x)	Mean of means	Std. Error	95% Confidence Interval	
				Lower Bound	Upper Bound
Quiz score	1	10.516	.179	10.164	10.868
	2	11.687	.175	11.343	12.031
	3	10.887	.205	10.484	11.290
	4	11.546	.173	11.205	11.887

Treatments: LM1 = Control, LM2=WBCT, LM3=dyads, LM4=Combined

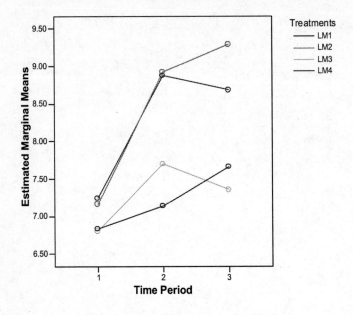

Treatments: LM1 = Control, LM2=WBCT, LM3=dyads, LM4=Combined

Figure 13: Satisfaction over Time

Table 17: Mean Estimates of Satisfaction

Measure	Treatments (LM-x)	Mean of means	Std. Error	95% Confidence Interval	
				Lower Bound	Upper Bound
Satisfaction	1	8.269	.228	7.821	8.716
(Reverse :	2	8.458	.222	8.021	8.895
lower scores	3	7.286	.261	6.773	7.798
better)	4	7.212	.221	6.779	7.646

Treatments: LM1 = Control, LM2=WBCT, LM3=dyads, LM4=Combined

5.4.1. Test of Hypothesis related to WBCT (H1)

H1: *Individuals in WBCT treatments will perform better on learning outcomes when compared to non-WBCT treatments.*

WBCT treatment was operationalized by training students using elementK. The effect using WBCT for training is analyzed by comparing learning outcome mean of vicarious treatment with WBCT treatment i.e. control (LM1) versus WBCT (LM2) and dyad (LM3) verses combined (LM4).

Table 18: Pair wise Comparisons for Testing Effect of WBCT

Measure	Treatment(I)	Treatment(J)	Mean Difference (I-J)	Std. Error	Sig.
Specific self-efficacy	1	2	-2.957	1.654	0.074
	3	4	-1.090	1.773	0.539
Self-efficacy	1	2	-0.787*	0.332	0.018
	3	4	-0.580	0.356	0.104
Quiz score	1	2	-1.171*	0.251	0.000
	3	4	-0.659*	0.269	0.015
Satisfaction	1	2	0.189	0.319	0.553
	3	4	-0.073	0.342	0.830

*p<0.05
Treatments: LM1 = Control, LM2=WBCT, LM3=dyads, LM4=Combined. Test results shown after taking into account the covariates discussed above.

Control (LM1) versus WBCT (LM2): A pair wise comparison of mean differences of individual treatments of non-WBCT treatment and WBCT treatment revealed a statistically significant difference for specific self-efficacy (p<.074), self-efficacy (p=.018) and quiz score (p<.0001) with WBCT treatments doing significantly better. Results for satisfaction were not significantly different.

Dyad (LM3) verses combined (LM4): A pair wise comparison of mean differences for self-efficacy of paired treatments of non-WBCT treatment and WBCT treatment revealed an insignificant differences (p<.104). Statistically significant mean difference was revealed for quiz score (p<.015), with WBCT treatments doing better. Results for mean differences for specific self-efficacy and satisfaction, were not statistically significant.

Overall, participants in WBCT treatment did significantly better for learning outcomes of self-efficacy and quiz score.

5.4.2. Test of Hypothesis related to Collaboration (H2)

H2: *Individuals in paired treatments will perform better on learning outcomes when compared to non-paired treatments*

Collaboration was operationalized by pairing students and following a reciprocal questioning methodology. The effect of pairing is analyzed by comparing learning outcome mean of non-paired treatments with paired treatments i.e. control (LM1) versus dyad (LM3) and WBCT (LM2) verses combined (LM4).

Control (LM1) versus dyad (LM3): A pair wise comparison of means between vicarious modeling treatments of individuals and pairs revealed a statistically significant difference for self-efficacy (p<.006) and satisfaction (p<.005) with the paired treatment showing higher learning outcomes. Results for differences in quiz scores, though higher for paired treatments, were not statistically significant.

WBCT (LM2) verses combined (LM4): A pair wise comparison of means between WBCT treatments of individual and pairs revealed a statistically significance difference for self-efficacy (p<.016) and satisfaction (p<.001) with paired treatments showing higher learning outcomes. The results for quiz scores did not show a statistically significant between the two treatments.

Table 19: Pair wise Comparisons for Testing Effect of Collaboration

Measure	Treatment(I)	Treatment(J)	Mean Difference (I-J)	Std. Error	Sig.
Specific self-efficacy	1	3	-3.381	1.793	0.060
	2	4	-1.514	1.624	0.352
Self-efficacy	1	3	**-0.999***	**0.360**	**0.006**
	2	4	**-0.792***	**0.326**	**0.016**
Quiz score	1	3	-0.371	0.272	0.174
	2	4	0.141	0.246	0.568
Satisfaction	1	3	**-0.983***	**0.346**	**0.005**
	2	4	**-1.246***	**0.313**	**0.000**
*p<0.05					
Treatments: LM1 = Control, LM2=WBCT, LM3=dyads, LM4=Combined					

Overall, paired treatments performed significantly better for learning outcomes of self-efficacy and satisfaction. Other measures of learning outcomes were not statistically significant.

5.4.3. Test of hypothesis related to Combined Treatment (H3)

H3: *Individuals in combined treatment will show higher levels of learning outcomes when compared to other treatments.*

This hypothesis compared the combined treatment (LM4) with the rest of the treatments i.e. base (LM1), collaboration (LM3) and technology (LM2) treatments. Significant differences on all learning outcomes with base treatment were observed (see Table 20). Additionally, the combined treatment performed significantly on self-efficacy and satisfaction when compared to technology-mediated treatment, on score when compared to collaboration treatment. Thus, this treatment resulted in the highest learning outcomes overall.

In summary, significant mean differences were found for most learning outcome constructs between hypothesized groups. Satisfaction was substantially higher for a combination of WBCT and paired treatment.

Table 20: Combined Treatment vs. Others

Measure	Treatment(J)	Mean Difference (4-J)	Std. Error	Sig.
Specific self-efficacy	1	4.47*	1.65	0.01
	2	1.51	1.62	0.35
	3	1.09	1.77	0.54
Self-efficacy	1	1.58*	0.33	0.00
	2	0.79*	0.33	0.02
	3	0.58	0.36	0.10
Score	1	1.03*	0.25	0.00
	2	-0.14	0.25	0.57
	3	0.66*	0.27	0.01
Satisfaction	1	1.06*	0.32	0.00
	2	1.25*	0.31	0.00
	3	0.07	0.34	0.83
* p<0.05				
Treatments: LM1 = Control, LM2=WBCT, LM3=dyads, LM4=Combined				

5.5. Statistical Analysis II: Stacked Latent Growth Model

The second statistical analysis uses structured equation modeling (SEM). Two important extensions to SEM will be used: Stacked group analysis and Latent growth modeling. Stacked models are models with multiple groups, but with subsequent groups being a subset of the fully identified group. Latent growth modeling (LGM) is a statistical technique with the ability to analyze a longitudinally measured variable by analyzing its constant and the growth effect (Lance et al. 2000).

Model correctness in SEM analysis is evaluated by comparing the model goodness-of-fit measures with the cut off values accepted in the research. These goodness-of-fit estimates are a result of comparing the variance/covariance matrix of the resulted model with the actual variance/covariance matrix. These cut-off values provide guidelines for evaluating model fit. Due to the lack of agreement on a single estimate, we use multiple goodness-of-fit estimates to infer model fit. Based on previous research (Hu et al. 1999; Tanaka 1993; Vandenberg 2002), we focus on the following goodness-of-fit estimates in evaluating model fit : χ^2 estimate, nonnormed fit index (NNFI > .90) comparative fit index (CFI > .90), root mean square error of approximation (RMSEA < .08) and standardized root mean square residual (SMR < 1.0). RMSEA estimates, however, show greater value in case of LGM analysis. Methodological expert (Vandenberg, conversation) suggest that as long as the other estimates satisfy the goodness-of-fit cut-off, a higher RMSEA value is acceptable. In this work, the above guidelines (except RMSEA) were used as a cut-off to judge model fit, subject to RMSEA value being close to the suggested guidelines. Please note that LISREL does not report SMR for multiple groups. .

To run this analysis, the following sequence of steps was followed. First, we determined measurement invariance across groups for the variables. Second, we analyzed for measurement invariance across time. Having established invariance, we performed a full analysis and describe the results of the analysis. LISREL 8.72 was used to conduct the analysis. LISREL uses correlations or covariance among the measured variables to estimate factor loadings, variance and error of latent constructs. LISREL's flexibility allows researchers to simultaneously estimate the relationships among latent variables with other latent variables.

5.5.1. Measurement Invariance

The establishment of measurement invariance across groups and time is a logical prerequisite for conducting substantive cross-group cross-time comparisons. Primarily, measurement invariance prevents against interpretational confounding (Anderson et al. 1988). Burt (1976) stated that interpretational confounding *"occurs as the assignment of empirical meaning to the unobserved variable which is other than meaning assigned to it by*

94

the individual a prior to the estimating unknown parameters." It is reflected by marked changes in the estimates of the pattern coefficients (Vandenberg 2002).

Vandenberg (2002) present an extensive review and framework to perform this analysis. In this research, since group mean differences exists, and differences are expected over time, we test for configural invariance, metric invariance and factor variance for each set of dependent and independent variables. The three tests are briefly described below:

Configural invariance: A test of configural invariance (Horn et al. 1992) is a test of "weak factorial invariance" where null hypothesis is that the same pattern of fixed and free factor loading is specified for each group. Configural invariance must be established in order for subsequent tests to be meaningful

Metric invariance ($\Lambda^{g/t}=\Lambda^{g+1/t+1}$): A test of metric invariance, or a test of strong factorial invariance (Horn et al. 1992), tests a null hypothesis that factor loadings for like items are invariant across time/group. At least partial metric invariance must be established in order for subsequent test to be meaningful.

Factor variance invariance ($\Phi_j^{g/t}=\Phi_j^{g+1/t+1}$): This is a test of the null hypothesis that factor variances are invariant across groups. This is a treatment in complement to metric invariance test, in which difference in factor variance were interpreted as reflecting group differences in calibration of true scores.

Configural invariance is evaluated based on model fit. Metric and factor invariance analysis, apart from looking at the model fit estimate, is done by comparing the value of Δ CHI for the changes in degrees of freedom from configural invariance. Below we report the invariance estimates across time followed by invariance estimates across group.

5.5.1.1. Measurement Invariance across Time

Measurement invariance across time captures the similarities of the construct across time for each of the groups. This is done by constraining the respective free estimates across groups. Table 21 shows the results of the goodness-of-fit indicators for different invariance tests across treatments. Since score and specific self-efficacy are single item variables, these were not included in the invariance tests. They were assumed to be perfectly measured with no measurement error. After comparing the values of the goodness-of-fit cut-off, the table shows a good level of metric invariance across time for all groups for the dependent variables, except for factor variance invariance for satisfaction construct after the second

95

training session. In this case, there was a significant increase in the chi-square when factor invariance constraints were imposed. However, when the factor variance for satisfaction for the second training period was freely estimated, the chi-square value was non-significant (see table 21). Thus, this factor was left to be freely estimated in subsequent tests.

Table 21: Measurement Invariance - Dependent Variables by Treatments

Dependent variables – Self efficacy and satisfaction								
LM4	df	CHI	NNFI	CFI	SRMR	RMSEA	delta df	Δ CHI
Configural	102	106.98	0.98	0.99	0.06	0.02		
Metric	110	128.84	0.97	0.98	0.08	0.04	8	21.86
Factor	114	140.32	0.96	0.97	0.09	0.04	4	11.48
LM3	df	CHI	NNFI	CFI	SRMR	RMSEA	delta df	Δ CHI
Configural	102	137.03	0.90	0.94	0.09	0.06		
Metric	110	146.90	0.90	0.93	0.09	0.06	8	9.87
Factor	114	150.73	0.90	0.93	0.11	0.06	4	3.83
LM2	df	CHI	NNFI	CFI	SRMR	RMSEA	delta df	Δ CHI
Configural	102	165.70	0.92	0.95	0.08	0.07		
Metric	110	179.23	0.92	0.94	0.08	0.07	8	13.53
Factor	114	202.78	0.91	0.93	0.12	0.08	4	23.55
Factor SATIS	113	186.36	0.92	0.94	0.10	0.07	3	7.13
LM1	df	CHI	NNFI	CFI	SRMR	RMSEA	delta df	Δ CHI
Configural	102	120.10	0.96	0.98	0.07	0.04		
Metric	110	129.89	0.96	0.97	0.07	0.04	8	9.79
Factor	114	140.05	0.91	0.97	0.10	0.05	4	10.16
Cut-offs			>.90	>.90	<.1	<.08		

Df=degrees of freedom, Goodness-of-fit guidelines - CHI=χ^2 value, delta df = changes in the degrees of freedom compared to the last test, Δ CHI = changes in χ^2 value from the previous test

Error! Not a valid bookmark self-reference. shows similar estimates for independent variables. The tables first show invariance across technology appropriation variables i.e. faithfulness and attitude towards technology use. These are done for LM4 and LM2. Next, it shows invariance estimates for collaboration construct across LM4 and LM3. In each case, a comparison of model goodness-of-fit estimates with the suggested values, leads us to conclude that a good level of measurement invariance across time.

In summary, both independent and dependent variables show good levels of measurement invariance across time.

Table 22: Measurement Invariance - Independent Variables by Treatments

Independent variables – Faithfulness and attitude of technology use								
LM4	df	CHI	NNFI	CFI	SRMR	RMSEA	delta df	Δ CHI
Configural	153	182.55	0.98	0.98	0.08	0.04		
Metric	163	192.51	0.98	0.98	0.08	0.04	10	9.96
Factor	167	210.42	0.97	0.98	0.10	0.05	4	17.91
LM2	df	CHI	NNFI	CFI	SRMR	RMSEA	delta df	Δ CHI
Configural	153	186.14	0.97	0.98	0.07	0.04		
Metric	163	193.34	0.98	0.98	0.08	0.04	10	7.20
Factor	167	202.49	0.97	0.98	0.09	0.04	4	9.15
Independent variable – collaboration								
LM4	df	CHI	NNFI	CFI	SRMR	RMSEA	delta df	Δ CHI
Configural	114	196.72	0.97	0.98	0.07	0.08		
Metric	124	218.39	0.97	0.97	0.09	0.08	10	21.67
Factor	126	220.50	0.97	0.97	0.13	0.08	2	2.11
LM3	df	CHI	NNFI	CFI	SRMR	RMSEA	delta df	Δ CHI
Configural	114	164.84	0.97	0.98	0.074	0.07		
Metric	124	196.04	0.97	0.97	0.10	0.08	10	31.20
Factor	126	202.48	0.96	0.97	0.16	0.086	2	6.44
Cut-offs			>.90	>.90	<.1	<.08		

Df=degrees of freedom, Goodness-of-fit guidelines - CHI=χ^2 value, delta df = changes in the degrees of freedom compared to the last test, Δ CHI = changes in χ^2 value from the previous test

5.5.1.2. Measurement Invariance across Groups

Having fixed the parameters across time for each group, we now tested the invariance across groups. These tests were done using the multi-group analysis feature of LISREL (running all groups simultaneously) and constraining parameters as discussed above.

Table 23 shows the results of the model goodness-of-fit estimates for all constructs across groups. When compared to the cut-off values, all constructs show good measurement invariance across groups. Please note that LISREL does not report SRMR for multi-group analysis.

In summary, all constructs show good measurement invariance across time and groups. We can thus, proceed with the latent group modeling for these groups.

Table 23: Measurement Invariance Goodness-of-Fit: Across Groups

Dependent variables – Self-efficacy and satisfaction							
	df	CHI	NNFI	CFI	RMSEA	delta df	Δ CHI
Configural	455	617.01	0.94	0.95	0.06		
Metric	467	661.08	0.93	0.95	0.06	12	44.07
Factor	518	719.59	0.93	0.94	0.06	51	58.51
Independent variables – faithfulness and attitude towards technology use							
	df	CHI	NNFI	CFI	RMSEA	delta df	Δ CHI
Configural	334	412.90	0.97	0.98	0.04		
Metric	339	430.53	0.97	0.97	0.05	5	17.63
Factor	356	472.70	0.97	0.97	0.05	17	42.17
Independent variables – Collaboration							
	df	CHI	NNFI	CFI	RMSEA	delta df	Δ CHI
Configural	252	422.99	0.97	0.97	0.08		
Metric	257	432.77	0.97	0.97	0.08	5	9.78
Factor	261	436.63	0.97	0.97	0.08	4	3.86
Cutoff			>.90	>.90	<.08		

Df=degrees of freedom, CHI=χ^2 value, delta df = changes in the degrees of freedom compared to the last test, delta CHI = changes in χ^2 value from the previous test

5.5.1.3. Latent Growth Model Parameterization

Table 24: Latent Growth Parameterization Goodness-of-Fit Estimates

Dependent variables – Self-efficacy and satisfaction					
DF	CHI	NNFI	CFI	SRMR	RMSEA
521	752.99	0.93	0.94	N/A	0.065
Independent variables – faithfulness and attitude towards WBCT use					
DF	CHI	NNFI	CFI	SRMR	RMSEA
363	515.31	0.96	0.96	N/A	0.06
Independent variables – Collaboration					
DF	CHI	NNFI	CFI	SRMR	RMSEA
260	432.1	0.97	0.97	N/A	0.081
Cutoff					
		>.90	>.90		<.80

Df=degrees of freedom, CHI=χ^2 value, NNFI= non-normed fit index, CFI=comparative fit index, SRMR=standardized root mean square residual, RMSEA = root mean square error of approximation

LGM provides a unified framework for modeling inter-individual differences in attributes for individual change trajectories. LGM produces two parameters: Intercept and Slope. The intercept corresponds to the initial status of the variable: the value of the variable just after the first training. The slope corresponds to the rate of change in the variable: The rate of increase or decrease over the training sessions. The task in the LGM analysis is to identify the appropriate growth curve that accurately and parsimoniously describes change over time (Chan 2002). Since the time periods for data collection were known, all models were run as specified multi-variate models, i.e., the growth model was specified.

Further standard assumptions of LGM are: (a) the means of all latent variables, error terms and factors have zero variance, (b) the variances of all latent variables are zero, (c) the means and variance of latent variables do not covary and (d) the error variance do not covary with each other or with any variables except the measured variables they directly affect (Duncan 1999). After parameterization, as obtained by the previous step, fit estimates for the model are obtained. Table 24 reports these estimates. A comparison with the cut-off values for these estimates shows good model fit.

Table 25: Latent Growth Parameter Mean Estimates (Alpha estimates)

	LM4	LM3	LM2	LM1
IN Faithfulness	1.69	NA	2.02	NA
Ch Faithfulness	0.13*	NA	0.08*	NA
IN Attitude	5.11	NA	5.03	NA
Ch Attitude	-0.27	NA	-0.27	NA
IN Collaboration	6.25	6.18	NA	NA
Ch Collaboration	-0.08	-0.12	NA	NA
IN Self-efficacy	3.07	2.9	2.89	2.6
Ch Self efficacy	0.27	0.28	0.23	0.2
IN Satisfaction	2.03	2.08	2.27	2.14
Ch Satisfaction	0.21	0.17	0.37	0.3
IN Score	9.98	8.93	10.06	8.98
Ch Score	1.59	1.95	1.58	1.57
IN SSE	24.87	24.33	22.69	21.55
CH SSE	20.38	18.98	19.02	17.81

* Insignificant (t-value <1.64)
IN = Initial Status, Ch= Change
Treatments: LM1 = Control, LM2=WBCT, LM3=dyads, LM4=Combined

Latent growth parameter means or alpha estimates for the initial status and change variables for each of the constructs generated from this analysis are reported in Table 25. All constructs show a significant change over time, except for faithfulness. This means that no significant changes in faithfulness were detected over time. Thus, in the subsequent analysis causal paths stemming from changes in faithfulness construct were not considered for interpretation.

5.6. Hypothesis Testing (H4 and H5)

Having established the measurement invariance and good model fits for latent growth parameters, the next step was to run the entire model together. The model was run as an all y-model. All four groups were estimated simultaneously, using the multi-group feature of LISREL (Chan 2002). Because the groups were stacked i.e. different in their treatments, the following updates were done the covariance matrix, the means vector, beta matrix, phi mate, theta-epsilon matrix. All of the changes, expect for the means vector, were based on Hayduk (1996) with necessary deviations for growth modeling. Hayduk (1996) recommendations are designed for estimation of paths alone. Since the current analysis also included estimation of latent means for latent growth parameters, means were also introduced. The LISREL code used in this analysis is in Appendix I. The steps in analysis were as follows:

1.   All covariance matrixes were made to have equal number of items but introducing dummy variables. The correlation of these items with observed items was fixed to zero, and the variance of the items was fixed to 1. The error of the item was fixed to zero.

2.   The variance of the dummy latent construct was fixed to 1. The factor loadings were fixed to 1 in groups without these variables.

3.   The beta values for the LGM parameterization was fixed to 1 in groups without these variables.

4.   Beta values of the causal path for the dummy variables were fixed to zero in groups without these variables.

5.   Latent means – alpha values- for the dummy variables was fixed to zero in groups without these variables.

6.   Model parameters discussed in the above sections were fixed to the estimates obtained from the analysis outlined earlier.

The causal paths in the analysis in SEM are modeled as beta values. The combined Treatment LM4 was modeled as a fully specified model, i.e., with path coefficients for faithfulness, attitude and collaboration (both initial states and change) to each of the dependent variables - self-efficacy, satisfaction, quiz score, and specific self-efficacy (both initial states and change). Treatments LM3 and LM2 were modeled similarly with path coefficient for collaboration and technology faithfulness & attitude respectively.

The beta paths for individual groups broadly showed similar values. Results are derived from a summary table showing the average values of the standardized estimates (Table 26). The Table also indicates the significance of the results. Figure 14 shows the second order structural model. Only path estimates found significant at p <0.05 are shown the Figure. The first order latent variables for each period are not shown to conserve space.

Below we discuss each hypothesis sets H4 and H5. The first hypothesis deals with the effect of the initial levels of appropriation, while the second one deals with the effect of the changes in appropriation.

Table 26: Completely Standardized Average Beta Values

H4: Path beta estimates for initial value of appropriation to initial value of learning outcomes			
	Faithfulness	Attitude towards WBCT	Collaboration
Self-efficacy	0.16	**0.73***	0.01
Satisfaction from process	**0.56***	**1.32***	0.165
Score	**0.50***	0.51	-0.04
Specific self-efficacy	0.0	-2.27	-0.695

H5: Path beta estimates for changes in appropriation to changes in learning outcomes			
	Faithfulness	Attitude towards WBCT	Collaboration
Self-efficacy	-0.13	0.255	0.075
Satisfaction from process	0.0	**0.525***	**0.51***
Score	0.25	0.20	0.2
Specific self-efficacy	0.0	-0.01	**0.16***

Post-hoc: Path beta estimates for initial value of appropriation to changes in learning outcomes			
	Faithfulness	Attitude towards WBCT	Collaboration
Self-efficacy	**0.93***	0.21	-0.23
Satisfaction from process	0.28	**0.79***	0.06
Score	0.06	0.17	-0.11
Specific self-efficacy	0.00	**0.38***	-0.05

* p< 0.05

H4: *Initial level of appropriation of structures in learning methods will have a positive correlation with initial levels of learning outcomes: a) technology-mediation, b) collaboration*

The summary table, i.e. Table 26, shows that the initial levels of faithfulness were significant in affecting initial levels of satisfaction and score. In addition, the initial levels of attitude have a significant effect on initial levels self-efficacy, satisfaction. No significant effects of initial levels of collaboration were found. Thus, the results support the hypothesis for technology-mediation but not for collaboration.

H5: *Increase in appropriation of structures in learning methods over time will have a positive correlation with changes in learning outcomes over time: a) technology-mediation, b) collaboration.*

Since faithfulness of technology did not have a significant change (see Table 25), no paths out of this variable were interpretable. Changes in attitude though, showed a strong correlation to changes in satisfaction. Changes in appropriation of collaboration structures showed a strong correlation with satisfaction and specific self-efficacy. Thus, the results show partial support for technology-mediation and a stronger support for the collaboration hypothesis.

5.7. Post-Hoc Tests

Two post-hoc tests were conducted. The first test compared the mean differences in the outcomes of dyads (LM3) and WBCT (LM2) treatments. The underlying question answered here is – *Between the technology-mediation and collaboration treatments, which treatment is better?* Significant differences were found in the difference between quiz score and satisfaction (see Table 27), with technology-mediated groups showing a higher quiz score and but lower satisfaction (since satisfaction is reverse scaled).

Table 27: Post-hoc test: Technology-mediated vs. Collaboration Treatment

Measure	Mean Difference (WBCT-Dyads)	Std. Error	Sig.
Specific self-efficacy	-0.42	1.777	0.81
Self-efficacy	-0.21	0.357	0.55
Score	0.80	0.270*	0.00
Satisfaction	-1.17	0.343*	0.00
* p<0.05			

The second post-hoc focuses on the downstream effects of initial levels of appropriation of structures. More specifically, we explored the following question – *Does initial level of appropriation have an effect on changes in the learning outcomes over time?* In case of a significant effect, focusing on initial levels of appropriation assume greater importance as it has continued impact over time. Results on this test can be drawn by looking at Table 26, which shows the beta coefficients from the initial levels of appropriation to the changes in specific learning outcomes. The results show that initial levels of attitude have a significant beta with changes on satisfaction and specific self-efficacy, while initial levels of faithfulness has a significant beta with changes in self-efficacy.

5.8. Summary

The chapter describes the use of two statistical techniques for testing five hypothesis. The entire process of data analysis was reported into seven major parts. The first part, results of which are described in Section 5.1, focused on establishing the assumption of equivalence of treatment groups. The test of this assumption was necessary especially because of the nature of sampling involved. The analysis proved that except for individual differences in gender between the four treatment groups, the groups were equivalents on the important biographical and affective constructs.

Section 5.2 focused on the measurement model underlying the first analysis. In this section, we focused on the validity and reliability concerns of information systems research. The validity and reliability results were presented for all the four periods. After removing items with low or cross loadings, sufficient reliability and validity was established.

The first technique used for testing the first three hypotheses is Repeated Measures Multivariate Analysis of Variance. Section 0 describes this technique, the assumptions, information on manipulation checks and the initial results MANOVA and ANOVA results. These results show a significant effect of treatment, both at an aggregate as well as individual construct levels. Initial levels of motivation, self-efficacy and gender were shown as significant covariates. The effect of these covariates on individual learning outcome constructs is also shown in this section.

Section 5.4 details the results of the first three sets of hypothesis. It also provides the mean estimates after effects of covariates. Overall, paired collaboration significantly improved self-efficacy and satisfaction, while WBCT effect was significant on self-efficacy and individual post treatment quiz score. Self-efficacy slopes were also different based on the treatments. Finally, the results also showed that the combined treatment was the most effective.

The second statistical technique used to test the last hypothesis is called Stacked Group Latent Growth Modeling. Section 5.5 describes this technique. An important assumption of stacked group analysis is measurement invariance across groups and for latent growth model is measurement invariance across time. Thus, configural, metric and factor invariance was tested across time and groups. Latent mean estimates for LGM parameterization for each group are also shown in the section. In each case, fit parameters are recorded.

Section 5.6 details the test of the last two hypothesis. H4, dealing with the effect of initial levels of appropriation on learning outcomes, showed a strong effect of technology appropriation, while no effect of collaboration was found. H5, dealing with the effect of changes in the levels of appropriation on changes in learning outcomes, showed a partial support for technology and a strong support for collaboration.

Two post-hoc tests were carried out in section 5.7. The first test compared the technology-mediated treatment with collaboration treatment concluding a significant score for technology-mediated treatment, but higher satisfaction for collaboration treatment. The second test, investigated the downstream effects of initial levels of appropriation of structures on learning outcomes. Results of this test are incorporated in Figure 14.

Figure 14 shows the relationships between the appropriation of learning method and learning outcomes. It summarizes the significant results of the SEM analysis. The latent variables shown are the initial status and changes in each case. For the purpose of clarity, only significant relationships are shown. For example, the initial status of faithfulness of e-learning has a significant relationship with changes in self-efficacy over time, and initial levels of satisfaction and quiz score.

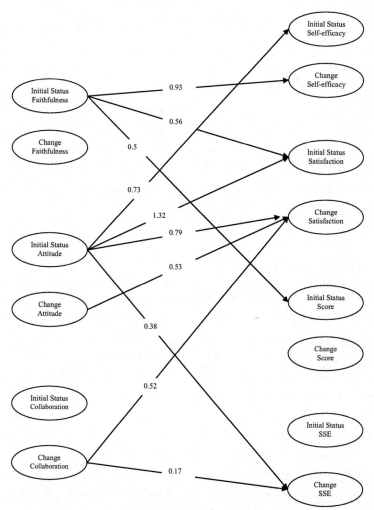

Figure 14: Completely Standardized Significant Beta Estimates

The next chapter discusses these findings and their implications.

6. Discussions, Implications and Conclusions

This chapter begins with an overview of the statistical findings presented in Chapter 5. The following sections will discuss specific findings for each major dependent variable and present the possible interpretations. Findings include hypothesis testing results as well as other interesting patterns observed in the data. We also incorporate some qualitative data to provide insights. The final four sections discuss the possible limitations of research, practical implications of the findings, suggested directions for future research and major conclusions.

6.1. Discussion and Interpretation of Research Findings

6.1.1. Overview of Findings

Five hypotheses were tested to determine the effectiveness of technology-mediated and collaboration as well as the impact of appropriation of each on learning outcomes: understanding (score), affective (self-efficacy, specific self-efficacy) and satisfaction levels. Table 28 presents a summary of the tested hypotheses. The first three hypotheses analyze the impact of web-based learning and paired treatments, the next hypothesis analyze the impact of initial levels of appropriation on initial levels of learning outcome variables and the final hypothesis test presents results of analysis of changes in appropriation of treatments on changes in dependent variables. The table also presents results of the second post-hoc test analyzing the impact of initial levels of treatments appropriation on changes in learning outcomes. Results of the first post-hoc test are included in the discussion. Using well-accepted criteria, the tests meeting $p < 0.05$ criteria are reported as significant.

In the following sections, we discuss the findings based on the above hypothesis test results. Discussion follows the outline in Table 28: treatment effects, followed by process effects, effect of time, and lastly the post-hoc tests results.

6.1.2. Treatment Effect

The experimental design helps us investigate the comparative effectiveness of each of the two treatments: enactive and vicarious learning embedded in technology and collaboration. Specific hypotheses were drawn supporting positive influence in both cases.

Finding 1: Technology embedding enactive learning in addition to vicarious learning has a positive effect on self-efficacy and quiz score (understanding).

Table 28: Summary of Tested Hypothesis

	Self-efficacy	*Specific Self-Efficacy*[*]	*Score (Understanding)*	*Satisfaction*
Treatment effect (H1-H3)				
Technology	Significant	Not significant	Significant	Not significant
Collaboration	Significant	Not significant	Not significant	Significant
Combined (compared to)	Significant (base+tech)	Significant (base)	Significant (base+collab)	Significant (Base+tech)
Process effect (H4)- Initial appropriation of treatments on initial dependent variables				
Technology -Faithfulness -Attitude	Not significant Significant	Not significant Not significant	Significant Not significant	Significant Significant
Collaboration	Not significant	Not significant	Not significant	Not significant
Longitudinal process effect (H5): Rate of change in appropriation on rate of change in dependent variables				
Technology -Faithfulness -Attitude	Not significant Not significant	Not significant Not significant	Not significant Not significant	Not significant Significant
Collaboration	Not Significant	Significant	Not significant	Significant
Post-hoc test: Effect of initial levels of appropriation on changes in dependent variables				
Technology -Faithfulness -Attitude	Significant Not significant	Not significant Not significant	Not significant Not significant	Not significant Significant
Collaboration	Not significant	Not significant	Not significant	Not significant
Note: "Significant" is based on meeting the p<0.05 criterion [*]*Results presented but not interpreted as explained earlier.*				

Web-based CBT (WCBT) treatments (LM2 and LM4) overall performed better than their non-WBCT counterparts on certain outcome measures. Comparison on each of the four learning outcome measures (shown in Table 29) showed a significant improvement in self-efficacy perceptions and quiz score. Specific self-efficacy was significantly better in case of individual learning.

Table 29: WBCT Treatment Effect Summary

	LM1 vs. LM2 (individual)	*LM3 vs. LM4 (collaboration)*
Specific Self-Efficacy*	**Significant**	Not significant
Self-Efficacy	**Significant**	**Significant**
Quiz Score	**Significant**	**Significant**
Satisfaction	Not significant	Not significant
Treatments: LM1 = Control, LM2=WBCT, LM3=dyads, LM4=Combined *Results presented but not interpreted as explained earlier.		

Interpretations of the preceding findings suggest that participants using WBCT gain substantially in their understanding. WBCT used in this study incorporated vicarious learning, followed by enactive learning in a micro-simulated environment. The context of learning was end-user training. More specifically, the WBCT environment led to improved perceptions of ability to master the end-user application as well as cognitive ability in terms of quiz scores. Student comments such as - "*...compounded with last week's training session, I am beginning to feel rather comfortable using Excel*" and "*... it (the WBCT) was quite intuitive and helped me gain knowledge and insight about charts I had not previously fathomed!*" - also support this finding.

There was a great variance in student satisfaction from the learning process (the standard deviation was 3.89 on a scale of 7 point scale on average, mean score was 3.7, with high of 7 and low of 2). Even though the main concern in using WBCT was the impersonalization of training, the overall impact of this on satisfaction was not significant. The variance is also captured in qualitative data gathered. One student commented "*I would prefer to be taught by a human being than by a computer...*" while other commented "*...it really helped me develop into a real go getter. Thanks Element K!*" This indicates that some participants were very satisfied with the use of e-learning, while some were not. However, as explored later, collaboration treatments showed a significantly higher satisfaction when compared to their individual counterparts. This indicates that interpersonal dynamics might play an important role in training satisfaction.

The data also indicates that certain individual difference constructs might play an important role in explaining this variance in satisfaction (Brown 2001). Three important individual difference constructs are explored in the literature: Attitude towards technology, learning style, and learning orientation. Attitude towards technology is discussed later. Learning style deals with how a person takes in, understands, expresses and remembers information (Kolb 1971) while learning orientations examines the comprehensive set of psychological factors (conative, affective, cognitive and social) that influence how individuals approach learning and manage the learning process (Martinez 1998). Both of these constructs capture the approach that participants take towards a learning process. Thus, these are expected to influence training satisfaction. Thus, overall individual difference constructs presents a very important area for future research.

This study can also help explain the inconsistent results of other studies using CBT. In this study, a theoretically grounded technology was used. Structural dimensions were outlined and their functional impact hypothesized. Thus, the learning outcomes were explained not by the technology used, but by the underlying structures of the technology. Earlier studies examining the impact of CBTs, however, have not looked at the underlying structural dimensions. Since different technologies were used across different studies, different set of dimensions were operationalized, resulting in varied results. Thus, an implication of the finding from this study is that the structural dimensions of WBCT determine its effect on learning outcomes. WBCT grounded in social cognitive theory show a significant improvement in learning outcomes in an end-user training scenario.

Finding 2: Paired learning method has positive effect on self-efficacy and satisfaction.

Paired learning treatments (LM3 and LM4) overall performed better than their individual counterparts on certain outcome measures. Comparison on each of the four learning outcome measures (shown in Table 30) showed a significant improvement in self-efficacy perceptions and satisfaction. Specific self-efficacy was significantly better in case of vicarious modeling.

Paired learning is a relatively new method of training in end-user training literature. This study used a much broader conceptualization of learning outcomes than the previous study, which looked at paired learning, in end-user training (Yi et al. 2001). Yi's study

109

measured only understanding, while this study also measured self-efficacy and satisfaction beyond the measure of understanding. When conceptualized this way, interpretation of the findings from this study shows that participants do indeed benefit from paired learning. Self-efficacy perceptions are improved and this may be due to the implicit comparison of skills between participants. In addition, participants were encouraged to teach each other. Pairs were also able to discuss and explore the software together as exemplified by this quote from a participant "*We were able to find new and cool charts through teamwork.*"

Table 30: Paired Learning Effect Summary

	LM1 vs. LM3 (VM)	*LM2 vs. LM4 (WBCT)*
*Specific Self-Efficacy**	Significant	Not significant
Self-Efficacy	Significant	Significant
Quiz Score	Not significant	Not significant
Satisfaction	Significant	Significant
Treatments: LM1 = Control, LM2=WBCT, LM3=dyads, LM4=Combined *Results presented but not interpreted as explained earlier.*		

Important implications exist in case of satisfaction. No external support was given to the participants, even in case of content questions. This is a realistic situation in WBCT situations. In case of paired learning, students were able to ask their partners about any queries or difficulties they had in creating their own mental models. For example, one student commented on the effectiveness of paired learning as "*…because when I was unsure of how to do something, my partner helped me figure it out.*" Consequently, collaboration enhanced satisfaction.

Interestingly, pairs did not help in enhancing the cognitive outcomes in terms of quiz scores. A couple of reasons could explain this. First, quiz scores focused on understanding based on individual performance. Earlier studies in education, however, have focused on group performance of learning task. Even though participants in this study were able to help each other during the learning task, some participants indicated that having partner was little value in learning context. Some in paired learning treatment alluded to this by saying "*…because I could learn it by myself without a partner.*"

Secondly, the experiment did not focus intensively on the development of initial team structures. In this study, teams were zero-history groups. The introduction session was used to introduce team participants to the collaboration guidelines and given 5 minutes to interact with each other. Though these operationalized the structures, no formal team development activities were conducted to enhance the team dimensions, i.e., develop the relationship between the partners. Although, the team interaction structural dimensions did show higher levels over time, the poor deign of collaboration treatment might have resulted in underdeveloped team dimensions that lead to no significant effect on understanding. Since quiz score require a higher level of cognitive knowledge, the impact of collaboration might be different at richer levels of team structural dimensions. This interpretation is also supported by findings 5, 8 and 9 outlined below. It not only explains our results but also helps us explain why earlier end-user training studies did not show a significant effect of collaboration on learning outcomes (Davis et al. 2004). These findings also indicate that more research is needed in exploring the cognitive effects of collaboration.

Finding 3: Combined (technology + collaboration) learning method has the most positive effect on learning outcomes when compared to other treatments.

Overall, the treatment effects support the usage of WBCT and paired learning together in end-user training by organizations. WBCT treatments positively influence self-efficacy and quiz outcomes while collaboration treatments influenced self-efficacy and satisfaction. Overall, the combined treatment was the most effective, influencing self-efficacy, quiz score and satisfaction when compared to technology or collaboration learning method separately. Technology enhanced quiz score, while collaboration influenced the other learning outcomes. This interpretation is also supported by the first post-hoc test. This is an important finding, especially for WBCT implementations. It suggests augmenting WBCT based training programs with collaboration to maximize training effectiveness satisfaction. This finding though, comes with a caveat in terms of the kind of WBCT used and paired learning methodology used. WBCT technology that embeds structures that positively influence learning and paired learning methods that encourage collaboration will lead to enhanced learning outcomes.

6.1.3. Process Effect

Hypothesis H4 and H5 focus on the learning process. The hypotheses focused on the appropriation of the learning method structures.

Finding 4: The initial level of technology appropriation has significant positive effect on initial level of learning outcomes.

Table 31: Process Effect of Technology Appropriation

	Faithfulness	*Attitude*
*Specific Self-Efficacy**	Not Significant	Not significant
Self-Efficacy	Not Significant	**Significant**
Quiz Score	**Significant**	Not significant
Satisfaction	**Significant**	**Significant**
Results presented but not interpreted as explained earlier.		

Hypothesis in this area were designed to study the core question of – *"how does technology influence learning?"* Given the positive results of the above treatment effect of technology, the focus here shifts on the conditions under which such effectiveness can be obtained. Appropriation of the WBCT was argued as the core condition for WBCT effectiveness. Findings from the study support this argument.

As shown in Table 31, faithfulness of technology used had a significantly path coefficient to quiz score and satisfaction, while attitude towards technology used had a significant path coefficient to self-efficacy and satisfaction perceptions. The interpretation of the influence of each technology appropriation construct on each learning outcome is almost intuitive. The more WBCT is used as designed the better the learning of skills. Interpreting this, one can conclude that if a well-designed WBCT is used as it is intended to be used; it will lead to higher understanding and more satisfaction.

Self-efficacy and satisfaction were both strongly influenced by attitude towards technology. This suggests that individual attitude towards technology is an important construct that needs to be focused on. A negative attitude towards technology acts as a barrier in enhancing the self-efficacy and satisfaction of participants. Satisfaction was also, though to a lesser degree, influenced by faithful use. The more diligently students used the system, the more satisfied they became.

Thus, it is important that the participants come in with an open mind for technology based training to be effective. Positive attitude and faithful use have a strong influence on learning outcomes and organizations should invest in developing and ensuring these before and during the training sessions.

Finding 5: The initial level of appropriation of collaboration has no significant effects on learning outcomes.

Contrary to expectations, the initial levels of collaboration had no significant effect on learning outcomes. This can be the result of two conditions. First, the initial session was comparatively easier when compared to the later sessions. It is possible that effects of paired learning are visible only at higher difficulty content level. However, the second condition relating to underdeveloped team dimensions, as explained in the discussion for finding 2, is more likely.

6.1.4. Longitudinal Impact

The study provides an in-depth view of the independent and dependent variables in over-time. Thus, a very important contribution of the study was to examine how appropriation of treatments changes over time as well as the impact of these changes on learning outcomes over time. This represents a real-world situation more closely where employees are constantly learning.

Finding 6: No significant changes were observed in faithfulness of WBCT use over time.

Finding 7: Significant changes were observed in attitude towards WBCT use over time.

Finding 8: The rate of changes in appropriation of technology over time had no significant effects on changes in any learning outcomes except satisfaction.

The LGM analysis showed non-significant changes in faithfulness over time, though significant changes were observed in attitude towards technology. The technology used in this experiment, elementK, is a fairly simple technology and was easy to use. Observations and experiment guidelines ensured that faithfulness of WBCT use was high from the first session. Thus, the finding of no significant change in faithfulness is not surprising.

Attitude towards technology however, is an affective reaction. A significant change in attitude, towards the positive, occurred as students used WBCT over time. Theoretically, this is an important finding showing how appropriation changes over time. For example, one student commented as *"elementK continued to be a help..."*.Thus, as students get positive

113

experience in their learning with technology, their attitude towards technology use in learning/training situations improves.

Most importantly, this change in attitude had a significant effect on improving certain learning outcomes over time. As attitude improved, students experienced higher levels of satisfaction with technology use.

Overall, in a real-world situation, faithfulness of use becomes very important. Corporations have various support structures like expert help, technology departments, etc. which can assist in faithful use. However, these are usually available only on request. Thus, participants choosing not to avail them might have lower faithfulness of use. In such a case, the effect of WBCT may be delayed depending on appropriation of structures. This will be more prominent for complex information system, where appropriation might be highly influenced by appropriation support. As appropriation gets more faithful, learning outcomes improve.

Finding 9: The level of collaboration changed significantly over time.

Finding 10: The rate of changes in extent of collaboration have significant effect on rate of changes in learning outcomes (satisfaction).

As expected, the level of collaboration showed significant improvement over time. As pairs spent increasing time with each other, they seem to have developed a working relationship around the guidelines presented to them. This also supports the earlier explanation suggesting that in this study team structural dimensions develop over time. An implication of this is that zero-history groups are likely to be less influential on learning outcomes than groups with positive history.

These changes in the extent of collaboration (or appropriation of team structures) were found to have a significant effect on satisfaction, and specific self-efficacy, with near support for effect on quiz score (see Table 28). This is a very important finding. The finding implies that when the effect of collaboration is viewed independent of the initial levels of collaboration, it does have a significant effect on learning outcomes.

This finding also explains the disparity between Education and end-user training results in collaborative learning. Development of team structural dimensions is important. The cross-sectional studies conducted in end-user training did not focus on these dimensions. As explained in the discussion of finding 2, this study also did not develop rich team

114

structures to begin with, however, as dyads continued to work together, these structures showed positive changes.

Education studies, which show a greater variance in results, also show a greater variance in time and team development. According to the results of this study, this variance can be explained by the possible variance in the levels of team structural dimensions.

It is important to note that time is only one of the mechanisms influencing the richness of structural dimensions. As argued earlier in Chapter 3, many different mechanisms can be employed to achieve higher levels of these structural dimensions.

6.1.5. Post-hoc Tests (Downstream Effects)

The above findings conclude that the learning method structures and their appropriation had an effect on learning outcomes. The study also provided evidence that emergent structures appropriation has an effect on changes in learning outcomes. However, adaptive structuration theory postulates that the initial appropriation of structures determines the future structuration potential, and thus, will continue to have an effect on changes in learning outcomes. Said differently, the study provides evidence that appropriation of learning method structures had an effect on learning outcomes, however, another question i.e. – *Does the initial level of appropriation have a continued effect on learning outcomes in the future?* remains unanswered. Drawing from the post-hoc tests carried out, this section explores answers to this question.

Finding 11: The effect of initial technology appropriation has a significant effect on changes in self-efficacy and satisfaction learning outcomes.

The initial level of appropriation of technology structures continued to have a lingering effect on satisfaction and self-efficacy perceptions. More specifically, attitude affected satisfaction while faithfulness affected self-efficacy (see Table 32).

Table 32: Initial Technology Appropriation Effect on Changes in Learning

	Faithfulness	*Attitude*
*Specific Self-Efficacy**	Not significant	Not significant
Self-Efficacy	Significant	Not significant
Quiz Score	Not Significant	Not significant
Satisfaction	Not Significant	Significant
Results presented but not interpreted as explained earlier.		

Interpreting this finding highlights two important implications. First, patterns of usage as well as notions about technology use change over time. However, the initial levels of these patterns continue to have an effect on learning outcomes over a longer duration. More importantly, the finding also shows that initial levels of appropriation are important. Practically, trainers and designers should focus more on getting the usage of a well designed WBCT correct the first time. This finding also suggests that important attitude development activities should be done in the pre-training or initial training session.

Finding 12: The initial level collaboration has no significant effect on changes in learning outcomes.

Similar to the effect of the initial level of appropriation of technology structures, the longitudinal effect of initial levels of collaboration structure appropriation was also tested. As expected, the initial levels of collaboration did not have any significant effect on any of the learning outcome variables. The explanation of this is consistent with the discussion on finding 2.

The implication of the findings on collaboration structure, in contrary to technology appropriation, shows that trainers/designers need to continuously reinforce and support the appropriation of collaboration structures over time. Rather than focusing only at the initial interaction, the focus in collaborative learning should be on continued interaction over time.

6.2. *Findings in an Adaptive Structuration Theory context*

Adaptive Structuration Theory (AST), presented by DeSanctis and Poole (1994), provided the basic framework for the work. One of the contributions of this work is the application of AST to learning and training context. In this section, we look at the work results from an AST lens. We outline and summarize some of the concepts that have transverse the work.

AST is a social theory aimed at explaining a broad range of interactions within organizational settings. Like earlier social theories (Structuration (Giddins 1984), Structuralism and Voluntarism (Parsons 1949)), AST presents an ontological arrangements of constructs in a defined system as well as how they interact. The theory recognizes the input constructs as internal and external structures of the system, while explaining the interaction through the role of actors. The theory does not, however, provide testable hypotheses as to the nature of the interaction and the consequent effect of the structures on the outcome from the system.

In this work, the focus has been on external structures, i.e., structures that are embedded in the learning method. Although AST has consistently talked about the spirit of design of the external structures, this is the first study that we know of that has explicitly defined the underlying constituents of spirit in a learning context (epistemological perspective and learning goals). Such analysis is very useful to explicitly understand the assumptions embedded in the external structures in all applications of AST. AST also argues that researchers need to focus on the underlying structures of a system. Earlier AST research has been restrictive in nature, applying the structural perspective only to technology. As shown in this work, though, the structural perspective can be extended to other structural elements as well.

As mentioned earlier, AST does not provide any hypotheses regarding the consequent effect of these structures. Drawing on this, we have argued that AST should be viewed as a meta-theory providing a research lens, while more specific theories should be used to understand the nature of structural impact. For example, in this study, we drew upon social cognitive theory (SCT) and social development theory (SDT) to understand and isolate the external structures that act as inputs to the learning system and for developing hypotheses. A similar argument can be made for internal structures. Internal structures, like individual differences, though not tested in this work, present a promising area for future research. Thus, the argument is that researchers should use AST as a meta-theory, embedding other relevant functional theories to explain the direction of impact of the structures.

In AST, actors (individual training participants in this study) in a social system are viewed from agency perspective, i.e., their behavior is goal-driven. This behavior influences the interaction among the various internal and external structures. DeSanctis et al. (1994) describe the underlying premise of the influence of such interaction on group processes (where groups were the collective actors) in a group decision support system's context in the following manner:

"Contextual and technology effect on group processes and outcomes are mediated by interactive structuring process, as reflected in the group's mode of appropriation"

Thus, AST challenges the deterministic perspective of functional theories by explicitly looking at the process. The process of using the structures is seen as an interpretive process through which the structures come into play, informing the actions of the actor and

117

getting shaped by the actions of the user i.e. appropriation. In this study, appropriation occurred as participants learned and adapted the structures of the learning method based on their interpretation of the spirit. It is important to remember that the functional theory through which the structures are guided provides the directionality of the mediation. As long as structures represent the critical structures of a functional theory (SCT and SDT in this case), a faithful appropriation of structures will positively mediate the outcomes. This work supports this assertion, especially in the case of the WBCT use. However, when the underlying structures are not well-designed, an ironic appropriation (or departure from the prescribed use) of the learning method might produce a better outcome.

The idea of an interactive structuration process embedded in AST permits researchers to also investigate the effect of purposeful actions of the actors as they interact with the system. This might result in the emergence of a new set of structures (that are later appropriated) or a change in the faithfulness of appropriation of existing structures (as was seen in this work). The ability to AST to capture the entire system of action provides researchers with a meta-theory for developing context or domain specific theoretical frameworks for investigation social systems. . For example, the e-learning model (See Chapter 3) developed in this dissertation used AST in this fashion.

Extensions of AST have also outlined the importance and role of appropriation support in enhancing the faithful appropriation structures (Clawson et al. 1996). Couched within the earlier discussion of the impact of the structures, appropriation support is likely to affect the faithfulness of appropriation, and represents an important area of future research. This dissertation has framed this important area for learning systems. In general, appropriation support has been a neglected AST area of research in IS.

In conclusion, AST is a meta-theory that provides a

- rich meta-theoretical view: an ontological arrangement of constructs in a system,
- set of meta-theoretical assumptions or propositions, and
- provides a template and a set of guidelines for creating context or system specific theoretical models (Poole and DeSanctis, 1994 and 2003)

AST brings together the deterministic and interpretive perspective together providing a core theory in post-modern paradigm (Kuhn 1996, Weber 2004). Other relevant theories need to be brought in to understand the impact of the structures and to state explicit hypotheses regarding the effect of the system on the expected outcomes. Findings of this study support the above discussion that AST presents an intuitive and appealing theoretical approach to understand the social learning process and outcomes involved in e-learning and collaboration. Future researchers are expected to draw on the idea of AST as a meta-theory to outline system (context) specific models as outlined here for the e-learning systems.

This work took a meta-theory view of AST and outlined how a domain specific model for e-learning can be made from it. We outlined the structures to draw upon learning theories to develop specific hypotheses. We also extended and clarified the underlying spirit of the structures in a learning context. The process of adaptive structuration was used to understand the process. Overall, the support for the hypotheses shows that such an AST-based approach is very useful.

6.3. Practical Implications

The study has substantial implications for practice. These implications can be broadly classified into implications for users, designers and educators. Table 33 summarizes these implications. They are further discussed below.

Table 33: Practical Consequences

Practical consequences
1. Well designed e-learning technology enhances self-efficacy and understanding (quiz score).
2. Initial technology appropriation has a significant effect on initial self-efficacy, understanding (quiz score) and satisfaction as well as downstream effects on self-efficacy and satisfaction.
3. Good collaboration needs rich team structural dimensions. Once they have been developed, they start positively influencing learning outcomes.
4. Collaboration between peers, when done well, improves self-efficacy and satisfaction especially in the long term.
5. Designers need to focus on learning theories when designing e-learning technology
6. Drawing on the model, designers need to focus on the structural dimensions of their design. AST provides a good model for understanding the possible influence of the design.
7. Since appropriation of learning method structures is an important determinant of the variance in learning outcomes, educators need to focus on appropriation support.

119

This study used two new training interventions in end-user training and tested its effectiveness. First, for users, web-based CBT represent a significant improvement in the potential to learn. These e-learning technologies provide an ability to learn any-time any-where and also provide a better mechanism for learners to test their mental models. The positive effect of e-learning technologies continues over time. This is a very encouraging result for users. E-learning embedding enactive learning in a simulated environment is positioned to revolutionize existing ways of learning (Aldrich 2004). The positive results from the micro-simulated environment are very encouraging for application of these technologies in training, especially end-user training applications. With the number of applications and the speed of change of end-user software, e-learning technology can provide a mechanism for fast-paced mass training. The study also has a direct application to universities, especially in their skill building courses. Results of the study show that e-learning technologies can be used in place of the instructor for skill development, with the instructor acting as a facilitator.

However, this result is contingent on the faithful use of e-learning technology by the users. Faithful use, especially positive attitude towards e-learning technology is a substantial influencer on the extent of learning. It is also found that over a period, attitudes towards e-learning technology become more favorable, improving learning outcomes. A practical implementation of this is to encourage participants to continue with e-learning solutions for a longer period, as experience helps in enhancing attitudes towards e-learning. More importantly, it shows the importance of developing a positive attitude upfront.

The second treatment, collaboration, also showed significant improvement in self-efficacy and satisfaction. However, as indicated by the results, users should not expect the benefit to be instantaneous. In this case, team structural dimensions took time to form, but once formed, they provide a significant benefit in learning. Practically, these structural dimensions can be enhanced in many different ways. This shows that not only is it necessary to have team development upfront, but a continued support is need to ensure enhanced learning outcomes.

From a designer's perspective, there are two important implications. First, e-learning technology designers need to shift their attention towards incorporating learning theories into their software i.e. focus on what learners need to successfully learn and how it is provided in the technology. For example, in this study, an e-learning technology incorporating social cognitive theory provided a basis for treatments. The focus of the technology treatment was to incorporate enactive learning in addition to vicarious learning in a simulated environment. With the growing investment in simulations by organizations, this study suggests that designers need to focus more on the realism and feedback structural dimensions for effective learning outcomes. However, more research is needed in the evolving simulation technology.

Secondly, designers need to focus on incorporating collaborative features in the training program. These can be included in the technology or can be outside the technology, but a well-structured collaboration improvement will lead to improvements. Finally, designers need to focus on appropriation support. Appropriation support mechanisms can be designed to enhance the faithfulness of appropriation of learning method structures, thus, influencing learning outcomes.

From an educator's perspective, this study also provides research evidence for investments in technology-based training programs. Business and consultants should, thus, be more proactive in exploring these options. More importantly, this study provides pedagogical guidelines for proper implementation of training programs. The importance of appropriation of e-learning technologies and collaboration structures highlights the future role of trainers. The future goal of trainers should be to include appropriation support to participants. Results suggest that technology appropriation support is needed early in the training program, while collaboration appropriation support might be more important after an initial relationship between collaborating individuals has been formed.

Overall, this study provides a richer view of designing contemporary training programs, both in-classrooms as well as virtually. These outcomes can be used not only by corporate businesses/ consultant/ trainers, but by instructors in K-12 and universities.

6.4. *Limitations of the Study*

Limitations of the study stem primarily from the context of the study and the nature of the research method. We address the latter first. The concerns about the limitations of a laboratory study have been well-documented (Campbell et al. 1966). These include external validity of results and experimenter bias and subject representativeness. Below we address each one of these.

6.4.1. External Validity:

Cook et al. (1979) define external validity as "...*the approximate validity with which we infer that the presumed causal relationship can be generalized to and across alternate measures of cause and effect and across different types of persons, settings and time*". The four primary threats to external validity in this case i.e. research method used, subjects, technology and target system are discussed below.

6.4.1.1. Laboratory Research

Laboratory research calls for the creation of situations that are analogous to situations encountered in the real work. In this research, two real work situations are targeted: academic institutions and corporate training.

Since the experiment is placed in an academic environment, using tools and participants from the academic environment, the realism of this research for academic institutions is high. Though most universities use instructor-led treatments (comparable to the baseline treatment in this study), some universities have started using technology-mediated learning for skill development. Thus, results from this study can easily be generalized to university environments.

Before generalizing the results to corporate training environment, however, two important concerns need to be recognized. First, subjects in the laboratory experiments tend not to take the tasks they perform very seriously, because of the lack of performance implications. In this study, however, subjects were concerned with learning as they had to take a final exam that was evaluated, though no implication of immediate performance existed. The task conducted, learning Excel, was a real task and the training simulated major training programs. Second, subjects are not free to appropriate WBCT in the way they see fit. Instead, subjects were broadly supervised by the experimenters to follow the guidelines. This lack of choice also reduces generalizability, as individuals typically decide to use e-learning technologies in any way they choose.

Another problem with experiments relates to experimental bias. In this case, only one other experimenter was used other than the primary researcher. Further, this experimenter would be assigned based on their availability rather than their training preference. The experimenter was only informed that the purpose of this study was to assess the quality of a training program. He was requested to keep journals to provide feedback to the researcher for this purpose. He was not informed of the specific hypotheses being examined. The experimenter was also given detailed structured scripts to reduce inter-experimenter variance. The researcher also acted as one of the experimenters, but caution was taken not to bias the results. A comparison of the sessions between the two experimenters did not show any significant differences in results.

There are other limitations of laboratory experiments (discussed below). However, it has been pointed out on several occasions that external validity is far more complex issue than has generally been acknowledged, and that a single study, whether it uses laboratory experiments or not, cannot achieve external validity (Greenberg 1987).

In conclusion, the laboratory research method suffers from several drawbacks, but at no more of a disadvantage than other research methods, which have their own specific drawbacks. It also has, like the other methods, several advantages. Prominent among these is the strength of internal validity of results. Thus, when used in a programmatic research, laboratory experiments provide a powerful means of triangulation. Thus, in spite of its drawbacks, laboratory experiments due to its strengths will provide continued utility in EUT and e-learning research. Also, in the interest of theory development and triangulation of methods, the results obtained though this study should serve as a basis for continued research in field settings.

6.4.1.2. Subject Representativeness

A very large subject population is required to perform this study under conditions which permit sufficient predictive power. Again, the university environment not only provided a representative setting for generalization to academic institutions, it also provided the large sample size.

For generalization to corporate training environments, the debate about suitability of the use of students subjects in behavioral research has raged for several years (Gordon et al. 1986). Opponents of the practice point out that it considerably reduces external validity (Gordon et al. 1986; Gordon et al. 1987), while its proponents have warned against taking a simplistic view of external validity (Greenberg 1987).

The use of student subjects certainly provides interesting challenges to experimental research, especially for end-user training. For one thing, the typical student in the study had limited had any experience in organizational settings (most participants were college

123

sophomores or juniors), and thus, was not in a position to venture an informed view of end-user training programs. However, since most training programs are conducted with employees who do not have a previous knowledge of the specific end-user training application, this is unlikely to bias the results.

Most organizations informally use some form of social network to enhance participant learning (Gordon et al. 1986). This study focuses on how a formalized collaborative network of dyads can be useful. This study uses ad-hoc, zero-history dyads for training. Thus, it must be noted that these findings may be generalized to ad-hoc or newly formed paired training only. This, though, resembles most training situations where participants are grouped together in dyads based on training need.

Another drawback in case of paired learning was the variance in existing knowledge between participants of the pairs in real world. In the study, homogeneity among partners was artificially imposed by elimination. Consequently, external validity may have suffered.

One implication of these limitations is that, as long as there is need for high sample sizes and controlled laboratory settings in e-learning and EUT research, there is the need for student subjects, primarily because of their availability. One change that might be made in the future designs is to investigate the effect of heterogeneity groups.

6.4.1.3. E-learning Technology

Various e-learning technologies exist in use by organizations currently. The use of WBCT as a technology-mediation is in line with the current training methods. However, not all WBCT share the same underlying theory (social cognitive theory), though a majority of these used in end-user training use vicarious modeling and enactive learning as tools of training. WBCT used in this study, elementK, emulates this and has gained rich acceptance among organizations and training institutions. The use of a tool accepted in both these realms increases the generalizability of this study to most scenarios. Another concern is the lack of control by the experimenter on WBCT. This though, might hamper internal validity, added to external validity by presenting a more realistic situation.

6.4.1.4. Target System

The main concerns here are the choice of end-user training application and the complexity thereof.

The software chosen for training is among one of the most extensive used end-user application in organizations, Microsoft Excel. This software has reasonable complexity that is confronted by users in post-industrialized world. Thus, the results of the study can be reasonably generalized to training of complex software packages.

Two factors make the use of Microsoft Excel as a good target system to be learned. First, groups were asked to go through a learning process. Since it was the process that was under investigation, it provided reasonable and sufficient degree of complexity. Secondly, the task complexity is usually subject to existing experience by the participants. The study was designed to resemble a situation where participants are trained on technology unknown to them. In this case, only subjects who had no prior knowledge of excel were included in the study, to provide a reasonable replication of the situation. A possible change in future designs is to introduce more complex task, and investigate interactions if any.

The limitations of the study steaming from the context of the study can also be viewed as areas of future research. Thus, they are addressed in the subsequent section.

6.5. Research Implications and Directions for Future Research

The ultimate outcome for line of research, initiated by this study, is to develop a specific collaborative e-learning model for end-user training. However, given the nomological validity of the AST based model used in this study, the model should be investigated in various other learning contexts. The propositions in Chapter 3 provide general guidelines for future research in this area. In this section, more specific areas are outlined.

For e-learning technologies, the research first clarifies the need to incorporate learning theory in the development of learning systems, especially learning-from-computer software. Technologies need to be described in terms of their underlying structures that reflect the underlying spirit or epistemological perspectives as well as the corresponding theoretical causes to correctly anticipate their effects. An important area of future research is the investigation of other epistemological perspectives (other than cognitive perspectives) as well as combination of structures from different perspectives. The results of this study can also be extended to other simulation technology uses. With simulation based learning set to revolutionize existing ways of learning (Aldrich 2004), it presents a very promising area for future research. However, and more importantly, this research states that the impact of simulation based study should be evaluated based on their structures and appropriation.

Collaboration learning method also showed a positive influence. The research details the various structural dimensions involved in teams. An important implication of the findings of this study is the need to focus on these structural dimensions. The study also developed an instrument to measure the richness of team structural dimensions, however, positive interdependence and individual accountability were implemented as separate structures, and the richness of appropriation was not measured. Thus, more research is needed in developing measures for these dimensions. This understanding can be used across research domains such as GSS and virtual teams. Next, the effects of team structural dimensions were found on self-efficacy and satisfaction, however, no effect was fond on cognitive outcomes. As highlighted earlier, an investigation into this area is important for future research.

Even though the study exclusively focused on learning-from-computers vis-à-vis traditional methods of teaching, the model presented is also applicable of learning-with-computers. With the ubiquity of computers, this is an important area of investigation. A wide area of research is the area of computer supported collaborative work (CSCW). However, a review of this research shows the inconsistency of results as well as a lack of analysis of the causes of the effect (collaboration or technology) (Gupta et al. 2004; Lehtinen et al. 2003; Strijbos et al. 2004). The model presented in this work is ideal for investigating the individual effect of collaboration or technology as well as the interaction effect of the two methods. Thus, an important stream of future research is analyzing the entire model in a learning-with-computer context. Such a stream would include analysis of the main, mediating and moderating effects shown in the model.

This research also opens up the black box of learning process not studied by earlier researchers. We find that appropriation of the learning method structures plays an important role in determining the learning outcomes. An important implication of this is that future researchers need to account for the level of appropriation in their studies. Future research needs to focus on early development of both technology and team structures through mechanisms outlined in Chapter 3. Such development should lead to initial effects of collaboration also. However, further empirical research is required in this area. Another important area for future research is a microlevel analysis of the reciprocal causation phenomenon outlined in the discussion. Such an analysis would focus on the embedded and emergent structures. Such a study would provide a significant contribution to theory of adaptive structuration.

The model describes various forms of appropriation support: procedural, meta-cognition, conceptual and strategic. Different appropriation support forms are likely to have different influences on the learning process. According to the model presented, appropriation support will have an indirect influence on learning outcomes by influencing appropriation support. Literature also states that the level of appropriation support changes over time, though no empirical work exists in this area. Thus, an important direction for future research is analyzing the impact of appropriation support measures on the structures embodied in learning methods. Mentoring in electronic domain also presents new challenges and opportunities (Salmon 2003). A study in this area would provide organizations and universities design guidelines to facilitate learning outcomes.

The study was carried out longitudinally, but one of the limitations of the study is that the periods selected were substantially close to each other. This might be true in a dedicated training session, but not necessarily true in continuous learning environments. Thus, future studies need to investigate the impact of larger duration of time. More interestingly, this study assumed a linear relationship for change over time. Researchers in other domains though, have suggested the existence of curve relationship between cohesiveness and performance (Katz 1982). Drawing from this, future research should examine the existence of quadratic relationships over time as well as with dependent variables. This is especially important for collaboration construct.

The learning outcomes in this study were multifaceted, but were measured immediately after the treatment. The immediate variables present the first true picture of training effectiveness. However, since the training programs are also aimed at long-term impact, researchers have suggested investigating the long-term influence of different learning methods. An important addition to learning outcomes would be to focus on delayed task performance (Santhanam et al. 1994; Sein et al. 1989; Sein et al. 1999b; Yi et al. 2003), especially in a job context. Other important learning outcomes that need to be studied are the differential effects of various training methods on adoption and subsequent use of the system. Since training has been found to have a significant effect on technology adoption (Igbaria et al. 1995), understanding the effects of various training methods on the TAM model presents a significant research opportunity (Yi et al. 2001). Both these areas suggest a need for field research to investigate this area, little of which has been done in end-user training literature.

Important influencers of learning outcomes are personality traits and states. With the increase in self-paced learning in organizations and the ability of customization e-learning,

127

further research is needed in this area. Considerable research has been done in this area; though the research continues to remain fragmented (Gupta et al. 2006). Also, none of this research has examined the impact of these differences in the area of collaborative e-learning. An important area for future research would include a framework for classification of individual differences in a collaborative e-learning environment. Such a study would provide substantial contribution in enhancing understanding of the learning process. An understanding of the impact of individual differences on learning outcomes will help designers design e-learning modules to cater to individual needs.

An important assumption in this study has been the fit between learning method structures. In this study, the researcher designed the fit. The design minimized overlap between technology-mediation and collaboration components of the experiment. It was also pilot tested. However, an important area for future research is to study the fit between structures. More importantly, the concept of technology adaptation in case of a design misfit needs to be further studied. Majchrzak et al. (2000) provides a lens to study this phenomenon by combining AST with adaptation of technology model (Leonard-Barton 1988).

In this study, we controlled for content across various experimental treatments. However, content variation is likely to have an impact on learning outcomes. Learning can also be conceptualized as appropriation of learning content. An expanded version of the model presented in Chapter 3 would provide a good starting guideline for investigating the impact of content. DeSousa (2004) shows that different job roles in using information systems need different kinds of knowledge. Such a spread of information systems coupled with the breath of job roles associated with software's provide a compelling need for such a study. This study primarily dealt with novice users. Very little research has been done on advanced users in end-user training and represents a promising future area of research.

This study has focused on 1 hour long learning modules. However, growing literature and technology capabilities are focusing on the area of learning objects (Brevern 2004; González-Martínez et al. 2004). A learning object is a digital resource that can be reused to support learning. The length of these objects can range from 15 minutes to 3 hours, while no guidelines exist about their lengths. Further, these can be combined in various ways to generate new modules. Various learning objects can be combined to create a training program. Such a property enhances the personalization structural dimension. Some research has been done in this area (Shayo et al. 2006), though the impact of increased personalization remains an important unexplored research issue.

Another area of substantial contribution is in the area of analysis of data. The research uses two techniques never used in IS literature and rarely used together in behavioral science. The first technique called stacked group analysis provides a method for comparison of nested groups. Unlike traditional techniques, which assume structural invariance between groups, this technique forces the researcher to explicitly test for these. With increased sophistication and complexity of research phenomena tested by experimental scientists, the study illustrates the use of stacked group analysis for IS researchers. The advantages of this method can be applied to future laboratory and field experiments. This study, thus, presents a good foundation study for using stacked group modeling for researchers.

Researchers also have not been very successful in analyzing change over time, and the shape of such change. Traditional techniques also do not control for issues of homosedacity and auto-regression. Latent Growth Modeling, the technique of analysis used in this work, presents a comprehensive technique of tacking these issues. Not only does this technique have a higher power than traditional techniques in detecting change over time (Fan 2003), it also specifically analyzes structural invariance over time. Researchers in IS have never tested these assumptions (e.g. Bhattacherjee et al. (2004) and Davis et al. (2004)) nor have they been able to analyze the nature of change. This study provides an overview to implement this technique in future studies.

6.6. Conclusions

The contributions to research from this study are many. It enriches our understanding of effectiveness of e-learning and collaboration. Most importantly, it provides a research framework for investigating e-learning and end-user training. The study extends our understanding of AST in a technology context, as well as the broader application in a collaboration context. The results provide contributions to both IS and Education fields. The analysis methods used in this study also provide a contribution in terms of experimental data analysis. Finally, future research directions provide a outlining a stream of research in this area.

There is a need for effective, efficient, rapid and dispersed training in end-user tools in organizations. This research explores the potential of two approaches to improving training. This study also found preliminary support for both approaches and for their combined application. The study provides guidelines for the development of training

129

programs to supplement technology-meditated training with collaboration to maximize effectiveness. The focus on the learning process exemplifies how learning outcomes vary depending on appropriation of learning method. Trainers and organizations, thus, need to start focusing on this. These findings lay the groundwork for future research in this area. In addition, the findings reported here provide optimism that it is possible to meet the demanding training needs in organizations.

7. Bibliography

Alavi, M. "Computer-Mediated Collaborative Learning: An Empirical Evaluation," *MIS Quarterly* (18:2) 1994, pp 159-174.

Alavi, M., and Liedner, D.E. "Research Commentary: Technology-Mediated Learning--A Call for Greater Depth and Breadth of Research.," *Information Systems Research* (12:1) 2001, pp 1-10.

Alavi, M., Marakas, G.M., and Yoo, Y. "A Comparative Study of Distributed Learning Environments on Learning Outcomes," *Information Systems Research* (13:4) 2002, pp 404-415.

Alavi, M., Wheeler, B.C., and Valancich, J.S. "Using IT to reengineer business Education: An exploratory investigation of collaborative telelearning," *MIS Quarterly* (19:3) 1995, pp 293-211.

Aldrich, C. *Simulations and the future of learning : an innovative (and perhaps revolutionary) approach to e-learning* Pfeiffer, San Francisco, 2004, pp. xi, 282.

Allen, I.E., and Seaman, J. "Sizing the Opportunity: The Quality and Extent of Online Education in the United States, 2002 and 2003," The Sloan Consortium.

Anderson, J.C., and Gerbing, D.W. "Structural equation modeling in practice: A review and recommended two-step approach," *Psychological Bulletin* (103:3) 1988, pp 411-423.

Anderson, J.R. "Acquisition of cognitive skill," *Psychological Review* (4) 1982, pp 369-406.

Arthur, W., Bennett, W., Edens, P.S., and Bell, S.T. "Effectiveness of Training in Organizations: A Meta-Analysis of Design and Evaluation Features," *Journal of Applied Psychology* (88:2) 2003, pp 234-245.

Bagozzi, R.P., and Phillips, L.W. "Representing and Testing Organizational Theories: A Holistic Construal.," *Administrative Science Quarterly* (27:3) 1982, pp 459-489.

Bagozzi, R.P., Yi, Y., and Phillips, L.W. "Assessing Construct Validity in Organizational Research," *Administrative Science Quarterly* (36:3) 1991, pp 421-458.

Bandura, A. "Self-efficacy: Toward a unifying theory of behavioral change," *Psychological Review*:84) 1977a, pp pp. 191-215.

Bandura, A. *Social learning theory* Prentice Hall, Englewood Cliffs, N.J., 1977b, pp. viii, 247 p.

Bandura, A. *Social foundations of thought and action : a social cognitive theory* Prentice-Hall, Englewood Cliffs, N.J., 1986, pp. xiii, 617.

Bandura, A. "SOCIAL COGNITIVE THEORY: An Agentic Perspective," *Annual Review of Psychology* (52:1) 2001, pp 1-26.

Bhattacherjee, A., and Premkumar, G. "Understanding changes in belief and attitude toward information technology usage: A theoretical model and longitudinal test," *MIS Quarterly* (28:2) 2004, pp 229-255.

Bilodeau, E.A. *Acquisition of skill* Academic Press, New York,, 1966, pp. xiii, 539.

Bligh, D.A. *What's the use of lectures?*, (3rd ed.) Penguin, Harmondsworth, England, 1972, p. 256.

Bohlen, G.A., and Ferratt, T.W. "End user training: An experimental comparison of lecture versus computer-based training," *Journal of End User Computing* (9:3) 1997, pp 14-27.

Bolt, M.A., Killough, L.N., and Koh, H.C. "Testing the interaction effects of task complexity in computer training using the social cognitive model," *Decision Sciences* (32:1) 2001, pp 1-20.

Bostrom, R.P. "Tutorial: E-Learning: Facilitating Learning through Technology," Americas Conference on Information Systems, Tampa, Florida, 2003, pp. 3159-3164.

Bostrom, R.P., and Heinen, J.S. "MIS Problems and Failures: A Socio-Technical Perspective. Part 1: The Causes," *MIS Quarterly* (1:3) 1977a, pp 17-32.

Bostrom, R.P., and Heinen, J.S. "MIS Problems and Failures: A Socio-Technical Perspective. Part II: The application of socio-technical theory," *MIS Quarterly* (1:4) 1977b, pp 11-28.

Bostrom, R.P., Olfman, L., and Sein, M.K. "The Importance of Learning Style in End-User Training," *MIS Quarterly* (14:1) 1990, pp 101-119.

Boudreau, M.-C., Gefen, D., and Straub, D.W. "Validation in Information Systems Research: A State of the Art Assessment," *MIS Quarterly* (25:1) 2001, pp 1-16.

Bowman, B.J., Grupe, F.H., and Simkin, M.G. "Teaching end-user applications with computer-based training: Theory and an empirical investigation," *Journal of End User Computing* (7:2) 1995, pp 12-18.

Brevern, H.v. "Cognitive and Logical Rationales for e-Learning Objects," in: *ITForum*, University of Bern, Institute of Information Systems, 2004.

Brown, K.G. "Using computers to deliver training: Which employees learn and why?," *Personnel Psychology* (54:2) 2001, pp 271-296.

Burt, R.S. "Interpretational Confounding of Unobserved Variables in Structural Equation Models," *Sociological Methods and Research* (5:1) 1976, pp 3-52.

Burton, J.K., Moore, D.M.M., and Magliaro, S.G. "Behaviorism and Instructional Technology," in: *Handbook of research for Educational communications and technology,* D.H. Jonassen (ed.), L. Erlbaum Associates, Mahwah, N.J., 2001, pp. 46-73.

Busch, T. "Gender, group composition, cooperation and self-efficacy in computer studies," *Journal of Educational Computing Research* (15:2) 1996, pp 125-135.

Campbell, D.T., Stanley, J.C., and Gage, N.L. *Experimental and quasi-experimental designs for research* R. McNally, Chicago,, 1966, pp. ix, 84.

Carmines, E.G., and Zeller, R.A. *Reliability and validity assessment* Sage Publications, Beverly Hills, CA, 1979.

Carroll, W.R., and Bandura, A. "Role of visual monitoring and motor rehearsal in observational learning of action patterns," *Journal of Motor Behavior* (17) 1985, pp 269-281.

Cats-Baril, W.L., and Huber, G.P. "Decision Support Systems of ill-structured problems: An empirical study," *Decision Sciences* (18:3) 1987, pp 350-372.

Chan, D. "Latent growth modeling," in: *Measuring and analyzing behavior in organizations : advances in measurement and data analysis,* F. Drasgow and N. Schmitt (eds.), Jossey-Bass, San Francisco, 2002, pp. 302-349.

Chi, M.T.H., Leeuw, N.D., Chiu, M.-H., and Lavancher, C. "Eliciting self-explanations improves understanding," *Cognitive Science* (18:3) 1994, pp 439-477.

Chidambaram, L., and Bostrom, R.P. "Group development(I): A review and synthesis of development models," *Group Decision and Negotiation* (6:2) 1996, pp 159-187.

Chidambaram, L., and Bostrom, R.P. "Group development(II): Implications for GSS research and practice," *Group Decision and Negotiation* (6:3) 1997, pp 231-254.

Chin, W., W., Gopal, A., and Salisbury, W.D. "Advancing the theory of adaptive structuration: The development of a scale to measure faithfulness of appropriation," *Information Systems Research* (8:4) 1997, pp 342-397.

Clawson, V.K., and Bostrom, R.P. "Research-driven facilitation training for computer-supported environments," *Group Decision and Negotiation* (5:1), Jan 1996, pp 7-29.
133

Cobanoglu, C., Warde, B., and Moreo, P.J. "A comparison of mail, fax and web-based survey methods," *International Journal of Market Research* (43:4) 2001, pp 441-452.

Cockburn, A., and Williams, L. "The costs and benefits of pair programming," in: *Extreme programming examined,* G. Succi and M. Marchesi (eds.), Addison-Wesley, Boston, 2001.

Cohen, E.G. "Restructuring the classroom: Conditions for productive small groups," *Review of Educational Research* (64:1) 1994, pp 1-35.

Cohen, J. *Statistical Power Analysis for behavioral Sciences*, Hillsdale, N. J., Erlbaum Associates (1988)

Collier, K.G. "Peer-Group learning in higher Education - The development of higher-order skills," *Studies in Higher Education* (5:1) 1980, pp 55-62.

Colquitt, J., LePine, J., and Noe, R. "Toward an Integrative Theory of Training Motivation: A Meta-Analytic Path Analysis of 20 Years of Research.," *Journal of Applied Psychology* (85:5) 2000, pp 678-707.

Compeau, D., Gravill, J., Haggerty, N., and Kelley, H. "Computer self-efficacy: A review," in: *Human-Computer Interaction in Management Information Systems,* D. Galletta and P. Zhang (eds.), M. E. Sharpe, Inc, 2005, pp. 1-87.

Compeau, D.R., and Higgins, C.A. "Application of Social Cognitive Theory to Training for Computer Skills.," *Information Systems Research* (6:2) 1995a, pp 118-143.

Compeau, D.R., and Higgins, C.A. "Computer Self-Efficacy: Development of a Measure and Initial Test," *MIS Quarterly* (19:2), June 1995b, pp 189-211.

Compeau, D.R., Olfman, L., and Sein, M.K. "End-user training and learning," *Communications of the ACM* (38:7) 1995c, pp 24-26.

Cook, T.D., and Campbell, D.T. *Quasi-experimentation : design & analysis issues for field settings* Rand McNally College Pub. Co., Chicago, 1979, pp. xii, 405.

Cooper, J., Prescott, S., Cock, L., and Smith, L. "Cooperative Learning and College Instruction," in: *Cooperative Learning Users' Group*, The California State University, Dominguez Hills, CA, 1990.

Coulson, A. "ERP training strategies: The role of knowledge levels in formation of accurate mental models," in: *Graduate Faculty of Information Science*, Claremont Graduate University, 2002.

Daft, R.L. "Why I recommended that your manuscript be rejected and what you can do about it," in: *Publishing in organizational sciences,* T.G. Cummings and Frost (eds.), Irwin, 1985, pp. 193-209.

Davis, F.D. "Perceived Usefulness, Perceived Ease of Use, and User Acceptance of Information Technology," *MIS Quarterly* (13:3) 1989, pp 319-339.

Davis, F.D., Bagozzi, R.P., and Warshaw, P.R. "User Acceptance of Computer-Technology - a Comparison of Two Theoretical-Models," *Management Science* (35:8), Aug 1989, pp 982-1003.

Davis, F.D., Bagozzi, R.P., and Warshaw, P.R. "Extrinsic and Intrinsic Motivation to Use Computers in the Workplace," *Journal of Applied Social Psychology* (22:14), Jul 16 1992, pp 1111-1132.

Davis, F.D., and Yi, M.Y. "Improving Computer Skill Training: Behavior Modeling, Symbolic Mental Rehearsal, and the Role of Knowledge Structures," *Journal of Applied Psychology* (89:3) 2004, pp 509-523.

Dekkers, J., and Donath, S. "The Integration of Research Studies on the Use of Simulation as an Instructional Strategy.," *Journal of Educational Research* (74:6) 1981, pp 424-427.

Dennis, A.R., Haley, B.J., and Vandenberg, R.J. "Understanding fit and appropriation effects in group support systems via meta-analysis," *MIS Quarterly* (25:2) 2001, pp 167-193.

Desai, M.S. "A Field Experiment: Instructor-Based Training vs. Computer-Based Training.," *Journal of Instructional Psychology* (27:4) 2000, pp 239-244.

Desai, M.S., and Richards, T. "End-user training: A meta model.," *Journal of Instructional Psychology* (26:2) 1999, pp 74-85.

DeSanctis, G., Fayard, A.-L., Roach, M., and Jiang, L. "Learning in Online Forums," *European Management Journal* (21:5) 2003, pp 565-577.

DeSanctis, G., and Gallupe, R.B. "A foundation for the study of group decision support systems.," *Management Science* (33:5) 1987, pp 589-609.

DeSanctis, G., and Poole, M.S. "Capturing the Complexity in Advanced Technology Use: Adaptive Structuration Theory.," *Organization Science* (5:2) 1994, pp 121-147.

Desiraju, R., and Gopinath, C. "Encouraging Participation in Case Discussions: A Comparison of the MICA and the Harvard Case Methods," *Journal of Management Education* (25:4) 2001, pp 394-408.

DeSousa, R.M.D. "Complex Information Technology Usage: Toward Higher Levels Through Exploratory Use - The ERP Systems Case," in: *Management Information Systems*, University of Georgia, Athens, GA, 2004.

Dossett, D.L., and Hulvershorn, P. "Increasing technical training efficiency: Peer training via computer assisted instruction," *Journal of Applied Psychology* (68) 1983, pp 552-558.

Duffy, T., and Cunningham, D.J. "Constructivism: Implications for design and delivery of instruction," in: *Handbook of research for Educational communications and technology*, D.H. Jonassen (ed.), L. Erlbaum Associates, Mahwah, N.J., 2001, pp. 170-198.

Duncan, T.E., *An introduction to latent variable growth curve modeling concepts, issues, and applications* L. Erlbaum Associates, Mahwah, N.J., 1999, pp. x, 197.

Dyer, L.D.C. "An investigation of the effects of cooperative learning on computer-monitored problem-solving," University of Minnesota, 1993, p. 232.

Fan, X. "Power of Latent Growth Modeling for Detecting Group Differences in Linear Growth Trajectory Parameters.," *Structural Equation Modeling* (10:3) 2003, pp 380-400.

Fenech, T. "Using perceived ease of use and perceived usefulness to predict acceptance of the World Wide Web," *Computer Networks and ISDN Systems* (30) 1998, pp 629-630

Fjermestad, J., Hiltz, S.R., and Zhang, Y. "Effectiveness for Students: Comparisons of "In-Seat" and ALN Courses," in: *Learning together online : research on asynchronous learning networks*, S.R. Hiltz and R. Goldman (eds.), Lawrence Erlbaum Associates, Mahwah, N.J., 2005, pp. 39-80.

Forman, E.A., and Cazden, C.B. "Exploring Vygotskian perspectives in Education: the cognitive value of peer interaction," in: *Culture communication, and cognition: Vygotskian perspectives*, J.V. Wertsch (ed.), Cambridge University Press, Cambridge Cambridgeshire ; New York, 1985.

Franklin, J.L., Wissler, A.L., and Spencer, G.J. *Survey-guided development : a manual for concepts training* Organizational Development Research Program Center for Research on Utilization of Scientific Knowledge Institute for Social Research University of Michigan, Ann Arbor, 1976, pp. vii, 202.

Financial Times, "Special Report: On the increasing focus on e-learning," London, 2005.

Fulk, J. "Social construction of communication technology," *Academy of Management Journal* (36:5) 1993, pp 921-950
136

Gardner, R.C. *Psychological statistics using SPSS for Windows* Prentice Hall, Upper Saddle River, N.J., 2001, pp. xi, 307.

Gartner " Forecast: E-Learning Software, Worldwide, 2002-2008 (Executive Summary)," Gartner, p. 2.

Gartner "Predicts 2005: Support Improves for Knowledge Workers," Gartner, p. 7.

Garud, R. "On the distinction between know-how, know-why and know-what in technological systems," in: *Advances in Strategic Management,* J.P. Walsh and A.S. Huff (eds.), JAI Press, Greenwich, Conn, 1997, pp. 81-101.

Gates, B. "Interview," in: *Microsoft Research Faculty Summit*, Redmond, Washington, 2005

Ge, X., and Land, S.M. "Scaffolding students' problem-solving processes in an ill-structured task using question prompts and peer interactions," *Educational Technology, Research and Development.* (51:1) 2003, pp 21-38

Giddens, A. *The constitution of society : outline of the theory of structuration* University of California Press, Berkeley, 1984, pp. xxxvii, 402.

Gist, M.E. "The effects of self-efficacy training on training task performance," Academy of Management, Ada, OH, 1986, pp. 376-416.

Gist, M.E. "The influence of training method and trainee age on acquisition of computer skills," *Personnel Psychology* (41:2) 1988, pp 255-265.

Gist, M.E., Schwoerer, C., and Rosen, B. "Effects of Alternative Training Methods on Self-Efficacy and Performance in Computer Software Training," *Journal of Applied Psychology* (74:6) 1989, pp 884-891.

González-Martínez, M.D., and Bermúdez, E. "Learning objects as facilitators of collaborative working in web based course development," 2004.

Goodhue, D.L. "Development and measurement validity of task-technology fit instrument for user evaluations of information systems," *Decision Sciences* (29:1) 1998, pp 105-138.

Gordon, M.E., Slade, L.A., and Schmitt, N. "The Science of the Sophomore Revisited - from Conjecture to Empiricism," *Academy of Management Review* (11:1), Jan 1986, pp 191-207.

Gordon, M.E., Slade, L.A., and Schmitt, N. "Student Guinea-Pigs - Porcine Predictors and Particularistic Phenomena," *Academy of Management Review* (12:1), Jan 1987, pp 160-163.

Gredler, M.E. "Educational games and Simulations: A technology in search of a (research) paradigm," in: *Handbook of research for Educational communications and*
137

technology : a project of the Association for Educational Communications and Technology, D.H. Jonassen (ed.), L. Erlbaum Associates, Mahwah, N.J., 2001, pp. 521-540.

Green, S.G., and Taber, T.D. "The effects of three social decision schemes on decision group process," *Organizational Behavior and Human Performance* (25) 1980, pp 97-106.

Greenberg, J. "The College Sophomore as Guinea-Pig - Setting the Record Straight," *Academy of Management Review* (12:1), Jan 1987, pp 157-159.

Grise, M.L., and Gallupe, R.B. "Information overload: Addressing the productivity paradox in face-to-face electronic meetings," *Journal of Management Information Systems* (16:3), Win 1999, pp 157-185.

Gundlach, M.J., and Thatcher, J.B. "Examining the Multi-Dimensionality of Computer Self-Efficacy: An Empirical Test," Florida State University, Tallahassee, 2000, p. 29.

Gupta, S. "Longitudinal Investigation of Collaborative e-Learning in an End User Training Context," in: *MIS department*, University of Georgia, Athens, GA, 2006.

Gupta, S., and Bostrom, R.P. "Collaborative e-learning: Information systems research directions," Americas Conference on Information Systems, New York, NY, 2004, pp. 3031-3039.

Gupta, S., and Bostrom, R.P. "End-User Training: What we know, What we need to know?," in: *University of Georgia*, Athens, GA, 2006 p. Working paper.

Hair, J.F. *Multivariate data analysis*, (5th ed.) Prentice Hall, Upper Saddle River, N.J., 1998, pp. xx, 730, I712.

Hannafin, M.J., Hannafin, K.M., Hooper, S.R., Rieber, L.P., and Kini, A.S. "Research on and research with emerging technologies," in: *Handbook of research for Educational communications and technology,* D.H. Jonassen (ed.), L. Erlbaum Associates, Mahwah, N.J., 2001, pp. 378-402.

Hannafin, M.J., Kim, M.C., and Kim, H. "Reconciling research, theory, and practice in web-based teaching and learning: The case for grounded design," *Journal of Computing in Higher Education* (15:2) 2004, pp 3-20.

Hashaim, S., Rathnam, S., and Whinston, A. "CATT: An Argumentation Based Groupware System For Enhancing Case Discussions In Business Schools," International Conference on Information Systems, New York, New York, 1991, pp. 371-385.

Hayduk, L.A. *LISREL issues, debates, and strategies* Johns Hopkins University Press, Baltimore, 1996, pp. xxii, 256.

Hevner, A.R., March, S.T., Park, J., and Ram, S. "Design science in Information Systems research," *MIS Quarterly* (28:1), Mar 2004, pp 75-105.

Hollenbeck, J.R., and Brief, A.P. "The effects of individual differences and goal origin on goal setting and performance," *Organizational Behavior and Human Decision Processes* (40) 1987, pp 392-414.

Horn, J.L., and McArdle, J.J. "A practical and theoretical guide to measurement invariance in aging research," *Experimental Aging Research* (18) 1992, pp 117-144.

Hron, A., and Friedrich, H.F. "A review of web-based collaborative learning: factors beyond technology.," *Journal of Computer Assisted Learning* (19:1) 2003, pp 70-79.

Hu, L.-t., and Bentler, P.M. "Cutoff Criteria for Fit Indexes in Covariance Structure Analysis: Conventional Criteria Versus New Alternatives," *Structural Equation Modeling* (6:1) 1999, pp 1-55.

Igbaria, M., Guimaraes, T., and Davis, G.B. "Testing the determinants of microcomputer usage via a structural equation model," *Journal of Management Information Systems* (11:4), Spring 1995 1995, p 87.

Jankowski, P., and Nyerges, T.L. *Geographic information systems for group decision making : towards a participatory, geographic information science* Taylor & Francis, London ; New York, 2001, pp. xiv, 273 , [278] of plates.

Jessup, L.M., and Valacich, J.S. *Group support systems : new perspectives* Macmillan New York, 1993, pp. xviii, 365.

Johnson, D.W., and Johnson, R.T. *Learning together and alone : cooperation, competition, and individualization* Prentice-Hall, Englewood Cliffs, N.J., 1975, pp. ix, 214.

Johnson, D.W., and Johnson, R.T. "Making Cooperative Learning Work," *Theory into Practice* (38:2) 1999, pp 67-74.

Johnson, D.W., Johnson, R.T., and Beth-Stanne, M. "Cooperative Learning Methods: A Meta-Analysis," 2003.

Johnson, D.W., Johnson, R.T., and Holubec, E.J. *Advanced cooperative learning*, (Rev. ed.) Interactive Book Co., Edina, Minn., 1992, p. 1 v. (various pagings).

Johnson, D.W., Johnson, R.T., and Holubec, E.J. *The new circles of learning : cooperation in the classroom and school* Association for Supervision and Curriculum Development, Alexandria, Va., 1994, p. 111 p.

Johnson, D.W., Johnson, R.T., and Smith, K.A. *Active learning : cooperation in the college classroom* Interaction Book Co., Edina, MN, 1991a, p. 1 v. (various pagings).

139

Johnson, D.W., Johnson, R.T., and Smith, K.A. *Cooperative learning : increasing college faculty instructional productivity* School of Education and Human Development The George Washington University, Washington, D.C., 1991b, pp. xix, 152.

Johnson, D.W., Maruyama, G., Johnson, R.T., Nelson, D., and Skon, N.L. "Effects of Cooperative, Competitive, and Individualistic Goal Structures on Achievement: A Meta-Analysis," *Psychological Bulletin* (89:1) 1981, pp 47-62.

Johnson, R.D., and Marakas, G.M. "Research Report: The Role of Behavioral Modeling in Computer Skills Acquisition--Toward Refinement of the Model," *Information Systems Research* (11:4) 2000, pp 402-417.

Jokela, P. "Peer-to-Peer Learning - an Ultimate Form of e-Learning," World Conference on E-Learning in Corp., Govt., Health., & Higher Ed., 2003, pp. 1624-1631.

Jonassen, D.H., and Reeves, T.C. "Learning with Technology: Using Computers as Cognitive Tools," in: *Handbook of research for Educational communications and technology : a project of the Association for Educational Communications and Technology,* D.H. Jonassen (ed.), L. Erlbaum Associates, Mahwah, N.J., 2001, pp. 693-719.

Jones, M. "Structuration Theory," in: *Rethinking management information systems : an interdisciplinary perspective,* W. Currie and R. Galliers (eds.), Oxford University Press, Oxford, 1999, pp. 103-135.

Kanfer, R. "Motivation theory and industrial and organizational psychology," in: *Handbook of industrial and organizational psychology,* M.D. Dunnette and L.M. Hough (eds.), Consulting Psychologists Press, Palo Alto, CA, 1991, pp. 75-170.

Kang, D., and Santhanam, R. "A longitudinal field study of training practices in a collaborative application environment," *Journal of Management Information Systems* (20:3), Win 2003, pp 257-281.

Katz, R. "The Effects of Group Longevity on Project Communication and Performance," *Administrative Science Quarterly* (27:1) 1982, pp 81-104.

Kelly, G.G., and Bostrom, R.P. "A Facilitator's General Model for Managing Socioemotional Issues in Group Support Systems Meeting Environments," *Journal of Management Information Systems* (14:3) 1997/98, pp 23-55.

King, A. "Enhancing Peer Interaction and Learning in the Classroom Through Reciprocal Questioning," *American Educational Research Journal* (27:4) 1990, pp 664-687.

King, A. "Facilitating Elaborative Learning Through Guided Student-Generated Questioning.," *Educational Psychologist* (27:1) 1992, pp 111-126.

Klassen, R.D., and Jacobs, J. "Experimental comparison of Web, electronic and mail survey technologies in operations management," *Journal of Operations Management* (19:6) 2001, pp 713-728.

Kogut, B., and Zander, U. "What firms do? Coordination, identity, and learning," *Organization Science* (7:5) 1996, pp 502-518.

Kolb, D.A. "Individual learning styles and the learning process," in: *Sloan School working paper*, Cambridge, MA, 1971.

Kovalchick, A., and Dawson, K. Education and technology : an encyclopedia ABC-CLIO, Santa Barbara, Calif., 2004, pp. 2 v. (xxi, 713).

Kuhn, T.S. *The structure of scientific revolutions*, (3rd ed.) University of Chicago Press, Chicago, IL, 1996, pp. xiv, 212.

Kulik, J.A. "Meta-Analytic studies of findings on computer-based instruction," in: *Technology assessment in Education and training*, E.L. Baker and H.F. O'Neil (eds.), L. Earlbaum Associates, Hillsdale, N.J., 1994, pp. 9-33.

Kulik, J.A., and Kulik, C.L.C. "College teaching," in: *Research on teaching: concepts, findings, and implications*, P.L. Peterson and H.J. Walberg (eds.), McCutcheon, Berkeley, CA, 1979.

Kulik, J.A., and Kulik, C.L.C. "Effects of ability grouping on student achievement," *Equity & Excellence in Education* (23) 1987a, pp 22-30.

Kulik, J.A., and Kulik, C.L.C. "Review of recent research literature on computer-based instruction," *Contemporary Educational Psychology* (12) 1987b, pp 220-230.

Kulik, J.A., and Kulik, C.L.C. *An Analysis of the Research on Ability Grouping: Historical and Contemporary Perspectives* National Research Center on the Gifted and Talented, Storrs, CT, 1991.

Lance, C.E., Vandenberg, R.J., and Self, R.M. "Latent Growth Models of Individual Change: The Case of Newcomer Adjustment," *Organizational Behavior and Human Decision Processes* (83:1) 2000, pp 107-140.

Learning-Circuits "Learning Circuits E-Learning Trends 2004."

Lehman, R.S. *Computer simulation and modeling: an introduction* Lawrence Erlbaum Associates Hillsdale, N.J., 1977, pp. xii, 411.

Lehtinen, E., Hakkarainen, K., Lipponen, L., Rahikainen, M., and Muukkonen, H. "Computer supported collaborative learning: A review," 2003.

Leidner, D.E., and Jarvenpaa, S.L. "The use of information technology to enhance management school Education: A theoretical view," *MIS Quarterly* (19:3) 1995, pp 265-291.

Leonard-Barton, D. "Implementation as Mutual Adaptation of Technology and Organization," *Research Policy* (17:5), Oct 1988, pp 251-267.

Lou, Y., Abrami, P.C., and d'Apollonia, S. "Small group and individual learning with technology: A meta-analysis," *Review of Educational Research* (71:3) 2001, pp 449-521.

Lou, Y., Abrami, P.C., Spence, J.C., Poulsen, C., Chanbers, B., and d'Apollonia, S. "Within-class grouping: A meta-analysis," *Review of Educational Research* (66:4) 1996, pp 423-458.

Lovie, A.D. "On the early history of ANOVA in the analysis of repeated measure designs in psychology," *British Journal of Mathematical and Statistical Psychology* (34) 1981, pp 1-15.

Lytras, M.D., Tsilira, A.A., and Themistocleous, M. "Technology Classification Framework for E-Learning Purposes from a Knowledge Management Perspective," Americas Conference on Information Systems, Tampa, FL, 2003, pp. 2573-2582.

MacCallum, R.C., Browne, M.W., and Sugawara, H.M. "Power analysis and determination of sample size for covariance structure modeling.," *Psychological Methods* (1:2) 1996, pp 130-149.

Majchrzak, A., Rice, R.E., Malhotra, A., King, N., and Ba, S. "Technology Adaption: The case of computer-supported inter-organizational virtual team," *MIS Quarterly* (24:4) 2000, pp 569-600.

Mao, J.-Y., and Brown, B.R. "The Effectiveness of Online Task Support vs. Instructor-Led Training," *Journal of Organizational and End User Computing* (17:3) 2005, pp 27-46.

Marakas, G.M., Johnson, R.D., and Yi, M.Y. "The importance of divergent validity in measurement development: Development of a measure of computer self-efficacy at general and task specific level," in: *Indiana University*, Bloomington, IN, 1999.

Marakas, G.M., Yi, M.Y., and Johnson, R.D. "The Multilevel and Multifaceted Character of Computer Self-Efficacy: Toward Clarification of the Construct and an Integrative Framework for Research.," *Information Systems Research* (9:2) 1998, pp 126-163.

Marcolin, B.L., Compeau, D.R., Munro, M.C., and Huff, S.L. "Assessing User Competence: Conceptualization and Measurement.," *Information Systems Research* (11:1) 2000, pp 37-61.

Martinez, M. "An investigation into successful learning--Measuring the impact of learning orientation, a primary learner-difference variable, on learning," Brigham Young University 1998.

Martocchio, J.J. "Effects of Conceptions of Ability on Anxiety, Self-Efficacy, and Learning in Training.," *Journal of Applied Psychology* (79:6) 1994, pp 819-826.

Martocchio, J.J., and Judge, T.A. "Relationship between Conscientiousness and Learning in Employee Training: Mediating Influences of Self-Deception and Self-Efficacy," *Journal of applied Psychology* (82:5) 1997, pp 764-773.

Martocchio, J.J., and Webster, J. "Effects of feedback and cognitive playfulness on performance in microcomputer software training.," *Personnel Psychology* (45:3) 1992, pp 553-578.

Maruyama, G. *Basics of structural equation modeling* Sage Publications, Thousand Oaks, Calif., 1997, pp. xvi, 311.

Masie, E. "TechLearn 2004," 2004.

Maynard, D.C., and Hakel, M.D. "Effects of objective and subjective task complexity on performance," *Human Performance* (10:4) 1997, pp 303-330.

McKeackie, W.J. *Learning, Cognition, and College Teaching* Jossey-Bass, San Francisco, CA, 1980.

Meredith, W., and Tisak, J. "Latent Curve Analysis," *Psychometrika* (55:1), Mar 1990, pp 107-122.

Moore, M.G. "Editorial: Learning the necessary principles," *American Journal of Distance Education* (16:3) 2002, pp 129-130.

Mowrer, R.R., and Klein, S.B. *Handbook of contemporary learning theories* Lawrence Erlbaum Associates, Mahwah, N.J., 2000, pp. x, 622.

Neter, J., Wasserman, W., and Kutner, M.H. *Applied linear statistical models : regression, analysis of variance, and experimental designs*, (2nd ed.) R.D. Irwin, Homewood, Ill., 1985, pp. xx, 1127.

Nunnally, J.C., and Durham, R.L. "Validity, reliability, and special problems of measurement in evaluation research," in: *Handbook of evaluation research*, E.L. Struening and M. Guttentag (eds.), Sage Publications, Beverly Hills, 1975.

143

Okada, T., and Simon, H.A. "Collaborative discovery in a scientific domain," *Cognitive Science* (21:2) 1997, pp 109-146.

Olfman, L., and Pitsatron, P. "End-user training research: Status and models for the future," in: *Framing the domains of IT management : projecting the future-- through the past,* R.W. Zmud (ed.), Pinnaflex Education Resources Inc., Cincinnati, Ohio, 2000, pp. 129-146.

Orlikowski, W.J. "The Duality of Technology: Rethinking the Concept of Technology in Organizations.," *Organization Science* (3:3) 1992, pp 398-427.

Orlikowski, W.J. "Using Technology and Constituting Structures: A Practice Lens for Studying Technology in Organizations," *Organization Science* (11:4) 2000, pp 404-428.

Papa, F., Perugini, M., and Spedaletti, S. "Psychological factors in virtual classroom situations: a pilot study for a model of learning through technological devices," *Behaviour & Information Technology* (17:4), Jul-Aug 1998, pp 187-194.

Parsons, T. *The structure of social action; a study in social theory with special reference to a group of recent European writers*, (2d ed.) Free Press, Glencoe, Ill., 1949.

Piccoli, G., Ahmad, R., and Ives, B. "Web-based Virtual learning environments: A research framework and a Preliminary assessment of effectiveness of basic IT skills training," *MIS Quarterly* (25:4) 2001, pp 401-426.

Poole, M.S., and DeSanctis, G. "Understanding the use of group decision support systems: The theory of adaptive structuration," in: *Theoretical approaches to information technologies in organizations,* C. Steinfield and J. Fulk (eds.), Sage, Beverly Hills, CA, 1989a.

Poole, M.S., and DeSanctis, G. "Use of group decision support systems as an appropriation process," Hawaii International Conference on System Sciences, 1989b.

Poole, M.S., and DeSanctis, G. "Understanding the use of group decision support systems: The theory of adaptive structuration," in: *Organizations and communication technology,* J. Fulk and C.W. Steinfield (eds.), Sage Publications, Newbury Park, Calif., 1990, pp. 175-195.

Poole, M.S., and DeSanctis, G. "Microlevel structuration in computer-supported group decision making," *Human Communication Research* (19:1) 1992, pp 5-49.

Poole, M.S., and DeSanctis, G. "Structuration theory in information systems research: Methods and Controversies," in: *The handbook of information systems research,* M.E. Whitman and A.B. Woszczynski (eds.), Idea Group Pub., Hershey, PA, 2003.

Popper, K.R. *The logic of scientific discovery,* (3d ed.) Hutchinson, London,, 1968, p. 480.

Rao, C.R. *Advanced statistical methods in biometric research* Wiley, New York,, 1952, p. 390.

Reeves, T.C., Herrington, J., and Oliver, R. "Design Research: A socially responsible approach to instructional technology research in higher Education," *Journal of Computing in Higher Education* (16:2) 2005, pp 97-116.

Reeves, T.C., and Reeves, P.M. "Effective dimensions of interactive learning on the world wide web," in: *Web-based instruction,* B.H. Khan (ed.), Educational Technology Publications, Englewood Cliffs, N.J., 1997, pp. 459-470.

Rigdon, E.E. "Calculating degrees of freedom in a structured equation model," *Structural Equation Modeling* (1:3) 1994, pp 274-278.

Roberts, J., and Scapens, R. "Accounting systems and systems of accountability: Understanding accounting practices in organizational contexts," *Accounting, Organisations and Society* (10:4) 1985, pp 443-456.

Roberts, J.M. "The story of distance Education: A practitioner's perspective," *Journal of the American Society for Information Science* (74:11) 1996, pp 811-816.

Rohrbeck, C.A., Ginsburg-Block, M.D., Fantuzzo, J.W., and Miller, T.R. "Peer-Assisted Learning Interventions With Elementary School Students: A Meta-Analytic Review," *Journal of Educational Psychology* (95:2) 2003, pp 240-257.

Rosenthal, T.L., and Zimmerman, B.J. *Social learning and cognition* Academic Press, New York, 1978, pp. xiv, 338.

Ryan, S.D., Bordoloi, B., and Harrison, D.A. "Acquiring conceptual data modeling skills: The effect of cooperative learning and self-efficacy on learning outcomes," *Data base for Advances in Information Systems* (31:4) 2000, pp 9-24.

Salas, E., and Cannon-Bowers, J.A. "THE SCIENCE OF TRAINING: A Decade of Progress," *Annual Review of Psychology* (52:1) 2001, pp 471-499.

Salmon, G. *E-moderating : the key to teaching and learning online,* (2nd ed.) RoutledgeFalmer, London ; New York, 2003, pp. xiv, 242.

Salomon, G., Perkins, D.N., and Globerson, T. "Partners in Cognition: Extending Human Intelligence with Intelligent Technologies," *Educational Researcher* (20:3) 1991, pp 2-9.

Sambamurthy, V. "Supporting group performance during stakeholder analysis: the effects of alternative computer-based designs," University of Minnesota, 1989.

Santhanam, R., and Sein, M.K. "Improving End-user Proficiency: Effects of Conceptual Training and Nature of Interaction.," *Information Systems Research* (5:4) 1994, pp 378-399.

Sarason, Y. "A model of organisational transformation: The incorporation of organizational identity into structuration framework," Academy of management, 1995, pp. 47-51.

Sasidharan, S., and Santhanam, R. "Technology-Based Training: Toward A Learner Centric Research Agenda," in: *Human-Computer Interaction and Management Information Systems,* P. Zang and D.F. Galletta (eds.), M. E. Sharpe, 2006.

Schunk, D.H. *Learning theories : an Educational perspective*, (4th ed.) Pearson/Merrill/Prentice Hall, Upper Saddle River, N.J., 2004, pp. xii, 532.

Sein, M.K., and Bostrom, R.P. "Individual differences and conceptual models in training novice users," *Human Computer Interaction* (4:3) 1989, pp 197-229.

Sein, M.K., Bostrom, R.P., and Olfman, L. "Rethinking End-user Training Strategy: Applying Hierarchical Knowledge-level Model," *Journal of End User Computing* (11:1) 1999a, pp 32-39.

Sein, M.K., Olfman, L., Bostrom, R.P., and Davis, S.A. "Visualization ability as a predictor to user learning success," *International Journal of Man-Machine Studies* (39:4) 1993, pp 559-620.

Sein, M.K., and Santhanam, R. "Research Report. Learning from Goal-Directed Error Recovery Strategy.," *Information Systems Research* (10:3) 1999b, pp 276-285.

Shayo, C., and Olfman, L. "The Learning Objects Economy: What Remains to be Done?," in: *Human-Computer Interaction and Management Information Systems: Applications,* P. Zang and D.F. Galletta (eds.), M. E. Sharpe, 2006.

Silver, M.S. *Systems that support decision makers : description and analysis* Wiley, Chichester ; New York, 1991, pp. xvii, 254.

Simon, S.J., and Werner, J.M. "Computer Training Through Behavior Modeling, Self-Paced, and Instructional Approaches:: A Field Experiment," *Journal of Applied Psychology* (81:6) 1996, pp 648-659.

146

Skarlicki, D.P., and Latham, G.P. "Leadership training in organizational justice to increase citizenship behavior within a labor union: a replication," *Personnel Psychology* (50:3) 1997, pp 617-633.

Skinner, B.F. *Science and human behavior* Macmillan, New York,, 1953, p. 461.

Slavin, R.E. "When does cooperative learning increase student achievement?" *Psychological Bulletin* (94) 1983, pp 429-445.

Slavin, R.E. *Cooperative learning : student teams*, (2nd ed.) National Education Asso., Washington, D.C., 1987, p. 31.

Slavin, R.E. "Cooperative Learning and Student Achievement," in: *School and classroom organization*, R.E. Slavin (ed.), L. Erlbaum Associates, Hillsdale, N.J., 1989.

Slavin, R.E., Sharon, S., Kagan, S., Hertz Larzarawitz, R., Webb, C., and Schmuck, R. *Learning to cooperate, cooperating to learn* Plenum Press, New York, 1985, pp. xiii, 472.

Smith-Jentsch, K.A., Salas, E., and Baker, D.P. "Training team performance-related assertiveness," *Personnel Psychology* (49:4) 1996, pp 110-116.

Strijbos, J.-W., Kirschner, P.A., and Martens, R. *What we know about CSCL and implementing it in higher Education* Kluwer Academic Publishers, Boston, Mass., 2004, pp. xiii, 262.

Tanaka, J.S. "Multifaceted conceptions of fit in structural equation models," in: *Testing Structural Equation Models,* K.A. Bollen and J.S. Long (eds.), Sage, Newbury Park, CA, 1993, pp. 10-39.

Taylor, M.W. *A computer simulation of innovative decision-making in organizations* University Press of America, Washington, D. C., 1978.

Training-magazine "Industry report," pp. 20-36.

Vandenberg, R.J. "Toward a further understanding of and improvement in measurement invariance methods and procedures," *Organizational Research Methods* (5:2), Apr 2002, pp 139-158.

Vedder, P., and Veendrick, A. "The Role of the Task and Reward Structure in Cooperative Learning," *Scandinavian Journal of Educational Research* (47:5) 2003, pp 529-542.

Venkatesh, V., and Speier, C. "Creating an effective training environment for enhancing telework," *International Journal of Human-Computer Studies* (52:6) 2000, pp 991-1005.

Vygotskiæi, L.S., and Cole, M. *Mind in society : the development of higher psychological processes* Harvard University Press, Cambridge, 1978, pp. xi, 159.

Vygotskiæi, L.S., and Hanfmann, E. *Thought and language* M.I.T. Press Massachusetts Institute of Technology, Cambridge,, 1962, pp. xxi, 168.

Webb, N.M. "Peer interaction and learning in cooperative small groups," *Journal of Educational Psychology* (74) 1982, pp 642-655.

Webb, N.M., and Palincsar, A.S. "Group processes in the classroom," in: *Handbook of Educational psychology,* D.C. Berliner and R.C. Calfee (eds.), Prentice Hall International, New York, 1996, pp. 841-873.

Weber, R. "The rhetoric of positivism versus interpretivism: A personal view," *MIS Quarterly* (28:1), Mar 2004, pp iii-Xii.

Webster, J., and Hackley, P. "Teaching effectiveness in technology-mediated distance learning," *Academy of Management Journal* (40:6) 1997, pp 1282-1309.

Weinstein, C.E., and Mayer, R.E. "The teaching of learning strategies," in: *Handbook of research on teaching,* M.C. Wittrock (ed.), Macmillan, New York, 1986, pp. 315-327.

Wertsch, J.V. *Culture communication, and cognition : Vygotskian perspectives* Cambridge University Press, Cambridge Cambridgeshire ; New York, 1985, pp. x, 379.

Wheeler, B.C., and Valacich, J.S. "Facilitation, GSS, and Training as Sources of Process Restrictiveness and Guidance for Structured Group Decision Making: An Empirical Assessment.," *Information Systems Research* (7:4) 1996, pp 429-450.

Wicker, R., Brown, G., Wiehe, J.A., and Shim, W. "Moods, goals, and measures for intrinsic motivation," *Journal of Psychology* (124) 1992, pp 75-86.

Williams, L., and Kessler, R.R. *Pair programming illuminated* Addison-Wesley, Boston, 2003, pp. xxi, 265.

Williams, L., Wiebe, E., Yang, K., Ferzli, M., and Miller, C. "In Support of Pair Programming in the Introductory Computer Science Course.," *Computer Science Education* (12:3) 2002, pp 197-213.

Winn, W., and Snyder, D. "Cognitive Perspectives in Psychology," in: *Handbook of research for Educational communications and technology,* D.H. Jonassen (ed.), L. Erlbaum Associates, Mahwah, N.J., 2001, pp. 112-142.

Wolfram, D. "Audio-Graphics for distance Education: A case study in students attitudes and perceptions," *Journal of Education for Library and Information Science* (35:3) 1994, pp 179-186.

Yi, M.Y., and Davis, F.D. "Improving computer training effectiveness for decision technologies: Behavior modeling and retention enhancement," *Decision Sciences* (32:3) 2001, pp 521-544.

Yi, M.Y., and Davis, F.D. "Developing and Validating an Observational Learning Model of Computer Software Training and Skill Acquisition.," *Information Systems Research* (14:2) 2003, pp 146-170.

Zhang, D., Zhao, J.L., Zhou, L., and Nunamaker Jr., J.F. "Can e-learning replace classroom learning," *Communications of the ACM* (47:5) 2004, pp 75-79.

Zigurs, L., and Buckland, B.K. "A theory of task/technology fit and group support systems effectiveness," *MIS Quarterly* (22:3) 1998, pp 313-334.

Zmud, R.Z. "Special Issue on Redefining the organizational Roles on Information Technology in Information Age," *MIS Quarterly* (26:3) 2002.

Appendix A: Pre-Test for Excel Knowledge

Note:
Items are randomly picked from blocks of questions from each post-training quiz to reflect the core concepts of each session.
The scoring of the pretest is shown at the end of the test.

Pretest for Excel Knowledge

Items for measuring Procedural knowledge from Session 1

1. To selects the contents of a cell:

    a. Click the cell
    *b. Double-click the cell, and then double click the cell again
    c. Double-click the cell
    d. Double-click the cell and then inside the formula bar
    e. I don't know

2. You want to move the active cell to the left after entering the data. You would use the following

    a. Hit the left arrow on the keyboard
    b. Hit the Enter key on the keyboard
    c. Click the Tab key
    *d. Click the Shift & Tab together
    e. I don't know

Items for measuring Declarative knowledge from Session 1

3. You have currently selected a cell. What happens when you click on another cell, while keeping the CTRL key pressed?

    a. Nothing happens – Excel gives you an Error
    b. It merges the two cells into one cell
    c. It copies data from the first cell into the second one
    *d. Selects both the cell.
    e. I don't know

4. A formula bar

    a. Appears below the toolbars
    b. Displays the contents of the active cell in a workbook
    *C. A & B
    D. None of the above
    E. I don't know

5. What is the primary advantage of learning how to use an electronic spreadsheet such as Excel

    *a. Helps you in making sound business decisions
    b. Helps you in using an application that would be available to you in the future
    c. Helps you in making better presentations of tabular information

d. Is an acceptable way of number crunching in the industry

e. None of the above

f. I don't know

Items for measuring Procedural knowledge from session 2

6. A firm is divided into six geographic regions. The Excel sheet you have contains the total sales from each region. To show the percentage sales in a visual format, you will do the following

    a. Calculate the percentage in Excel and show it in a Bar chart

    b. Draw a line chart, and choose percentage in the chart options dialog box

    *c. Draw a pie chart, and choose percentage in the chart options dialog box

    d. Calculate the percentage in Excel and show it in a pie chart

    e. I don't know

7. In an Excel sheet, you want to display an organizational chart. To do that, you would do the following

    a. Use the cells in Excel to show the organizational chart

    *b. Choose Insert-->Diagram → Organizational Chart

    c. Choose Tools-->Insert Diagram → Organizational Chart

    d. Create the diagram in word and copy it to Excel

    e. I don't know

Items for measuring Declarative knowledge from session 2

8. When would you use a diagram

    a. To show the relationship among different elements that are related to worksheet data

    b. To illustrate a concept or enhance a document

    c. To visually represent data

    *d. A & b

    e. A & B & C

    f. I don't know

9. By default, a chart contains the following items

    a. Data Table

    b. Gridlines

    c. Legend

    *d. B & C

    e. All of the above

    f. I don't know

10. Which of the following statements about data labels is true?

    a. They can be typed into the chart wizard dialog box
    b. They can point to cell references
    c. They are typed in below each axis
    *d. A & B
    e. A & B & C
    f. I don't know

Items for measuring Procedural knowledge from session 3

11. What would be the outcome of the following expression entered into Excel =2+4^2*3

    a. 4098
    b. 108
    *c.50
    d. 128
    e. I don't know

12. To copy a formula or function to create a new value, you first copy , then paste from / in the relevenet cells. The next step is

    a. Double-click the cell(s) bounded by the selection marquee to activiate the selection marquee
    b. Press Enter to copy the formula
    *c. The steps are done
    d. None of the above
    e. I don't know

Items for measuring Declarative knowledge from session 3

13. Which of the following statements is true

    a. Relative references are used when you want to copy a formula or function, and you wish that the cell reference should automatically be updated
    b. All formula's and functions need to contain relative references
    c. Absolute references are used when you want to copy a formula or function , and you wish that the cell reference should not automatically be updated
    *d. A & C
    e. A & B
    f. All of the above
    g. I don't know

14. Cell F6 contains the formula = F3-D$3. What will be the contents of cell F7 if the entry in cell F6 is copied to cell F7

*a. = F3- D$3
b. = G3 – E$3
c. = F4 – D$4
d. = G4 – E$4
e. I don't know

15. You would use absolute formulas because

a. You will only have to change data in one place rather than multiple places (each formula) as common data changes
b. Its makes it easier to copy formulas which use common data
c. That is the correct way of writing formulas
*d. A & B
e. B & C
f. I don't know

Scoring the pretest
The pretest will be scored on the number of questions correctly answered by the participant. It will give two scores:
1. Procedural knowledge = No. of items that the particpant gets right from questions 1,2, 6,7, 11 & 12
2. Declarative knowledge = No. of items that the particpant gets right from questions 3, 4, 5, ,8, 9, 10, 13, 14 & 15

Appendix B: Content and Instructor Scripts

1. For Session 1 – Working with existing workbooks
2. For Session 2 – Analyzing and managing data
3. For Session 3 – Advanced Formula

Note:

These scripts will be used to create videos

Working with Existing workbooks

Lesson Introduction

Hi, I am Mark Huber, and I'll be your instructor for this session.

You would never use a computer without first having a basic understanding of its components and how it operates. Understanding the basic components of Excel prior to using it will give you familiarity with the application and make you a more efficient user

An overview of excel

{open Excel, sheet 1 session 1 and move your mouse to the respective regions as you describe them below}

A spreadsheet is a form used to store and manipulate numbers, text, and non-alphanumeric symbols. All spreadsheets consist of a grid of columns and rows that intersect to form a cell. Cells store the data entered into a spreadsheet. Columns appear vertically and are identified by letters; rows appear horizontally and are identified by numbers. Some spreadsheets are paper-based, others can be stored electronically. Spreadsheets differ from one another based upon their associated business needs and data requirements.

When you open Excel, two windows are displayed, one within the other. The outer window is the main application window, and the inner window is the workbook window. The application window usually fills the entire screen and provides a place for you to interact with Excel. The workbook window appears within the application window and displays a workbook in which to enter and store data.

The formula bar appears below the toolbars and displays the contents of the active cell in a workbook. The name box appears above the column A heading and displays the name of the current or active cell. The Active cell is the currently selected cell. Worksheet tabs appear at the bottom of the workbook and allow you to move from one worksheet to another. Tabs scrolling buttons appear to the left of the sheet tabs and allow you to scroll the display of the worksheet tabs one at a time, or display the first or last grouping of sheet tabs within a workbook.

An Excel worksheet is an electronic spreadsheet. By default, Excel designates column headings with letters running across the top of the worksheet. Column headings begin with the letter A and continue through the letter Z. After the 26th column (column Z), headings become double letter, from AA to IV.

Row headings are designated by numbers running down the left border of the worksheet. Row headings begin with the number 1 and continue though the number 65536. An Excel workbook is a repository of related worksheets. The default workbook contains three worksheets named Sheet1 though Sheet3. An Excel workbook file can contain up to 255 separate worksheets. The worksheet names appear on tabs at the bottom of the workbook.

In this topic, you received an introductory overview of spreadsheets and the Excel application environment\. This overview helped familiarize you with some Excel's basic concepts that you won't be lost when you fully deploy the application.

Navigate in Excel

{show the navigation in the current window as you go thru it}

In this topic, you will navigate through the Excel environment.

There are a number of ways to move around Excel. One way to move to a specific cell or range of cells is to use the mouse. To move the worksheet display up or down one row per click,

click vertical scroll arrow. To move the worksheet display left to right one per column per click, click a horizontal scroll arrow. To continuously move the worksheet display horizontally or vertically, continuously click the mouse button while pointing at a horizontal or vertical scroll arrow.

To move the worksheet display one screen at a time, click between the scroll box and scroll arrow of either the horizontal or vertical scroll bar. To move rapidly, either vertically or horizontally, though the worksheet area, drag the scroll boxes. To move to the cell specified in the cell reference, click in the Name Box, type the cell reference, and press Enter.

Another way to move to a specific cell or range of cells is to use the keyboard. To move the active cell one cell at a time to the left, right, up or down, press the corresponding arrow keys. To move the active cell to a column A of the current row, press Home. To move the active cell down or up by one screen's worth of rows, press Page Down or Page Up. To move the active cell to the right, one cell at a time, press Tab.

To move the active cell to the left, one cell at a time, press Shift+Tab. To move the active cell to cell A1 in the active worksheet, press Ctrl+Home. To move the active cell one screen to the right, press Alt+Page Down. To move the active cell one screen to the left, press Alt+Page Up.

In this topic, you practiced navigating in the Excel environment using both mouse and keyboard action. This practice navigating in Excel helps you understand this terrain, thus, making it easier for you to use the application.

Select Data

{Demonstrate various methods of selecting data, in the current sheet}
In this topic, you will select data.

There are many ways to select data in Excel worksheet. To select a single cell, click the cell. To select the contents of a cell, you can double-click the cell to place the insertion point inside the cell, and then double-click again to select the contents of the cell. Or you can click the cell, then select the contents of the Formula Bar. To select a contiguous range, navigate to the last cell in the range, press and hold Shift, and then click the last cell to select the full range. Or you can click and drag from the first cell to the last cell. To select a noncontiguous range of cells, click the first cell in the range, navigate to the next cell in the range, press and hold Ctrl, and click cell. You can combine Shift-click and Ctrl-click methods if necessary. To select an entire worksheet, click the blank box immediately below the Name Box.

In this topic, you learned how to select data in an Excel worksheet. Before you can manipulate any data that already exists in worksheet, you must fist know how to select that data.

Enter Data

In this topic, you will enter data.
To enter data into an Excel spreadsheet
1. Either create a new workbook or open an existing workbook
2. Select the cell in which you want to enter data (A3)
3. Type the data you want the cell to contain (Type – Class session)
4. Either press Enter or Tab to place the data into the cell and move the insertion point to a new cell.
   a. Press tab to move down one cell
   b. Press tab to move right one cell

In this topic, you learned how to enter data into Excel worksheet. Knowing how to enter data into a worksheet is the difference between using Excel to help you make a sound business decisions and purchasing a software application you never use.

Save a workbook

In this topic, you will save a workbook

Both the Save and Save As commands can be used to save a file to disk. However, the Save and Save As commands are used in slightly different situations. Use Save when you want to save a brand new file you've never saved before or to resave an existing file when you do not need to change the file's name, type, or directory location. Use Save As when you want to resave an existing file with a new name, with a new file type, in a new directory. Don't be alarmed when you use the File->Save command or click the save button to save a file for the first time and the Save As dialog box opens. This only happens when you save the file that has never been saved before. The Save As dialog box opens because you are changing the name of the file from the default name to the name you need to use.

To save a new workbook

5. With a new workbook open in Excel, choose File→Save to open the Save As dialog box.
6. Navigate to the directory where you want to save the file
7. Name the file
8. Click Save

To save an existing workbook, follow these steps

9. With an existing workbook open in Excel, choose File→ Save As to open the Save As dialog box
10. Navigate to the directory where you want to save the file
11. Rename the file
12. Click Save

In this topic, you learned how to save a workbook. By saving your work regularly, you make that work accessible beyond your current work session.

Obtain Help

In this topic, you will obtain help using Excel's Help system.

To obtain help

13. Choose Help - > Microsoft Excel Help
14. In the Search text box, type the subject of your search
15. Click Start Searching button
16. Review the returned list of links, and then click the link that corresponds to your search.

In this topic, you learned how to obtain help from Excel's Help system. By accessing the Help system, you can find information that shows you how to complete the task you are working on.

Lesson Follow Up

In this lesson, you got started with Excel by familiarizing yourself with Excel environment and interacting with some of its components. Because you have familiarized yourself with Excel, you can be more efficient user.

Creating and modifying charts

Hi, I am Mark Huber and I'll be teaching this session.
In this lesson, you will create and modify charts

Create a Chart

{open Excel}
Sometimes, when you look at large amount of data, row after row of numbers can seem endless. Even worse, it is nearly impossible to draw any meaningful conclusion from the vast amount of data. When you use a chart, however, you can consolidate data into a visual format that is easily understandable. By looking at the information this way, you can quickly compare the data and possibly find information you would not have noticed otherwise.

In this topic, you will create a chart
A chart is a visual representation of information based on data in the worksheet. A chart contains:

❑ Data range – The range of cells that contains the actual data being charted
❑ Data point – One item of data (one cell) in a data range.
❑ Data Row – A row of cells that each contain a unique piece of information such as item, cost and quantity. A data row contains several different data points
❑ Data Series – One column containing the same data point (piece of information) for each data row
❑ Data Markers – The graphic representation of a data point in a chart such as one bar in a bar chart or one slice in a pie chart.

There are a variety of chart types. A chart type you choose depends on how you want to analyze the data. Charts can contain additional items such as a title and a legend for more clarification

{Click insert -> chart. As you go through the list below, click on each graph type}
There are a variety of chart types. The data analysis you want to perform determines the chart type you will use.

Chart Type	Description
Column	Compares values across categories.
Bar	Compares values across categories.
Line	Displays trends over time or categories.
Pie	Displays the contribution of each value to a total.
XY (Scatter)	Compares values of pairs.
Area	Displays the trend of the contribution of each value over time or categories.
Doughnut	Displays the contribution of each value to a total but can contain multiple series.
Radar	Displays changes in values relative to a center point.
Surface	Shows trends in values across two dimensions in a continuous curve.
Bubble	Compares sets of three values.
Stock	Displays several series of data in a specific order, which includes open, high, low, close, and volume.
Cylinder	A column or bar chart with a cylindrical shape.

| Cone | A column or bar chart with a conical shape. |
| Pyramid | A column or bar chart with a pyramid shape. |

Create a Column, Bar, or Line Chart

{open file sheet 1 for session 2. Perform the following actions as well as speak them. Specific actions are noted in brackets below}}

To create a column, bar, or line chart:

1. Choose Insert→Chart. This begins the Chart Wizard.
2. On the Standard Types page, select Column, Bar, or Line chart. {Select column}
3. {just speak} If necessary, select the appropriate Chart Sub-type.
4. Click Next.
5. On the Data Range page:
   - Select the range of cells containing the data you want to chart. {$B$6:$E$13}
   - Select whether the series is in Rows or Columns. {Columns}
6. On the Series page:
   - Enter a name for each data series by typing text or selecting a cell. {B5, C5, D5, E5}
   - {Just speak} If necessary, select the range of cells represented by each data series.
   - Enter a label for the category (X) axis by typing text or selecting a range of cells. {A6:A13}
7. Click Next.
8. On the Titles page:
   - Enter a Chart title. {Robin's Pet Place}
   - Enter a category (X) axis title. {Store number}
   - Enter a value (Y) axis title. {Sales in US Dollar}

{Just speak the following}

9. If necessary, on the Axes page, select Automatic, Category, or Time-scale for the category (X) axis.
10. If necessary, on the Gridlines page, select major and minor gridlines for both the category (X) axis and value (Y) axis.
11. If necessary, on the Legend page, change the placement of the legend.
    Note: You can choose to eliminate the legend completely by unchecking the Show Legend check box.
12. If necessary, on the Data Labels page, choose data labels containing the series name, the category name, the value, or any combination of these. If you choose multiple data labels, you can indicate a separator such as a space, comma, semicolon, or separate line.
13. If necessary, on the Data Table page, check the Show Data Table check box.

{Act the following, as well as speak}

14. Click Next.
15. In the Place Chart area, select a location for the chart from either:

- As A New Sheet and name the new sheet. {Stores by quarter}
- {Just speak} As A New Object and select any of the worksheets in the workbook.
16. Click Finish.

Create a Pie Chart

{open file sheet 1 for session 2. Perform the following actions as well as speak them. Specific actions are noted in brackets below}}

To create a pie chart:

1. Choose Insert→Chart. This begins the Chart Wizard.
2. On the Standard Types page, select Pie.
3. If necessary, select the appropriate Chart Sub-type. {5th sub type}
4. Click Next.
5. On the Data Range page:
   - Select the range of cells containing the data you want to chart. {=Sheet1!$A$5:$E$5,Sheet1!$A$14:$E$14}
   - Select whether the series is in Rows or Columns. {Rows}
6. Click Next.
7. If necessary, on the Data Labels page, choose data labels containing the series name, the category name, the value, or any combination of these. {Percentage}
8. Click Next.
9. In the Place Chart area, select a location for the chart from either:
   - As A New Sheet and name the new sheet. {Quarter totals}
10. Click Finish.

In this topic, you created a chart. When you show your data in a chart, you can analyze the data by comparing visual information instead of row upon row of data.

Change the Chart Type

In this topic, you will format chat items

There are a variety of chart items. The chart items you add to chart depend on the areas of the chart that might need more explanation or clarification. The chart title describes what the overall chart represents. The chart title describes what the overall chart represents. In charts displaying multiple data series, the X axis shows the data series in each category, and the Y axis shows how the data is measured (dollar amounts, time and others). The Category (x) Axis Title describes what the Y axis represents. Each of the X and Y axis can display both major and minor gridlines. The ledge indicates what color represents which particular data series. Data labels indicate the numeric value, the percentage, or the name of a single data point. The data table displays the worksheet data the chart is based on in a table below the chart.

Modify Chart Items

{open file sheet 2 for session 2. Perform the following actions as well as speak them. Specific actions are noted in brackets below}}

To modify chart items:

1. Right-click in any blank area of the chart and choose Chart Options.

161

2. Select the appropriate page for the item you want to modify and make the changes {Click on Legend – select top. Click on Data labels, uncheck percentage and check the value box}
3. Click OK.

Format Chart Items

{Continue with the same sheet}
To format chart items:

1. Right-click an item and choose Format. {right click on the title of the chart – quarter totals}
2. Make the necessary change to the item. {Change font to Verdana , Size to 28}
3. Click OK.

In this topic, you learned how to format chat items so each item enhances and clarifies the chart data.

Change the chart type

In this topic, you will change the chart type.
{open file sheet 3 for session 2. Perform the following actions as well as speak them. Specific actions are noted in brackets below}}
To change the chart type:
1. Right-click and choose chart type.
2. Select the appropriate chart type. {Choose a bar chart , second sub type}
3. Click OK. You many need to modify or format some chat items to appear correctly in the new chart type.

In this topic, you changed the chart type. In the event that the original chart type you choose does not show the data as you want, you can change it to a different type.

Create a diagram

In this topic, you will create a diagram
A diagram is a graphic that is placed on a worksheet to illustrate a concept, show a relationship, or enhance the document. Diagrams are not numerically based, they are not created directly from worksheet data. Diagrams have a drawing border and sizing handles that allow you to customize the diagram. A diagram is created by selecting a template from the diagram gallery.
{Choose insert – Diagram to show them the various diagram options}
The diagram you choose is determined by the relationship of the information you need to display.

- ❑ Organization chart – Shows hierarchical relationship
- ❑ Cycle diagram – Shows a continuous process cycle
- ❑ Radial diagram – Shows the relationship of core elements to other elements
- ❑ Pyramid diagram – Shows foundation-based relationships
- ❑ Venn diagram – Shows areas of overlap between elements
- ❑ Target diagram – Shows steps towards a goal

{Continue with the same file as open, Go to a new blank sheet}
To create a diagram:

1. Select the location for the diagram.
2. Choose Insert→Diagram.
3. Select the diagram type. {Organizational chart}
4. Enter text. {Enter Robin Peterson as the head, - The sub headings would be West, Central and East}
5. Add additional objects. {Select Insert Shape - > Subordinate, enter text "#53 Brian Wilson". Select insert shape -> coworker. Enter text "#72 Jim Francis"}
6. Save and Exit

In this topic, you created a diagram. Although a diagram is not directly based on the data in a worksheet, the information contained in a diagram can show the relationship among different elements that are related to the worksheet data.

Lesson follow-up

In this lesson, you learned how to display data in a graphical manner through charts. These charts allow you to observe a large amount of data and draw relevant conclusions quickly.

Advanced Formulas

Hi, I am Mark Huber and I am going to be your instructor for this lesson. In this lesson, you will perform calculations

You have a spreadsheet containing sales data. Your manager has asked you for the total sales for all reps for the month of February. Would you like to calculate by hand? Calculating by hand is inefficient. Excel can do this for you.

Create Basic Formulas

In this topic, you will create basic formulas.

A formula is a set of mathematical instructions that performs calculations. Formulas can contain any mathematically sound combination of numbers and symbols. Some common mathematical symbols include the plus sign for addition, the minus sign for subtraction, the asterisk for multiplication, the front slash for division, the caret symbol for exponents, and the open and close parentheses to group computation instructions.

An order of operations is a sequence of computations that a formula follows to arrive at a desired result. The order of operations follows this sequence. Computations enclosed in parentheses are performed first, no matter where they appear in a formula. Computations involving exponents are performed second. Computations involving multiplication and division are performed third. Excel performs these calculations in the order in which it encounters them, from left to right. Computations involving addition and subtraction are performed last. Excel performs these calculations in the order in which it encounters them, from left to right.

In Excel, all formulas begin with an equal sign (=). Additionally, you can write formulas using cell reference rather than numbers. If cell A1 contains the value 2, and cell A2 contains the value 5, you can write a formula that reads =A1+A2 in any cell and that new cell will contain the result of the calculation: "7"

{open file sheet 1 session 3}
To create a basic formula
1. Click the cell in which you would like the formula to appear {Click cell c13}
2. In the formula bar, type an equal sign, and then type the formula you would like to perform { =c7+c8+c9+c10 , press enter}
{drag the handle from this cell to cell F13}
{click cell c14, type =(c7+c8+c9+c10)/4 in the formula bar }
{drag the handle from this cell to cell F14}
3. Press Enter

In this topic, you created basic formulas. Creating basic formulas helps you gather valuable information from the data you've entered into a worksheet.

Calculate with Functions

In this topic, you will calculate with functions.

A function is a built-in formula in Excel. Functions start with an equal sign and generally have two components: the function name or an abbreviation of that name, and the arguments, which are required data enclosed in parentheses. Excel provides over 200 built-in functions. You can use a function by itself or in conjunction with other formulas or functions.

{Using the same sheet}
To calculate with functions:

1. Click the cell in which you would like the function to appear. {cell H7}
2. If you are only going to sum a range of cells, click the AutoSum button. Otherwise, choose Insert→Function to open the Insert Function dialog box. {Click insert->function, select all functions , click on sum, click okay}
3. On the Select A Function list, double-click the function you would like to use.
4. On the worksheet, select the cells you want to include in the function. { C7:f7}
5. In the Function Arguments dialog box, click OK to insert the function into the cell and populate the cell with the results of the function.

{drag the handle in cell H7 to H10}
In this topic, you performed calculations with functions. Functions help speed up the development of calculations because they contain built-in formulas that you don't have to write out by hand.

Copy formulas and functions

In this topic, you will copy formulas and functions.

A relative reference is a cell reference that is automatically updated by Excel whenever a formula or function is compiled from an original cell to a destination cell. Relative references include only a cell's column and row identification.

Copy a Formula or Function to Maintain the Original Value

When you want to copy a formula or function from an originating cell to a destination cell, and you want the destination cell to contain the same value as the originating cell:

1. Select the cell that contains the formula you want to copy. {select cell C13}
2. Select the contents of the Formula Bar.
3. Choose Edit→Copy and then press Enter.
4. Select the cell that you want to copy the formula to. {c19}
5. Choose Edit→Paste.

In this topic, you copied formulas and functions. By copying formulas and functions, you can reuse some of the formulas and functions in other cells, and your calculations will contain fewer error because you aren't manually keying the formulas and functions.

Create an absolute reference

In this topic, you will create an absolute reference.

An absolute reference is a cell reference in a formula what doesn't change when you copy the formula. All absolute references include dollar sign ($) either before both the column and row headings or before either the column or row headings. You can convert any relative cell reference to an absolute reference by adding a dollar sign in front of the cell's column and row headings. By identifying a cell as an absolute reference, a change made to that cell will automatically update other cells using that reference.

Create an Absolute Reference

{Create a formula in cell I7 = H7*H4}
To create an absolute reference:

1. Select the cell that contains the formula you want to add the absolute reference to. {cell I7}
2. Type a dollar sign ($) in front of the column heading and row heading for each column and row you want to refer to absolutely. For example, to create an absolute reference to cell B3 in a formula, you would change B3 to $B$3. {cell H4}
3. Press Enter to activate the absolute reference(s).

In this topic, you created an absolute reference. By identifying cells with absolute references, you will only have to change data in one place rather than in multiple places (each formula) as the common data changes.

In this lesson, you performed calculations on existing data. By using Excel to perform calculations on your data, you remove the inefficiency of calculating by hand.

Appendix C: Experiment Scripts

Note:

The appendix contains scripts for the first session for all four treatments. The rest of the session scripts are similar, and thus, not attached.

Experiment Protocol: LM1

Trainer Name: _____   Room: _____ _____

Date: _____   Starting time: _____

Experimental Procedure:

Subjects will enter the lab, and then be seated at any available computer.
Once all subjects are seated, begin the following script.

Script

<<Record the current time: _____ : _____ >>

Hello, thank you for talking the time to participate in this research study. My name is _____. I will be leading this training session. This study is to understand how people acquire computer software skills. By participating in this study, you will have an opportunity to improve your computer software skills, particularly, using Microsoft Excel.

You will receive credit for your participation and prizes for the outstanding performers. You will get _____ credit for faithfully participating in the research. Prizes are based on your performance on the quizzes at the end of each session. Three gift cards of $50, $30 and $20 will be awarded to the top three performers.

Excel training will be conducted in three training sessions. For the research to be successful as well as get credit for participation, you need to participate in all three sessions and restrict yourself to the contents of the training i.e. Do not access ElementK outside the experimental setting.

Microsoft Excel is one of the best-selling spreadsheet programs of all times. The beauty of a spreadsheet program such as Excel is that everything's built in—the rows and columns, formatting controls, and mathematical functions are all right there for you, ready to use. Excel can turn anyone into an instant analyst in various fields like Accounting, Management, Real estate etc. You don't have to be a math wizard, and you don't need an MBA—all you need are a spreadsheet program and a little instruction, and soon you'll be crunching numbers into complex formulas and calculations, balancing budgets, keeping statistics on your softball team—and doing other high-profile tasks.

Today, *you are going to learn basic usage of Excel (changes based the session).* You will go through a video demonstrating the various Excel functions. While you listen to the video, please do not work with the computer. You will be given practice time to practice your skills after the video. Throughout the training, you will not be allowed to work with other students. You should not discuss with other students and you should not look at other student computers.

You have been handed out a booklet. Please fill in the details on the first page and proceed to the online questionnaire in the next section. You will use the Internet to fill out the questionnaires. Your data will be kept strictly confidential and will be known only to the researcher. Data will be used only as aggregate for research purposes. Thus, you can and need to be very honest. We need honest responses in order for the study to come up with good training guidelines for helping people learn software. Please complete step 1 of your booklet.

<<After 3 mins>>

Let's move on to step 2. As we go through the video, you are all allowed and advised to take notes. Use the pages in the worksheet provided for taking notes. At the end of the training, a quiz will be conducted to measure how much you have learned. If you have any questions, please raise your hand. I will not

167

answer any question regarding Excel. I will answer any questions related to the learning process, questionnaires or technology.
<<answer questions if asked>>

We will now start the video.
<<Start the video>>
<< After the video finishes >>

Now we have finished with the video. You can now start Excel and practice what you have learned i.e. Step 3.

<<After 15 minutes >>

Please close Excel now. It will not be used any further. Please proceed to fill the online questionnaire. The questionnaire will be followed by a quiz. The quiz will help us see how much we have learned. Please proceed to step 4.

<<After 10 mins. Record the current time: _____:_____>>

Time is up. Please return the training workbook. You are now free to leave. You will receive the results of your performance after the final session of the experiment. Please make sure that you attend the next training session at _____. I thank you for your participation.

Space for Trainer / Experimenter Notes _____

Experimental Protocol : LM2

Trainer Name: _____   Room: _____ _____
Date: _____   Starting time: _____

Experimental Procedure:

Subjects will enter the lab, and then be seated at any available computer.
Once all subjects are seated, begin the following script.

Script

<<Record the current time: _____: _____>>
Hello, thank you for talking the time to participate in this research study. My name is _____. I will be leading this training session. This study is to understand how people acquire computer software skills. By participating in this study, you will have an opportunity to improve your computer software skills, particularly, using Microsoft Excel.

You will receive credit for your participation and prizes for the outstanding performers. You will get _____ credit for faithfully participating in the research. Prizes are based on your performance on the quizzes at the end of each session. Three gift cards of $50, $30 and $20 will be awarded to the top three performers.

Excel training will be conducted in three training sessions. For the research to be successful as well as get credit for participation, you need to participate in all three sessions.

Microsoft Excel is one of the best-selling spreadsheet programs of all times. The beauty of a spreadsheet program such as Excel is that everything's built in—the rows and columns, formatting controls, and mathematical functions are all right there for you, ready to use. Excel can turn anyone into an instant analyst in various fields like Accounting, Management, Real estate etc. You don't have to be a math wizard, and you don't need an MBA—all you need are a spreadsheet program and a little instruction, and soon you'll be crunching numbers into complex formulas and calculations, balancing budgets, keeping statistics on your softball team—and doing other high-profile tasks.

Throughout the training, you will not be allowed to work with other students. You should not discuss with other students and you should not look at other student computers.

You have been handed out a booklet. Please fill in the details on the first page and proceed to the online questionnaire in the next section. You will use the Internet to fill out the questionnaires. Your data will be kept strictly confidential and will be known only to the researcher. Data will be used only as aggregate for research purposes. Thus, you can and need to be very honest. We need honest responses in order for the study to come up with good training guidelines for helping people learn software. Please complete step 1 of your booklet.

<<After 3 mins>>

For the purpose of training we will be using an online training program called ElementK. I will now give you a quick demo of how to enter ElementK. You can follow the guidelines in step 2 of the workbook. Please let me know if you are having trouble logging in.

<<Use the steps in the workbook attached to provide a quick demo of how of ElementK. Follow the instructions in the element K guide. Show them all the screens on the overhead projector using the faculty computer. >>

<<After the demo – Make sure that all groups are logged in>>

You are all allowed and advised to take notes. Use the pages in the worksheet provided for the same. At the end of the training, tests will be conducted to measure how much you have learned. If you have any questions, please raise your hand. I shall answer any questions related to the learning process, questionnaires or technology. I shall not answer any question regarding Excel.

<<answer questions if asked>>

You may now start your lesson plan. Please make sure that you use the worksheet in step 3 of your workbook. Please make sure that you stop at the first lesson level lab. You should print out your lab once you are done. That is step 4 of your workbook.

<< After 45 mins ElementK, everybody should have completed the task. Move to the next part >>

Please close Excel now. It will not be used any further. Please proceed to fill the online questionnaire. The questionnaire will be followed by a test. The test will help us see how much we have learned. Please complete step 5 of your workbook.

<<After 10 mins. Record the current time: _____:_____ >>

Time is up. Please return the training workbook. You are now free to leave. You will receive the results of your performance after the final session of the experiment. Please make sure that you attend the next training session at _____. I thank you for your participation.

Space for Trainer / Experimenter Notes
_____

Experiment protocol: LM3

Trainer Name: _____   Room: _____ _____
Date: _____   Starting time: _____

Experimental Procedure:

Subjects will enter the lab, and then be seated at any available computer.
Once all subjects are seated, begin the following script.

Script

<<Record the current time: _____:_____>>
Hello, thank you for talking the time to participate in this research study. May name is _____.
I will be leading this training session. This study is to understand how people acquire computer software skills. By participating in this study, you will have an opportunity to improve your computer software skills, particularly, Microsoft Excel.

You will receive credit for your participation and prize for your performance later. Excel training will be conducted in three training sessions. For the research to be successful as well as get credit for participation, you need to participate in each session and restrict yourself to the contents of the training. You will get _____ credit for faithfully participating in the research. Prize for participation is based on your performance on the quizzes at the end of each session. Three gift cards of $60, $30 and $25 will be awarded to the top three performing groups.

Microsoft Excel is one of the best-selling spreadsheet programs of all times. The beauty of a spreadsheet program such as Excel is that everything's built in—the rows and columns, formatting controls, and mathematical functions are all right there for you, ready to use. Excel can turn anyone into an instant analyst in various fields like accounting, Management, Real estate etc. You don't have to be a math wizard, and you don't need an MBA—all you need are a spreadsheet program and a little instruction, and soon you'll be crunching numbers into complex formulas and calculations, balancing budgets, keeping statistics on your softball team—and doing other high-profile tasks. Today, *you are going to learn an basic usage of Excel (changes based the session).*

You will be working in pairs. You should be sitting next to your pre-designated partner. You are supposed to work closely with your partner, but only with your partner. Please check with me if you don't know who your partner is.

<<Answer questions>>

You have been handed out a booklet. Please fill in the details on the first page and proceed to the online questionnaire in the next section. You will use the Internet to fill out the questionnaires. Your data will be kept strictly confidential and will be known only to the researcher. Data will be used only as aggregate for research purposes. Thus, you can and need to be very honest. We need honest responses in order for the study to come up with good training guidelines for helping people learn software. Please complete step 1 of your booklet.

<<After 3 mins>>

Next, you have been provided with a collaboration guide in your workbook. Let us go through it. It is step 2 in your workbook.

171

<<go through the collaboration guide, attached below. Read each one the collaboration guidelines as scripted below with the bold text to be emphasized>>

Collaboration Guidelines

Both partners in the team are supposed to work together. **Learning in a team enhances learning for each participant. This is because each partner can bring in their own personal perspective and help the other partner understand the content better. The following are guidelines that you need to follow to benefit from your mutual learning experience.**

1. You will be both learning from the video.
2. As you go through the sessions, each of you have the following responsibilities
   i.   Listen & see attentively and learn
   ii. If your partner has any trouble understanding, help and support your him/her i.e. If your partner doesn't understand a topic, he or she should ask you about it.
   iii. Take notes in your workbook in the space provided
   iv. Write down at least **three** comprehensive questions in the training workbook in the space provided regarding the lesson that you have just gone through. These questions will be used for discussion with your partner later on. As a guide, step 3 provides generic question stems that can be used to make questions. Questions examples are like – Why would I use Excel? How to enter data in Excel? Etc.
3. **Once the video has completed and before you start practicing, each partner needs to ask the other the questions that he/she has noted down. So together, you discuss 6 questions minimum, 3 asked by each partner. If the answer to the question is not correct, you and your partner need to discuss it till you come up with a common answer and understanding. This discussion is oral in nature and need not be written.**
4. After the discussion, you should practice what you have learned with your partner.

Lessons are followed by individual tests. Your rewards will be based on the total score of both individuals in the all tests put together.

Any questions on the guidelines ?

<end of collaboration guideline. Answer questions >>

Lets move on to step 3. For the purpose of training we will be using a video demonstration of using Excel. As we go through the video, you are all allowed and advised to take notes. Use the pages in the worksheet provided for the same. At the end of the training, tests will be conducted to measure how much you have learned. If you have any questions, please raise your hand. I shall answer any questions related to the learning process, questionnaires or technology. I shall not answer any question regarding Excel.

<<answer questions if asked>>

We will now start the video.

<<Start the video>>

<< After the video finishes >>

Now we have finished with the video. You should now discuss your discussion questions (Step 3) and practice (Step 4) in Excel as instructed in the collaboration guidelines.

<<after 15 minutes>>

Please close Excel now and return back to your individual computers. It will not be used any further. Please proceed to fill the online questionnaire. The questionnaire will be followed by a test. The test will help us see how much we have learned. Please complete step 5 of your workbook.

<<After 10 mins. Record the current time: _____:_____>>

Time is up. Please return the training workbook. You are now free to leave. You will receive the results of your performance after the final session of the experiment. Please make sure that you attend the next training session at _____. I thank you for your participation.

Space for Trainer / Experimenter Notes
_____

Experiment Protocol: LM4

Trainer Name: _____   Room: _____ _____
Date: _____   Starting time: _____

Experimental Procedure:

Subjects will enter the lab, and then be seated at any available computer.
Write on the whiteboard, PLEASE SIT NEXT TO YOUR PAIR.

Once all subjects are seated, begin the following script.

Script

<<Record the current time: _____:_____>>

Hello, thank you for talking the time to participate in this research study. My name is _____. I will be leading this training session. This study is to understand how people acquire computer software skills. By participating in this study, you will have an opportunity to improve your computer software skills, particularly, using Microsoft Excel.

You will receive credit for your participation and prizes for the outstanding group performances. You will get _____ credit for faithfully participating in the research. Prizes are based on your performance on the quizzes at the end of each session. Three gift cards of $60, $30 and $25 will be awarded to the top three performing groups.

Excel training will be conducted in three training sessions. For the research to be successful as well as get credit for participation, you need to participate in all three sessions and restrict yourself to the contents of the training i.e. Do not access ElementK outside the experimental setting.

Microsoft Excel is one of the best-selling spreadsheet programs of all times. The beauty of a spreadsheet program such as Excel is that everything's built in—the rows and columns, formatting controls, and mathematical functions are all right there for you, ready to use. Excel can turn anyone into an instant analyst in various fields like Accounting, Management, Real estate etc. You don't have to be a math wizard, and you don't need an MBA—all you need are a spreadsheet program and a little instruction, and soon you'll be crunching numbers into complex formulas and calculations, balancing budgets, keeping statistics on your softball team—and doing other high-profile tasks.

Today, *you are going to learn basic usage of Excel (changes based the session)*. You will be working in pairs. You should be sitting next to your pre-designated partner. You are supposed to work closely with your partner, but only with your partner. Please check with me if you don't know who your partner is.

<<Answer questions>>

You have been handed out a booklet. Please fill in the details on the first page and proceed to the online questionnaire in the next section. You will use the Internet to fill out the questionnaires. Your data will be kept strictly confidential and will be known only to the researcher. Data will be used only as aggregate for research purposes. Thus, you can and need to be very honest. We need honest responses in order for the study to come up with good training guidelines for helping people learn software. Please complete step 1 of your booklet.

<<After 3 mins>>

174

Next, you have been provided with a collaboration guide in your workbook. Let us go through it. It is step 2 in your workbook.

<<go through the collaboration guide, attached below. Read each one the collaboration guidelines as scripted below while putting emphasis on the bolded text>>

Collaboration Guidelines

Both partners in the team are supposed to work together. Even though ElementK was initially designed to be used by individuals, more and more organization are now using collaborative or team-based learning. **Learning in a team enhances learning for each participant. This is because each partner can bring in their own personal perspective and help the other partner understand the content better. The following are guidelines that you need to follow to benefit from your mutual learning experience**.

1. You will both be working on separate computers. Once you have finished the first three modules, you will stop and wait for your partner to complete the same.
2. As you go through the sessions, each of you have the following responsibilities
   a. Listen & see attentively and learn
   b. If your partner has any trouble understanding, help and support your him/her. If your partner doesn't understand a topic, he or she should ask you about it.
   c. Take notes in your workbook in the space provided
   d. Write down at least **three** comprehensive questions in the training workbook in the space provided regarding the lesson that you have just gone through. These questions will be used for discussion with your partner later on. As a guide, step 4 provides generic question stems that can be used to make questions. Questions examples are like – Why would I use Excel? How to enter data in Excel? Etc.
3. **Once both of you have completed the lesson and before you do your lesson level lab, each partner needs to ask the other the questions that he/she has noted down. So together, you discuss 6 questions minimum, 3 asked by each partner. If the answer to the question is not correct, you and your partner need to discuss it till you come up with a common answer and understanding. This discussion is oral in nature and need not be written.**
4. The lesson is followed by a lesson level lab. In the lesson level lab, do the following
   a. Do the lab together. One person acts as the keyboard and mouse operator. You and your partner need to discuss how to get the correct answer, before the taking the actions. Remember, the lab is a joint work for both partners.
   b. A hardcopy of the activity steps for doing the lab is given to you. Data files (if any) are in your _____ folder. You do not need to download them from ElementK.
5. Lessons are followed by individual tests. Your rewards will be based on the lab output and the total score of individuals in the all tests put together.

Is the collaboration guide clear?
<<end of collaboration guide – answer questions >>

For the purpose of training we will be using an online training program called ElementK. I will now give you a quick demo of how to enter ElementK. You can follow the guidelines in step 3 of the workbook.
Lets start your ElementK sessions. Please follow the guidelines in your workbook, as I give you a quick demo. Please let me know if you are having trouble logging in or have questions as I am doing the demo.

<<Use the steps in the workbook attached to provide a quick demo of how of ElementK. Follow the instructions in the Element K guide. Show them all the screens on the overhead projector using the faculty computer. >>

<<After the demo – Make sure that all individuals are logged in>>

You are all allowed and advised to take notes. Use the pages in the worksheet provided for the same. At the end of the training, a quiz will be conducted to measure how much you have learned. If you have any questions, please raise your hand. I shall answer any questions related to the learning process, questionnaires or technology. I shall not answer any question regarding Excel.

<<answer questions if asked>>

You may now start your lesson plan. Please make sure that you use the worksheet in step 4 of your workbook. Please make sure that you stop at the first lesson level lab, but before you start your lab. You need to collaborate your partner, so just wait for instructions after you reach the first lesson level lab. Remember, before you do your labs, you need to discuss the questions and then do the labs together.

<< After 45 mins ElementK, everybody should have completed the task. Move to the next part >>

Now we have finished going through ElementK. You should discuss your discussion questions (Step 4) and lesson level lab (Step 5) in Excel as instructed in the collaboration guidelines. You should print your lab after you are done.

<<After 5 mins >>

Okay, its' time to see how much we have learned. Please move to the next section in your workbook and answer the questions in the quiz online. You have 10 mins.

<<After 10 mins. Record the current time: _____:_____>>

Please close Excel now and return back to your individual computers. It will not be used any further. Please proceed to fill the online questionnaire. The questionnaire will be followed by a test. The test will help us see how much we have learned. Please complete step 6 of your workbook.

<<After 10 mins. Record the current time: _____:_____>>

Time is up. Please return the training workbook. You are now free to leave. You will receive the results of your performance after the final session of the experiment. Please make sure that you attend the next training session at _____. I thank you for your participation.

Space for Trainer / Experimenter Notes
_____

Appendix D1: Introduction Training Workbooks

For the introductory training session
- Workbook for treatment LM1 (white)
- Workbook for treatment LM2 (blue)
- Workbook for treatment LM3 (yellow)
- Workbook for treatment LM4 (green)

Note:
1. The first set of workbooks were used in the first training session
2. The last three training sessions used similar workbooks.
3. Books were color coded by the color shown in parenthesis.

Step 1: Fill out the consent form

That was page 1 that you just signed.

Step2: Overview Guidelines

We will be using a video to learn to learn Excel. **The following are guidelines as you go through the training.**

- As you go through the video, you have the following responsibilities
  - Listen & see attentively and learn
  - Take notes in your workbook in the space provided
  - Do not access your computer when the video is going on
  - Practice time will be given after the video
- Lessons are followed by individual tests. Your rewards will be based on your score of these tests.

Step 3: Fill out the surveys

Please perform the following activities as instructed by the instructor.

- Fill the attached survey. Next page.
- Start internet explorer and go to
  - http://arches.uga.edu/~gupta

  - And click on the color **WHITE** (your group color & the color of your workbook). Fill the survey that comes up.

- At the end of the survey, you will be directed to a new survey. It is the learning orientation survey. Follow the instructions on the last page to create a login and fill the survey.

Step 1: Fill out the consent form

That was page 1 that you just signed.

Step2: Overview Guidelines

We will be using a state of the art training system, ElemenK, to learn Excel. This is a system used by most organizations now-a-days. **The following are guidelines as you go through the training.**

- As you go through the sessions, you have the following responsibilities
  - o Listen & see attentively and learn
  - o Take notes in your workbook in the space provided
- The lesson is followed by a lesson level lab. In the lesson level lab, do the following
  - o Do the lab
  - o A hardcopy of the activity steps for doing the lab is given to you. Data files (if any) are in your **W:\classes\MIST2090\Excel** folder. You do not need to download them from ElementK. Let your TA know if you don't know how to access the W: drive.
- Lessons are followed by individual tests. Your rewards will be based on your score of these tests.

Step 3: ElementK Manual

This part shows you how to access ElementK. Please use the steps below to access ElementK.

1. Open internet explorer and go to http://my.uga.edu.

2. Enter your UGA My ID and password. This is the same you use for accessing your email.

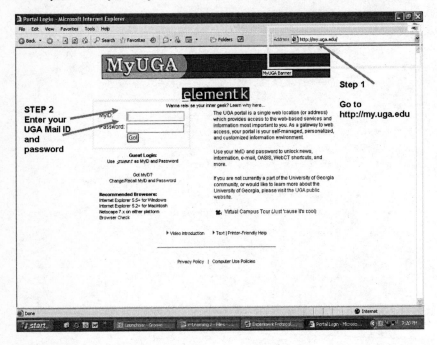

3. This is your UGA portal. Click on ElementK icon. A new window will open up once your click this icon

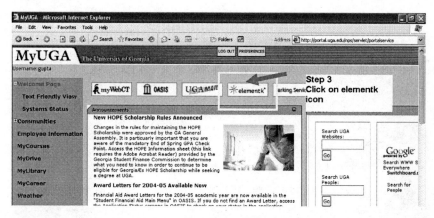

4. Enter the following search phrase that will be given to you in each session in the search catalog text box.

For the purpose of this demo: we will use the term

Excel 2003: Manipulating workbooks

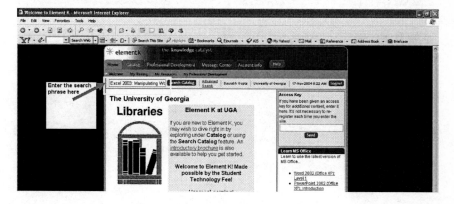

5. The next page would be the search results page. Click on the search result.

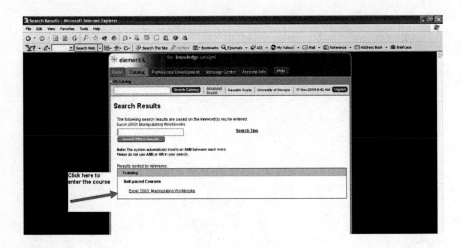

5. Click on Course Content to access the course organizer.

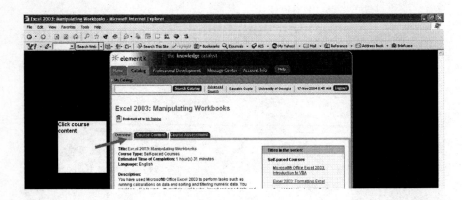

7. You will see multiple lessons in the course. To access a lesson click "begin" for the first line of the module.

Please wait for your trainer to instruct you when to click begin.

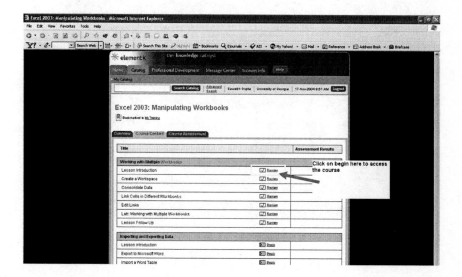

7. A new window will open and will take you through the training session for the first sub-section. Maximize this window. To navigate, use the buttons on the bottom.

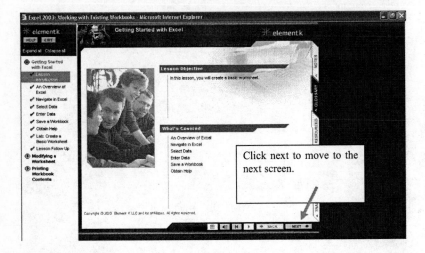

8. Some screens will ask you to launch a Demo and launch activity. Please do both in the order shown: Launch demo first, then activity

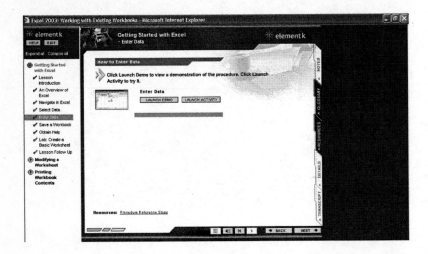

9. Each lesson ends with a Lesson level lab. These screens describe a scenario for the exercise. The activity sheets would be printed and provided in your workbook.

Data files and solution files (if any) will be located in the **W:/Classes/MIST2190/Excel/** folder . Data files are needed to solve the scenario. Solution files are for you to cross check your answer.

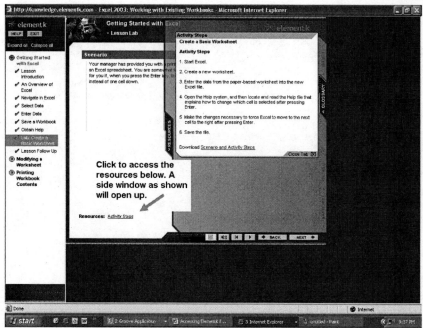

Very important Notes!!!
1. **ElementK will continue on without a break. You need to be careful that you exit ElementK as soon as you reach the lesson level lab**
2. **Labs are done outside ElementK. You will exit ElementK and use Excel on your computer to perform the activities of the lab.**
3. **Because of multiple people logging in, ElementK might get a bit slow sometimes. Just give it time.**
4. **In some very rare cases, ElementK stops giving sound. In such a case – Change computers if available or reboot.**

Step 4: Fill out the surveys

Please perform the following activities as instructed by the instructor.

- Fill the attached survey. Next page.
- Start internet explorer and go to
    - http://arches.uga.edu/~gupta

    - And click on the color **BLUE** (your group color & the color of your workbook). Fill the survey that comes up.

- At the end of the survey, you will be directed to a new survey. It is the learning orientation survey. Follow the instructions on the last page to create a login and fill the survey.

Step 1: Fill out the consent form and find your partner

That was page 1 that you just signed.

STUDENT PAIRS - PLEASE FIND YOUR PARTNER AND SIT WITH HIM/HER

Last name	First name	Last name	First name
Listed the pairs			

Step 2: Collaboration guidelines

Both partners in the team are supposed to work together. Even though most learning is designed to be for individuals, more and more organizations are now using collaborative or team-based learning. **Learning in a team enhances learning for each participant. This is because each partner can bring in their own personal perspective and help the other partner understand the content better. The following are guidelines that you need to follow to benefit from your mutual learning experience.**

6. You will both be watching the video till it ends. During this period, do not access your computer.
7. As you go through the video, each of you have the following responsibilities
   a. Listen & see attentively and learn
   b. If your partner has any trouble understanding, help and support your him/her. If your partner doesn't understand a topic, he or she should ask you about it.
   c. Take notes in your workbook in the space provided
   d. Write down at least **three** comprehensive questions in the training workbook in the space provided regarding the lesson that you have just gone through. These questions will be used for discussion with your partner later on. As a guide, the next lab workbook will provide generic question stems that can be used to make questions. Questions examples are like – Why would I use Excel? How to enter data in Excel? Etc.
8. **Once the video ends and before you start practicing, each partner needs to ask the other the questions that he/she has noted down. So together, you discuss 6 questions minimum, 3 asked by each partner. If the answer to the question is not correct, you and your partner need to discuss it till you come up with a common answer and understanding. This discussion is oral in nature and need not be written. Remember, your can also demonstrate activities to your partner using the computer.**
9. The video is followed by time for practice.
   c. Practice what you have learned in the video as a team.

187

10. Lessons are followed by individual tests. Your rewards will be based on the total score of individuals on all three tests.

Step 3: Fill out the surveys

Please perform the following activities as instructed by the instructor.

1. Fill the attached survey. Next page.
2. Start internet explorer and go to
   http://arches.uga.edu/~gupta

   And click on the color **YELLOW** (your group color & the color of your workbook). Fill the survey that comes up.

3. At the end of the survey, you will be directed to a new survey. It is the learning orientation survey. Follow the instructions on the last page to create a login and fill the survey.

Step 1: Fill out the consent form

That was page 1 that you just signed.

Step 2: Collaboration guidelines

Both partners in the team are supposed to work together. Even though the learning software, ElemenK, discussed later was initially designed to be used by individuals, more and more organizations are now using collaborative or team-based learning. **Learning in a team enhances learning for each participant. This is because each partner can bring in their own personal perspective and help the other partner understand the content better. The following are guidelines that you need to follow to benefit from your mutual learning experience.**

11. You will both be working on separate computers. Once you reach the lab portion of the lab, you will stop and wait for your partner to complete the same.
12. As you go through the sessions, each of you have the following responsibilities
     a. Listen & see attentively and learn
     b. If your partner has any trouble understanding, help and support your him/her. If your partner doesn't understand a topic, he or she should ask you about it.
     c. Take notes in your workbook in the space provided
     d. Write down at least **three** comprehensive questions in the training workbook in the space provided regarding the lesson that you have just gone through. These questions will be used for discussion with your partner later on. As a guide, the next lab workbook will provide generic question stems that can be used to make questions. Questions examples are like – Why would I use Excel? How to enter data in Excel? Etc.
13. **Once both of you have completed the lesson and before you do your lesson level lab, each partner needs to ask the other the questions that he/she has noted down. So together, you discuss 6 questions minimum, 3 asked by each partner. If the answer to the question is not correct, you and your partner need to discuss it till you come up with a common answer and understanding. This discussion is oral in nature and need not be written. Remember, your can also demonstrate activities to your partner using the computer.**
14. The lesson is followed by a lesson level lab. In the lesson level lab, do the following
     d. Do the lab together. One person acts as the keyboard and mouse operator. You and your partner need to discuss how to get the correct answer, before the taking the actions. Remember, the lab is a joint work for both partners.

e. A hardcopy of the activity steps for doing the lab is given to you. Data files (if any) are in your **W:\classes\MIST2090\Excel** folder. You do not need to download them from ElementK. Let your TA know if you don't know how to access the W: drive.

15. Lessons are followed by individual tests. Your rewards will be based on the lab output and the total score of individuals on all three tests.

Step 3: ElementK Manual

As shown in the previous handbook.

Step 4: Fill out the surveys

Please perform the following activities as instructed by the instructor.

- Fill the attached survey. Next page.
- Start internet explorer and go to
  - http://arches.uga.edu/~gupta

  - And click on the color **GREEN** (your group color & the color of your workbook). Fill the survey that comes up.

- At the end of the survey, you will be directed to a new survey. It is the learning orientation survey. Follow the instructions on the last page to create a login and fill the survey.

Appendix D2: Training Workbooks for Excel Session

For subsequent training sessions
- Workbook for treatment LM1 (white)
- Workbook for treatment LM2 (blue)
- Workbook for treatment LM3 (yellow)
- Workbook for treatment LM4 (green)

Note:
1. The first set of workbooks were used in the first training session
2. The last three training sessions used similar workbooks.
   Books were color coded by the color shown in parenthesis.

MICROSOFT EXCEL 2003

Working with Workbooks

PLEASE FILL THE FOLLOWING

First Name:	Last Name:

This workbook provides you guidelines for going though the experiment.

Training workbook

Training overview guidelines

We will be using a video to learn to learn Excel. **The following are guidelines as you go through the training.**

16. As you go through the video, you have the following responsibilities
    a. Listen & see attentively and learn
    b. Take notes in your workbook in the space provided
    c. Do not access your computer when the video is going on

Space to take notes

Step 2: Practice

1. The video is followed by time for practice.
    f. Practice what you have learned in the video.

Step 3: Post-Training Questionnaire & Quiz

Please wait for instructor instructions before proceeding

Got to http://www.arches.uga.edu/~gupta and fill the Post-training questionnaire. Some questions might seem repetitive, but answer them to the best of your ability. The answers are vital to the success of the research.

Click on **White.** You are group white

See you next time!

Please submit this workbook to the experimenter. **Make sure the page 1 is completed.**

Thank you for participation in this session. Credit for participation will be given later. Make sure that you attend the next lab.

Blue.1

MICROSOFT EXCEL 2003

Working with Workbooks

PLEASE FILL THE FOLLOWING

First Name:	Last Name:

This workbook provides you guidelines for going though the experiment.

Training workbook

Overview of guidelines for the training session

Instructions to access ElementK lesson. This is as was shown to you in the introductory lab.

A. Open internet explorer and go to http://my.uga.edu.

B. Enter your UGA My ID and password. This is the same you use for accessing your email.

C. This is your UGA portal. Click on ElementK icon. A new window will open up once your click this icon

D. Enter the following search phrase in the search catalog text box.

Excel 2003: Working with existing workbooks

   The next page would be the search results page. Click on

Excel 2003: Working with existing workbooks

E. Click on Course Content to access the course organizer.

F. You will see multiple lessons in the course. To access a lesson click "begin" for the first line of the first module.

This is STEP 1 – next page - of your workbook

G. A new window will open and will take you through the training session for the first sub-section. Maximize this window. To navigate, use the buttons on the bottom.

H. Some screens will ask you to launch a Demo and launch activity. Please do both in the order shown: Launch demo first, then activity

I. Once you reach the lesson level lab. These screens describe a scenario for the exercise.

The activity sheets are printed and provided in your workbook.
This is STEP 2 of your workbook

J. Once you are done with the lab, you are finished with your training session and should wait for more instructions.

Step 1: Lab worksheet

Fill in the following worksheet as you go thought the training session.

Start time : _____

Check mark the appropriate box below based on the extent of completion of each module.

Module (steps shown for lab 1 only)	Completed	Partially Completed	Not started
An overview of Excel			
Navigate in Excel			
Select Data			
Enter Data			
Save a workbook			
Obtain help			
Lab exercise (activities printed in the workbook – Step 2)			
Lab: Create a basic worksheet			

End time : _____

Very important Notes!!!

5. ElementK will continue on without a break. You need to be careful that you exit ElementK as soon as you reach the lesson level lab

6. Labs are done outside ElementK. You will exit ElementK and use Excel on your computer to perform the activities of the lab.

7. Because of multiple people logging in, ElementK might get a bit slow sometimes. Just give it time.

8. In some very rare cases, ElementK stops giving sound. In such a case – Change computers if available or reboot. **Let the researcher know this.**

Space to take notes

Step 2: Lab session

The lesson is followed by a lesson level lab. In the lab sessions, do the following
NOTE: Labs are done outside ElementK, in Excel installed on your computer

    a. A hardcopy of the activity steps for doing the lab is given below.

    b. Print your lab (just click print)

Scenario: (for lab 1)

Your manager has provided you with a printed document. She would like the paper document converted to an Excel spreadsheet. You are somewhat familiar with Excel, and you have found that it would be easier for you if, when you press the Enter key, the insertion point moves one cell to the right (like the Tab key) instead of one cell down.

Activity Steps:

- Start Excel.
- Create a new worksheet.
- Enter the data from the paper-based worksheet into the new Excel file. (Worksheet shown below the instructions)
- Open the Help system, and then locate and read the Help file that explains how to change which cell is selected after pressing Enter.
- Make the changes necessary to force Excel to move to the next cell to the right after pressing Enter.
- Save the file on the computer desktop. Name – Book and beyond.xls

Book and Beyond - Northeastern Region
5/12/2002

Employee ID	January	February	March	April
123456789	110.25	175.65	140.96	125.15
234567890	200.75	210.63	240.82	205.79
345678901	210.34	185.11	195.14	310.44
456789012	220.15	195.37	185.66	250.15

Scenario: (for lab 2)

As a high school math teacher, you have entered all your students' names and their quiz grades into a worksheet. You want to create a bar chart that compares the average grade for each quiz. Each data series should be labeled with the appropriate quiz number. You decide to title the chart First Marking Period Average Quiz Score so the students will know what information the chart represents. After you create the chart, you want to make some formatting changes including deleting the legend and the category (X) axis title, adding the series name and value to the data labels, making the title font larger, and adding a light purple background.

Activity Steps:

- In Math Class Chart workbook on Worksheet1, insert a bar chart.
- Select the average quiz grades as the data series.
- Select the quiz number for each series name.
- Enter First Marking Period Average Quiz Score for the title.
- Place the chart as a new sheet named 1QAvg.
- Delete the legend and the X Axis label.
- Add the series name and value to the data labels.
- Change the background color to light purple.
- Increase the font size of the title to 16pt.
- Save the workbook as **My Math Class Chart** in My Document Folder and exit Excel.

Scenario: (for lab 3)

Management has provided you with a financial worksheet. You have been asked to calculate the Total Income, Net Income, Taxes, and Profit After Tax.

Activity Steps:

1. For 2003
    1. In cell B8, use a function to calculate the Total Income.
    2. In cell B12, write a basic formula to calculate the Net Income. This is the amount derived from subtracting the Expenses from the Total Income.
    3. In cell B14, use an absolute reference to calculate the Taxes. This is the amount derived from multiplying the Net Income by the Tax Rate.
    4. In cell B16, copy a formula that helps you calculate the Profit After Tax. This is the amount derived from subtracting the Tax value from the Net Income.
2. Copy the formulas to 2004 to complete that column also.
3. Save the workbook as **TierOneCalculations.xls** in My Documents and exit Excel

---

Step 3: Post-Training Questionnaire & Quiz

Please wait for instructor instructions before proceeding

Got to http://www.arches.uga.edu/~gupta and fill the Post-training questionnaire. Some questions might seem repetitive, but answer them to the best of your ability. The answers are vital to the success of the research.

Click on **Blue.** You are group Blue

See you next time!

Please submit this workbook to the experimenter. **Make sure pages 1 and 3 are completed.**

Thank you for participation in this session. Credit for participation will be given later. Make sure that you and your partner attend the next lab.

Group

Yellow.1

MICROSOFT EXCEL 2003

Working with Workbooks

PLEASE FILL THE FOLLOWING

First Name:	Last Name:

MAKE SURE YOU ARE SITTING NEXT TO YOU PARTNER

YOU NEED TO FOLLOW THE COLLABORAITON GUIDELINES DISCUSSED IN THE FIRST LAB

This workbook provides you guidelines for going though the experiment.

Training workbook

Training overview guidelines

Both partners in the team are supposed to work together. Even though most learning is designed to be for individuals, more and more organizations are now using collaborative or team-based learning. **Learning in a team enhances learning for each participant. This is because each partner can bring in their own personal perspective and help the other partner understand the content better. The following are guidelines that you need to follow to benefit from your mutual learning experience.**

17. You will both be watching the video till it ends. During this period, do not access your computer.

18. As you go through the video, each of you have the following responsibilities
    a. Listen & see attentively and learn
    b. If your partner has any trouble understanding, help and support him/her. If your partner doesn't understand a topic, he or she should ask you about it.
    c. Take notes in your workbook in the space provided
    d. Write down at least **three** comprehensive questions in the training workbook in the space provided regarding the lesson that you have just gone through. These questions will be used for discussion with your partner later on. As a guide, the next lab workbook will provide generic question stems that can be used to make questions.

Page to take Notes and discussion questions

1. Write down at least **three** comprehensive questions in the training workbook in the space provided regarding the lesson that you have just gone through. These questions will be used for discussion with your partner later on. As a guide, the next lab workbook will provide generic question stems that can be used to make questions. Questions would be like – Why would I use Excel? How to enter data in Excel? Etc.

2. **Once the video ends and before you start practicing, each partner needs to ask the other the questions that he/she has noted down. So together, you discuss 6 questions minimum, 3 asked by each partner. If the answer to the question is not correct, you and your partner need to discuss it till you come up with a common answer and understanding. This discussion is oral in nature and need not be written. Remember, your can also demonstrate activities to your partner using the computer.**

Generic question stems to guide to guide the development of your discussion questions.	
What is the use of ....?	Explain how do I do .... ?
How would you use .... to ... ?	How does .... affect ... ?
What would happen if ....?	What is the meaning of ...?
What do we already know about .... ?	Why is ... important?
How does ... tie in with what we learned before?	What is the difference between ... and ...?
Explain why I should do .... ?	Do you agree or disagree with this statement .... ? Support your answer.

Question 1

Question 2

Question 3

More questions

Space to take notes

Step 2: Practice

1. The video is followed by time for practice.
   - Practice what you have learned in the video as a team.

Step 3: Post-Training Questionnaire & Quiz

Please wait for instructor instructions before proceeding

Got to http://www.arches.uga.edu/~gupta and fill the Post-training questionnaire. Some questions might seem repetitive, but answer them to the best of your ability. The answers are vital to the success of the research.

Click on **Yellow.** You are group Yellow

NOTE - Your rewards will be based the total score of individuals in all the tests put together.

See you next time!

Please submit this workbook to the experimenter. **Make sure that page 1 is completed.**

Thank you for participation in this session. Credit for participation will be given later. Make sure that you and your partner attend the next lab.

GREEN.1

MICROSOFT EXCEL 2003

Working with Workbooks

PLEASE FILL THE FOLLOWING

First Name:	Last Name:

MAKE SURE YOU ARE SITTING NEXT TO YOU PARTNER

YOU NEED TO FOLLOW THE COLLABORAITON GUIDELINES DISCUSSED IN THE FIRST LAB

This workbook provides you guidelines for going though the experiment.

Training workbook

Overview of guidelines for the training session

Instructions to access ElementK lesson. This is as was shown to you in the introductory lab.

A. Open internet explorer and go to http://my.uga.edu.

B. Enter your UGA My ID and password. This is the same you use for accessing your email.

C. This is your UGA portal. Click on ElementK icon. A new window will open up once your click this icon

D. Enter the following search phrase in the search catalog text box.

Excel 2003: Working with existing workbooks

The next page would be the search results page. Click on

Excel 2003: Working with existing workbooks

E. Click on Course Content to access the course organizer.

F. You will see multiple lessons in the course. To access a lesson click "begin" for the first line of the first module.

This is STEP 1 – next page - of your workbook

G. A new window will open and will take you through the training session for the first sub-section. Maximize this window. To navigate, use the buttons on the bottom.

H. Some screens will ask you to launch a Demo and launch activity. Please do both in the order shown: Launch demo first, then activity

I. Once you reach the lesson level lab – **Stop**. These screens describe a scenario for the exercise.

The activity sheets are printed and provided in your workbook.
This is STEP 2 of your workbook

J. Once you are done with the lab, you are finished with your training session and should wait for more instructions.

.

Step 1: Lab worksheet

Both partners in the team are supposed to work together. Even though ElementK was initially designed to be used by individuals, more and more organization are now using collaborative or team-based learning. **Learning in a team enhances learning for each participant. This is because each partner can bring in their own personal perspective and help the other partner understand the content better. The following are guidelines that you need to follow to benefit from your mutual learning experience.**

1. You will both be working on separate computers. The training session you go through will contain the following modules. Fill the following worksheet as you go through it. Once you reach the lesson level lab, you will stop and wait for your partner to complete the same.

2. As you go through the sessions, each of you have the following responsibilities

   e. Listen & see attentively and learn

   f. If your partner has any trouble understanding, help and support your him/her

   g. Take notes in your workbook in the space provided

   h. Write down at least **three** comprehensive questions in the training workbook in the space provided (next page) regarding the lesson that you have just gone through. These questions will be used for discussion with your partner later on.

Fill in the following worksheet as you go thought the training session.

Start time : _____

Check mark the appropriate box below based on the extent of completion of each module.

Module (steps shown for lab 1 only)	Completed	Partially Completed	Not started
An overview of Excel			
Navigate in Excel			
Select Data			
Enter Data			
Save a workbook			
Obtain help			
Lab exercise (activities printed in the workbook – Step 2)			
Lab: Create a basic worksheet			

End time : _____

Very important Notes!!!

- ElementK will continue on without a break. You need to be careful that you exit ElementK as soon as you reach the lesson level lab
- Labs are done outside ElementK. You will exit ElementK and use Excel on your computer to perform the activities of the lab.

- Because of multiple people logging in, ElementK might get a bit slow sometimes. Just give it time.
- In some very rare cases, ElementK stops giving sound. In such a case – Change computers if available or reboot. **Let the researcher know this.**

Page to take Notes and discussion questions

1. Write down at least three comprehensive questions in the training workbook in the space provided (below) regarding the lesson that you have just gone through. These questions will be used for discussion with your partner later on. Below is a generic question stems that can be used to make questions.

2. Once both of you have completed the lesson and before you do your lesson level lab, each partner needs to ask the other the questions that he/she has noted down. If the answer to the question is not correct, you and your partner need to discuss it till you come up with a common answer and understanding. This discussion is oral in nature and need not be written. Remember: you can demonstrate activities to your partner using the computer too.

Generic question stems to guide to guide the development of your discussion questions.	
What is the use of ....?	Explain how do I do .... ?
How would you use .... to ... ?	How does .... affect ... ?
What would happen if ....?	What is the meaning of ...?
What do we already know about .... ?	Why is ... important?
How does ... tie in with what we learned before?	What is the difference between ... and ...?
Explain why I should do .... ?	Do you agree or disagree with this statement .... ? Support your answer.

Question 1

Question 2

Question 3

More questions

Page to take notes

Step 2: Lab session

Steps after discussing the questions

The lesson is followed by a lesson level lab. In the lab sessions, do the following

NOTE: Labs are done outside ElementK, in Excel installed on your computer

- Do the lab together. One person acts as the keyboard and mouse operator. You and your partner need to discuss how to get the correct answer, before the taking the actions. Remember, the lab is a joint work for both partners.
- A hardcopy of the activity steps for doing the lab is given below.
- **Print your lab (just click print)**

Scenario: (for lab 1)

Your manager has provided you with a printed document. She would like the paper document converted to an Excel spreadsheet. You are somewhat familiar with Excel, and you have found that it would be easier for you if, when you press the Enter key, the insertion point moves one cell to the right (like the Tab key) instead of one cell down.

Activity Steps:

- Start Excel.
- Create a new worksheet.
- Enter the data from the paper-based worksheet into the new Excel file. (Worksheet shown below the instructions)
- Open the Help system, and then locate and read the Help file that explains how to change which cell is selected after pressing Enter.
- Make the changes necessary to force Excel to move to the next cell to the right after pressing Enter.
- Save the file on the computer desktop. Name – Book and beyond.xls

---

Book and Beyond - Northeastern Region
5/12/2002

Employee ID	January	February	March	April
123456789	110.25	175.65	140.96	125.15
234567890	200.75	210.63	240.82	205.79
345678901	210.34	185.11	195.14	310.44
456789012	220.15	195.37	185.66	250.15

Scenario: (for lab 2)

As a high school math teacher, you have entered all your students' names and their quiz grades into a worksheet. You want to create a bar chart that compares the average grade for each quiz. Each data series should be labeled with the appropriate quiz number. You decide to title the chart First Marking Period Average Quiz Score so the students will know what information the chart represents. After you create the chart, you want to make some formatting changes including deleting the legend and the category (X) axis title, adding the series name and value to the data labels, making the title font larger, and adding a light purple background.

Activity Steps:

- In Math Class Chart workbook on Worksheet1, insert a bar chart.
- Select the average quiz grades as the data series.
- Select the quiz number for each series name.
- Enter First Marking Period Average Quiz Score for the title.
- Place the chart as a new sheet named 1QAvg.
- Delete the legend and the X Axis label.
- Add the series name and value to the data labels.
- Change the background color to light purple.
- Increase the font size of the title to 16pt.
- Save the workbook as **My Math Class Chart** in My Document Folder and exit Excel.

Scenario: (for lab 3)

Management has provided you with a financial worksheet. You have been asked to calculate the Total Income, Net Income, Taxes, and Profit After Tax.

Activity Steps:

4. For 2003
    1. In cell B8, use a function to calculate the Total Income.
    2. In cell B12, write a basic formula to calculate the Net Income. This is the amount derived from subtracting the Expenses from the Total Income.
    3. In cell B14, use an absolute reference to calculate the Taxes. This is the amount derived from multiplying the Net Income by the Tax Rate.
    4. In cell B16, copy a formula that helps you calculate the Profit After Tax. This is the amount derived from subtracting the Tax value from the Net Income.
5. Copy the formulas to 2004 to complete that column also.
6. Save the workbook as **TierOneCalculations.xls** in My Documents and exit Excel

Step 3: Post-Training Questionnaire & Quiz

Please wait for instructor instructions before proceeding

Got to http://www.arches.uga.edu/~gupta and fill the Post-training questionnaire. Some questions might seem repetitive, but answer them to the best of your ability. The answers are vital to the success of the research.

Click on **GREEN.** You are group GREEN

NOTE - Your rewards will be based on the lab output and the total score of individuals in all the tests put together.

See you next time!

Please submit this workbook to the experimenter. **Make sure the pages 1, 3 and 4 are completed.**

Thank you for participation in this session. Credit for participation will be given later. Make sure that you and your partner attend the next lab.

Appendix E: Pre-training Questionnaire

Note:

The questionnaire shown below shows measures for all items in the pre-training survey.
The questions for each construct are shown together, with reliability from previous instruments indicated in the title.
Scoring for the constructs used in MANOVA is shown at the end of the questionnaire.

Pre-Training Questionnaire

The following questions are designed to understand your basic background. Your answers to these questions are strictly confidential and will only be shared as an aggregate with other researchers. Please answer them honestly. Some questions might appear to be similar, but please answer them all.

1. First Name. _____   2. Last Name. _____

3. Major. _____ (drop down box containing a list of majors)

4. Current cumulative GPA. _____   5. Gender. _____

The following questions were asked for paired groups only

6. Your partners Name. _____

7. How long have you known your partner before this session? Answer in number of months. _____

8. How would you rate your working relationship with your partner so far?
   1(very bad) – 5 (neutral) – 10 (very good)

Items for measuring computer self-efficacy (Reliability in Compeau et al. 1995 = 0.93)
NOTE: Scale modified for Excel and items updated for current time. Scale is also updated to for web-based survey. For MANOVA, construct scored by adding the rating of the confidence scale. 'Cannot complete' was rated as zero

9. Excel is a complex application and can be used for many tasks. For the following questions, imagine that you have to perform an UNFAMILIAR TASK THAT REQUIRES THE USE OF AN UNFAMILIAR EXCEL CAPABILITY.

For each of the statements below, if you think you can do the task, rate your confidence in your ability to complete the task given the condition by clicking a number between 1 to 10, where 1 indicates 'Not at all confident', and 10 indicates 'totally confident'

For each condition you think you cannot do the task, click "cannot complete" (the box to the right of '10')

Now, please rate the following statements.

As of today, I could complete the UNFAMILIAR TASK THAT REQUIRES THE USE OF AN UNFAMILIAR EXCEL CAPABILITY...

Code	Questions	Confidence Scale	Cannot complete
CSE1	... if there was no one around to tell me what to do	1(Not at all confident) – 10(Totally confident)	( )
CSE2	... if I had never used software capability like it before	1(Not at all confident) – 10(Totally confident)	( )
CSE3	... if I had only the internet for reference	1(Not at all confident) – 10(Totally confident)	( )
CSE4	... if I had seen someone using it before trying myself	1(Not at all confident) – 10(Totally confident)	( )
CSE5	... if I could get in touch with someone for help if I got stuck	1(Not at all confident) – 10(Totally confident)	( )
CSE6	... if someone else helped me get started	1(Not at all confident) – 10(Totally confident)	( )

CSE7	... if I had a lot of time to complete the job for which I was using Excel	1(Not at all confident) – 10(Totally confident)	( )
CSE8	... if I had just the built-in help facility for assistance	1(Not at all confident) – 10(Totally confident)	( )
CSE9	... if someone showed me how to do it first	1(Not at all confident) – 10(Totally confident)	( )
CSE10	... if I had used similar capability like this one before for a different task	1(Not at all confident) – 10(Totally confident)	( )

Items for measuring motivation to learn
For MANOVA, construct scored by adding the rating on the agreement scale.

10. For each question below, circle the number to the right that best fits your opinion on the importance of the issue using the scale shown.

Code	Questions	Agreement Scale
Outcome expectations (Reliability in Gopal et al. 1992/3 = 0.94)		
OE1	Learning Excel would improve my performance in the class and future jobs	1(Strongly Agree) – 7(Strongly Disagree)
OE2	Learning Excel would improve my productivity in the class and future jobs	1(Strongly Agree) – 7(Strongly Disagree)
OE3	Learning Excel would enhance my effectiveness in the class and future jobs	1(Strongly Agree) – 7(Strongly Disagree)
OE4	I would find learning Excel useful	1(Strongly Agree) – 7(Strongly Disagree)
Intrinsic motivation (Reliability in Davis et al 1992 = 0.81)		
IM1	I would find learning Excel enjoyable	1(Strongly Agree) – 7(Strongly Disagree)
IM2	Learning Excel would be pleasant	1(Strongly Agree) – 7(Strongly Disagree)
IM3	I would have fun learning Excel	1(Strongly Agree) – 7(Strongly Disagree)

Branching question: (the next few questions and the quiz was only surveyed if the students had any knowledge of Excel)

11. Do you have any specific knowledge of Excel or similar application? YES/NO

**Items for measuring specific self-efficacy (Formative measure). No reliability estimate available
NOTE: Last 3 questions have been added to the existing measure to more accurately reflect the
content of the current study. Scale is also updated to for web-based survey. For MANOVA, construct
scored by adding the rating of the confidence scale. 'Cannot complete' was rated as zero**

12. This question asks your perception for a specific spreadsheet software like Excel

Each statement asks you to rate your ability to use a specific Excel capability. For each capability that you think
you have the ability to use, rate your confidence in your ability by clicking a number between 1 to 10, where 1
indicates "not at all confident', and 10 indicates "Totally confident"

For each capability that you think you do not have the ability to use, click "Do not have the ability" (the box next
to '10')

All statements ask you to rate your CURRENT ability

Now please rate the following statements.

AS OF TODAY, I believe I have the ability to

Code	Questions	Confidence Scale	Cannot complete
SSE1	... to use and understand the cell references in Excel	1(Not at all confident) – 10(Totally confident)	( )
SSE2	.. to enter and manipulate numbers in Excel spreadsheet	1(Not at all confident) – 10(Totally confident)	( )
SSE3	... to use Excel to communicate and share numeric information to others on different computers	1(Not at all confident) – 10(Totally confident)	( )
SSE4	... to write a simple formula in Excel to perform mathematical calculations	1(Not at all confident) – 10(Totally confident)	( )
SSE5	... to summarize numeric information using Excel spreadsheet	1(Not at all confident) – 10(Totally confident)	( )
SSE6	... to use Excel to display numbers as graphs	1(Not at all confident) – 10(Totally confident)	( )
SSE7	... to use Excel to assist me in making decisions	1(Not at all confident) – 10(Totally confident)	( )
SSE8	... to use the in-built help in Excel if I need to get more information regarding the task	1(Not at all confident) – 10(Totally confident)	( )
SSE9	... to use Excel to display diagrams	1(Not at all confident) – 10(Totally confident)	( )
SSE10	... to use in-built functions in Excel to perform mathematical calculations	1(Not at all confident) – 10(Totally confident)	( )
SSE11	... to navigate in Excel using keyboard and mouse	1(Not at all confident) – 10(Totally confident)	( )

Items for measuring self-efficacy (Reliability in Hollenbeck et al. 1987 = 0.89)
For MANOVA, construct scored by adding the rating of the confidence scale. 'Cannot complete' was rated as zero

13. The following questions ask you to rate your CURRENT ability regarding using Excel. Please rate your level of agreement with the following statements

Code	Questions	Agreement Scale
SE1	I have mastered Excel use	1(Strongly agree) – 7(Strongly disagree)
SE2	I cannot yet use Excel as well as I would like	1(Strongly agree) – 7(Strongly disagree)
SE3	I am able to perform tasks using Excel well	1(Strongly agree) – 7(Strongly disagree)
SE4	It is not yet possible for me to use Excel at the level I like	1(Strongly agree) – 7(Strongly disagree)
SE5	I think my ability to use Excel can be improved substantially	1(Strongly agree) – 7(Strongly disagree)

Appendix F: Post-Training Questionnaire

Note:
The questionnaire shown below shows measures for all items. Only scales appropriate for the treatment group will be administered in each case.
The questions for each construct are shown together, with reliability from previous instruments indicated in the title.

Post-Training Questionnaire

The following questions are designed to understand your attitude for today's training session. The answers to these questions are kept strictly confidential. **Please answer them honestly. Some questions might appear to be similar, but please answer them all.**

1. First Name. _____   2. Last Name. _____

2. Did you use Excel between the last lab and today? Yes / No

3. If yes, enter the approximate no. of minutes you sued Excel between the last lab and today? _____

For ElementK users only

4. The following statements ask you about your use of ElementK between the training session(s)/Lab(s). Please select all the statements that best described your use of ElementK between lab(s).

( ) I did not access ElementK outside the lab
( ) I was just browsing through it
( ) I did the lab(s) again
( ) I did a different lesion, but not in Excel
( ) I continued with last lab(s) at home/dorm
( ) I did a different lesson in Excel

For Paired groups only

5. The following statements ask you about your interactions with your partner outside the training/lab session. Please select all the statements that best describe your interaction with your partners between lab sessions

( ) I did not interact with my partner outside the lab(s)
( ) I casually interacted with my partner
( ) I worked with my partner on a different assignment for a different class
( ) I worked with partner using Excel, but on the contents of the previous lab(s)
( )I worked with my partner using Excel, but on new Excel features

6. If you spent anytime with your partner outside the class, please enter (in minutes) the amount of time you spent with your partner in the last week outside the lab. _____

Items for appropriation of technology (for ElementK users only)
For MANOVA, construct scored by adding the ratings on the agreement scale.

7. These questions relate to your experience with ElementK. For each question below, circle the number to the right that best fits your opinion on the importance of the issue. Use the scale above to match your opinion.

Code	Question	Agreement Scale
Faithfulness of technology appropriation (Reliability in Chin et al. 1997 = 0.93)		
Faith1	I probably used elemenK improperly	1(Strongly Agree) – 7(Strongly Disagree)
Faith2	The instructor of ElementK would view my use of the system as inappropriate	1(Strongly Agree) – 7(Strongly Disagree)
Faith3	I failed to use ElementK as it should have been used	1(Strongly Agree) – 7(Strongly Disagree)
Faith4	I did not use ElementK in most appropriate fashion	1(Strongly Agree) – 7(Strongly Disagree)

Attitude: Degree of respect for technology (Reliability in Gopal et al. 1992/3 = 0.82)		
Rspt1	I am not in favor of computer-based training, because it is another step towards depersonalization of learning	1(Strongly Agree) – 7(Strongly Disagree)
Rspt2	Using a computer system for learning seems like a good idea to me	1(Strongly Agree) – 7(Strongly Disagree)
Rspt3	I don't like ElementK	1(Strongly Agree) – 7(Strongly Disagree)
Rspt4	ElementK was more of a hindrance in the process of learning	1(Strongly Agree) – 7(Strongly Disagree)
Attitude: Level of comfort with technology (Reliability in Gopal et al. 1992/3 = 0.82)		
Comf2	Using ElementK was fun	1(Strongly Agree) – 7(Strongly Disagree)
Comf3	While using ElementK, I felt comfortable	1(Strongly Agree) – 7(Strongly Disagree)
Comf4	I enjoyed using ElementK	1(Strongly Agree) – 7(Strongly Disagree)

8. Do you think learning from ElementK has helped you in learning Excel? If yes, how? If No, why not?

Items for appropriation of collaborative learning (for paired groups only)
For MANOVA, construct scored by adding the ratings on the agreement scale.

9. For each question below, circle the number to the right that best fits your opinion on the importance of the issue. Use the scale above to match your opinion.

Code	Question	Agreement Scale
Collab1	My partner was friendly and easy to approach	1(Strongly Agree) – 7(Strongly Disagree)
Collab2	My partner paid attention to what I was saying	1(Strongly Agree) – 7(Strongly Disagree)
Collab3	My partner encouraged us to work together	1(Strongly Agree) – 7(Strongly Disagree)
Collab4	My partner emphasized learning	1(Strongly Agree) – 7(Strongly Disagree)
Collab5	My partner helped me enhance my learning	1(Strongly Agree) – 7(Strongly Disagree)
Collab6	My partner encouraged me to give my best effort	1(Strongly Agree) – 7(Strongly Disagree)

10. Do you think learning in pairs has helped you in learning Excel? If yes, how? If No, why not?

218

Items for measuring perceived task difficulty
For MANOVA, construct scored by adding the ratings on the agreement scale.

11. For each question below asks about your feelings regarding the lesson you just learned. For each statement, rate the degree to which you agree or disagree the statements.

Code	Question	Agreement Scale
Diff1	I found this to be a complex lesson	1(Strongly Agree) – 7(Strongly Disagree)
Diff2	This lesson was mentally demanding	1(Strongly Agree) – 7(Strongly Disagree)
Diff3	This lesson required a lot of thought and problem-solving	1(Strongly Agree) – 7(Strongly Disagree)
Diff4	I found this to be a challenging lesson	1(Strongly Agree) – 7(Strongly Disagree)

Items for measuring satisfaction from learning process
Reliability in Chin et al. 1997 = 0.82, Green et al 0.88
For MANOVA, construct scored by adding the ratings on the agreement scale.

12. How would you describe your learning process on the scale below? The two ends of the scale represents the two ends of a continuum.

Code	Question	Agreement Scale	
Satis1	Efficient	1(Strongly Agree) – 7(Strongly Disagree)	Inefficient
Satis2	Coordinated	1(Strongly Agree) – 7(Strongly Disagree)	Uncoordinated
Satis3	Fair	1(Strongly Agree) – 7(Strongly Disagree)	Unfair
Satis4	Confusing	1(Strongly Agree) – 7(Strongly Disagree)	Understandable
Satis5	Satisfying	1(Strongly Agree) – 7(Strongly Disagree)	dissatisfying

Appendix G: Post-Test for Excel Knowledge

1. Administered at the end of Session 1
2. Administered at the end of Session 2
3. Administered at the end of Session 3

Note:

Scoring for each quiz is shown at the end of the quiz

Items for measuring Procedural knowledge

1. In Excel, to move one page to the right or left, you will do the following?

    a. Press Page Up / Page Down
    b. Press Enter
    c. Click the downward scroll arrow
    *d. Press ALT+Page Up / ALT+Page Down
    e. I don't know

2. To selects the contents of a cell:

    a. Click the cell
    *b. Double-click the cell, and then double click the cell again
    c. Double-click the cell
    d. Double-click the cell and then inside the formula bar
    e. I don't know

3. What do you press to go to the very end of your data on your worksheet?

    a. Ctrl+Home
    b. Ctrl+A
    c. Alt+Shift+End
    d. Ctrl+Page Down
    *e. Ctrl+End
    f. I don't know

4. You want to slect the entire worksheet. What will you do?

    *a. A. Click the box below the name box
    b. B. Goto the top most cell, right click, then select "Select all data"
    c. C. Double click cell A1
    d. D. Got to the frist cell. Next, while keeping the shift key pressed, click the last cell of your data
    e. A or B or C or D– All are correct ways of doing it.
    f. I don't know

5. To open the Excel help system, choose

a. File->Open->Help
*b. Help->Microsoft Excel Help
c. Window-> Help
d. Help -> Window
e. I don't know

6. You want to move the active cell to the left after entering the data. You would use the following

    a. Hit the left arrow on the keyboard
    b. Hit the Enter key on the keyboard
    c. Click the Tab key
    *d. Click the Shift & Tab together
    e. I don't know

Items for measuring Declarative knowledge

7. What is the primary advantage of saving an Excel spreadsheet

    a. Makes your work assessable beyond your current session
    b. Helps you in the process of transporting an Excel spreadsheet
    c. Helps you make sound business decisions later
    d. All of the above
    *e. A & B
    f. I don't know

8. The primary method to find information that shows you how to complete the task you are working on

    a. Open Excel help. A window showing the answer will pop up
    *b. You type the subject of your search in the search text box of the help window
    c. You start working on the task. Microsoft Excel will prompt you on the right path
    d. You search the internet or ask for help
    e. I don't know

9. You have currently selected a cell. What happens when you click on another cell, while keeping the CTRL key pressed?

    a. Nothing happens – Excel gives you an Error
    b. It merges the two cells into one cell
    c. It copies data from the first cell into the second one
    *d. Selects both the cell.
    e. I don't know

10. Which is not a basic element of a spreadsheet?

  *a. Paragraph
  b. Column
  c. Row
  d. Cell
  e. I don't know

11. A formula bar

  a. Appears below the toolbars
  b. Comes up when writing an Excel formula
  C. Displays the contents of the active cell in a workbook
  *D. A & C
  e. A & B & C
  E. I don't know

12. The cell at the intersection of the second column and the third row is

  *a. B3
  b. 3B
  c. C2
  d. 2C
  e. I don't know

13. What is the primary advantage of learning how to use an electronic spreadsheet such as Excel

  *a. Helps you in making sound business decisions
  b. Helps you in using an application that would be available to you in the future
  c. Helps you in making better presentations of tabular information
  d. Is an acceptable way of number crunching in the industry
  e. None of the above
  f. I don't know

14. What are the possible uses of a spreadsheet

  a. Manipulate numbers, text and non-alphanumeric numbers
  b. To make tables for computation
  c. To store data, such as class schedule
  *d. All of the above
  e. None of the above

f. I don't know

15. An Excel workbook is a

     a. A single sheet, containing multiple rows and columns
     b. A set of worksheets to store information about the entire business
     *c. Repository of worksheets containing similar data
     d. All of the above
     e. I don't know

Scoring the Posttest
Each of the above quizzes will give two scores
1. Procedural knowledge score = No. of items correctly responded to in questions 1-6
2. Declarative knowledge score = No. of items correctly responded to in questions 7-15.

1. To format a chart item, right-click the item and choose

    a. Edit
    *b. Format
    c. Insert
    d. Change
    e. I don't know

2. A firm is divided into six geographic regions. The Excel sheet you have contains the total sales from each region. To show the percentage sales in a visual format, you will do the following

    a. Calculate the percentage in Excel and show it in a Bar chart
    b. Draw a line chart, and choose percentage in the chart options dialog box
    *c. Draw a pie chart, and choose percentage in the chart options dialog box
    d. Calculate the percentage in Excel and show it in a pie chart
    e. I don't know

3. You cannot make a chart without

    a. Selecting a chart area on the worksheet
    b. Without having a Data Series
    *c. Without having a Data range
    d. B & C
    e. All of the above
    f. I don't know

4. How do you change the font size of the text along the axis of the chart

    a. Choose Source Data from the Chart menu. Select the tab labeled Axes and adjust the font.
    b. Right-click the chart area and choose Properties. Select the tab labeled Axes and adjust the font.
    c. Click anywhere on the chart and rerun the Chart Wizard choosing the appropriate font settings when asked.
    d. Choose Chart Options from the Chart menu. Select the tab labeled Axes and adjust the font.
    *e. Select the text, choose Format Axis title>Selected Axis, click the Font tab and adjust the font settings.

f. I don't know

5. In an Excel sheet, you want to display an organizational chart. To do that, you would do the following

    a. Use the cells in Excel to show the organizational chart
    *b. Choose Insert-->Diagram → Organizational Chart
    c. Choose Tools-->Insert Diagram → Organizational Chart
    d. Create the diagram in word and copy it to Excel
    e. I don't know

6. You want to display the trend of the contribution of each value over time. So, you decide to insert a chart. To create the appropriate chart, you choose:

    a. File-->New Chart → Area
    *b. Insert-->Chart → Area
    c. Data-->New Chart → Bubble
    d. Tools-->Insert Chart → Line
    e. I don't know

Items for measuring Declarative knowledge

7. When would you use the process of making a chart

    a. When you want to consolidate data
    b. When you want to make a visual comparison
    c. When you want to find information that you would not have noticed otherwise
    d. When you want to draw meaningful conclusions from vast amount of data
    *e. All of the above
    f. I don't know

8. When would you use a diagram

    a. To show the relationship among different elements that are related to worksheet data
    b. To illustrate a concept or enhance a document
    c. To visually represent data
    *d. A & b
    e. A & B & C
    f. I don't know

9. You have created a line chart that displays trend over time. You now want to use the same data to create chart that compares values across categories. To do this, you would

a. Create a new chart
b. Save the worksheet with a new name
c. Right-click the chart and choose Format
*d. Right-click and choose chart type
e. I don't know

10. By default, a chart contains the following items

a. Data Table
b. Gridlines
c. Legend
*d. B & C
e. All of the above
f. I don't know

11. A chart is made from

a. Data Range
b. Data Point
c. Data Row
*d. All of the above
e. None of the above
f. I don't know

12. A diagram

a. Uses number
b. Is based directly from worksheet data
*c. has a drawing border and sizing handles that allow you to customize the digram
d. All of the above
e. I don't know

13. A pyramid diagram

a. Shows a hierarchical relationship
b. Shows a continuous process cycle
c. Shows a relationship of core elements to other elements
*d. Shows foundation-based relationships
e. Shows areas of overlap between elements

14. Which of the following statements about data labels is true?

    a. They can be typed into the chart wizard dialog box
    b. They can point to cell references
    c. They are typed in below each axis
    *d. A & B
    e. A & B & C
    f. I don't know

15. You want to show a comparison between two paired data series. You would

    a. Use the radial diagram to show the relationship
    b. Use the Venn diagram to show the overlap
    c. Use a bar chart to show the comparison
    *d. Use a scatter plot
    e. None of the above
    f. I don't know

Scoring the Posttest
Each of the above quizzes will give two scores
1. Procedural knowledge score = No. of items correctly responded to in questions 1-6
2. Declarative knowledge score = No. of items correctly responded to in questions 7-15.

1. The active cell is A7. You want to calculate the sum of values in cell A1 through A6. Which of the following procedures is a valid procedure in Excel

    a. Clicking on Σ on the toolbar
    b. Typing =SUM(A1:A6) in the active cell
    c. Typing =+A1:A6 in the active cell
    d. Typing =A1+A2+A3+A4+A5+A6 in the active cell
    e. All of the above are valid
    f. A & B & C
    *g. A& B & D
    h. I don't know

2. What would be the outcome of the following expression entered into Excel =2+4^2*3

    a. 4098
    b. 108
    *c. 50
    d. 128
    e. I don't know

3. What is the effect of typing F5+F6 into a cell without a beginning equal sign?

    a. The entry is the same as the formula =F5+F6
    b. The cell will display the contents of cell F5 plus cell F6
    *c. The entry will be treated as a constant and display the literal value F5+F6.
    d. The entry will be rejected by Excel, which will signal an error message.
    e. I don't know

4. To calculate with functions, you first click in the cell you would like the function to appear. The next step is

    a. Type the function
    *b. Choose Insert --> Function to open the Insert Function dialog box
    c. Open the Function Arguments dialog box
    d. None of the above
    e. I don't know

5. The first step in copying a formula or function from one cell to another cell is to select the cell that contains the formula or function. What is the second step?

     a. Press Copy
     b. Select the contents of the Formula Bar.
     *c. Choose Edit-->Paste
     d. Choose Copy-->Formula or Function.
     e. I don't know

6. To copy a formula or function to create a new value, you first copy , then paste from / in the relevant cells. The next step is

     a. Double-click the cell(s) bounded by the selection marquee to activate the selection marquee
     b. Press Enter to copy the formula
     *c. The steps are done
     d. None of the above
     e. I don't know

Items for measuring Declarative knowledge

7. Which of the following statements is true

     a. Relative references are used when you want to copy a formula or function, and you wish that the cell reference should automatically be updated
     b. All formula's and functions need to contain relative references
     c. Absolute references are used when you want to copy a formula or function , and you wish that the cell reference should not automatically be updated
     *d. A & C
     e. A & B
     f. All of the above
     g. I don't know

8. When you want to reuse a formula's and functions, but want to reflect the calculation based on new data, you use the following procedure

     a. Copy a formula or function to maintain the original value
     *b. Copy a formula or function to create a new value
     c. Create an absolute reference
     d. Create a new formula
     e. Create a relative reference
     f. I don't know

9. In which of the following circumstances would you use relative reference exclusively

    *a. You want to calculate A2 * B2 in cell C2. Next, you want to calculate A3* B3 in cell C3
    b. You want to calculate A2 * B2 in cell C2. Next, you want to calculate A2* B3 in cell C3
    c. You want to calculate A2 * B2 in cell C2. Next, you want to calculate A2* B2 in cell C3
    d. All of the above
    e. None of the above
    f. I don't know

10. After typing an equal sign (=) in an empty cell, what happens when you select another cell?

    a. The function wizard opens.
    b. An error message pops up.
    c. A smart tag is displayed in the cell that you selected.
    *d. The address of the selected cell is entered into the formula after the equal sign.
    e. A smart tag is displayed in the cell in which you typed "=".
    f. I don't know

11. In Excel, which of the following has the lowest order of precedence

    *a. Addition and Subtraction
    b. Parenthesis
    c. Exponential
    d. Division and multiplication
    e. I don't know

12. Cell F6 contains the formula = F3-D$3. What will be the contents of cell F7 if the entry in cell F6 is copied to cell F7

    *a. = F3- D$3
    b. = G3 – E$3
    c. = F4 – D$4
    d. = G4 – E$4
    e. I don't know

13. You would use absolute formulas because

    a. You will only have to change data in one place rather than multiple places (each formula) as common data changes
    b. Its makes it easier to copy formulas which use common data

c. That is the correct way of writing formulas
*d. A & B
e. B & C
f. I don't know

14. The advantage of using functions and formulas is

  a. Creating formulas helps you gather valuable information from your data
  b. Speed up development of calculations
  c. Reduces errors
  *d. All of the others
  e. None of the above
  f. I don't know

15. A function can use the following components

  a. Other functions and formulas
  b. Relative and absolute cell references
  c. Each function is unique in its requirements
  *d. A & B
  e. B & C
  f. I don't know

Scoring the Posttest
Each of the above quizzes will give two scores
1. Procedural knowledge score = No. of items correctly responded to in questions 1-6
2. Declarative knowledge score = No. of items correctly responded to in questions 7-15.

Appendix H: Consent Form

CONSENT FORM

I, _____(participant name). agree to participate in a research study titled "Longitudinal investigation of collaborative e-learning in an end-user training context" conducted by Saurabh Gupta from the Department of MIS at the University of Georgia (542-4665) under the direction of Dr. Robert Bostrom, Department of MIS, University of Georgia (542-3559). I understand that my participation is voluntary. I can stop taking part without giving any reason, and without penalty. I can ask to have all of the information about me returned to me, removed from the research records, or destroyed.

The reason for this study is to find out the effectiveness or various end-user training methods currently used by industry.

If I volunteer to take part in this study, I will be asked to do the following things:
1)   Answer questions regarding my ability to use computers.
2)   Participate in three training sessions of two hours each to learn a computer application.
3)   Answer questions regarding my interactions with others and technology
4)   Answer a quiz at the end of each session.
5)   Someone from the study may call me to clarify my information
6)   My responses will be stored and analyzed

I will receive a credit points for participating in the study. If I do not wish to participate in this study, I may receive my extra credit by doing an alternative assignment that does not involve participation in research but involves comparable effort and duration to research participation. I may ask my course instructor about pursuing this option

I will also be eligible of a monetary cash reward (Gift card of $30, $20, $15) based on my performance on the post training quiz. The monetary reward will be given to the best performer on three quizzes combined, for each group of participants. There are four groups, with each around 70 participants. The benefits for me are learning a new computer application, using procedures and process that are currently used by the industry, thus, giving me an early introduction to professional life.

No risk is expected from participating in this experiment.

No information about me, or provided by me during the research, will be shared with others without my written permission, except as required by law. Data will only be available to the researcher and will be used as aggregates for research purposes only.

The investigator will answer any further questions about the research, now or during the course of the project (542-4665).

I understand that I am agreeing by my signature on this form to take part in this research project and understand that I will receive a signed copy of this consent form for my records.

__Saurabh Gupta_____   _____   _____

Name of Researcher   Signature   Date
Telephone: __542-4665_____
Email: _gupta@terry.uga.edu__

_____   _____   _____

Name of Participant   Signature   Date

Sign both copies, keep one, and return the other to the researcher
Additional questions or problems regarding your rights as a research participant should be addressed to Chris A. Joseph, Ph.D. Human Subjects Office, University of Georgia, 612 Boyd Graduate Studies Research Center, Athens, Georgia 30602-7411; Telephone (706) 542-3199; E-Mail Address IRB@uga.edu

234

Appendix I: LISREL syntax

```
TI Configural Invariance Test GRP 4
DA NI=483 NO=119 NG=4 MA=CM
CM FI='C:\projects\thesis\may25\group4D.cov'
ME FI='C:\projects\thesis\may25\group4D.me'
!RA FI='C:\projects\thesis\may25\group3C.psf'
SE
1 2 3 4 5 6 7 8 9 10
11 12 13 14 15 16 17 18 19 20
21 22 23 24 25 26 27 28 29 30
31 32 33 34 35 36 37 38 39 40
41 42 43 44 45 46 47 48 49 50
51 52 53 54 55 56 57 58 59 60
61 62 63 64 65 66/
LA
B_SE2_R B_SE4_R B_SE5_R C_SE2_R C_SE4_R C_SE5_R D_SE2_R D_SE4_R D_SE5_R
B_SATIS2 B_SATIS4 B_SATI_A C_SATIS2 C_SATIS4 C_SATI_A D_SATIS2 D_SATIS4
D_SATI_A B_FAITH1 B_FAITH2 B_FAITH3 B_FAITH4 C_FAITH1 C_FAITH2 C_FAITH3
C_FAITH4 D_FAITH1 D_FAITH2 D_FAITH3 D_FAITH4 B_RSPT2 B_RSPT3 B_COMF1 B_COMF3
C_RSPT2 C_RSPT3 C_COMF1 C_COMF3 D_RSPT2 D_RSPT3 D_COMF1 D_COMF3 B_COLL_A
B_COLL_B B_COLL_C B_COLL_D B_COLL_E B_COLL_F C_COLL_A C_COLL_B C_COLL_C
C_COLL_D C_COLL_E C_COLL_F D_COLL_A D_COLL_B D_COLL_C D_COLL_D D_COLL_E
D_COLL_F b_A_score C_A_score D_A_score B_A_SSE
C_A_SSE D_A_SSE/

!151 152 153 254 255 256 360 361 362 127 128 129 230 231 232 336 337 338
!90 91 92 93 193 194 195 196 299 300 301 302/

MO NY=66 NE=35 LY=FU,FI BE=FU,FI PS=SY,FI TE=SY,FI AL=FI TY=ZE

LE
B_SE C_SE D_SE B_SATIS C_SATIS D_SATIS IN_SE CH_SE IN_SATIS CH_SATIS
b_FAITH C_FAITH D_FAITH IN_FAITH CH_FAITH
B_ATTI C_ATTI D_ATTI IS_ATTI CH_ATTI
b_collAB C_COLLAB D_COLLAB IN_COLLAB CH_COLLAB
b_score C_score D_score IN_SCORE CH_SCORE
B_sse C_sse D_sse IS_SSE CH_SSE/

FR LY 2 1 LY 3 1
FR LY 5 2 LY 6 2
FR LY 8 3 LY 9 3

FR LY 11 4 LY 12 4
FR LY 14 5 LY 15 5
FR LY 17 6 LY 18 6

!FAITHFULNESS ITEMS

FR LY 20 11 LY 21 11 LY 22 11
FR LY 24 12 LY 25 12 LY 26 12
FR LY 28 13 LY 29 13 LY 30 13

FR LY 32 16 LY 33 16 LY 34 16
FR LY 36 17 LY 37 17 LY 38 17
FR LY 40 18 LY 41 18 LY 42 18

!COLLABORAITON ITEMS
```

```
FR LY 44 21 LY 45 21 LY 46 21 LY 47 21 LY 48 21
FR LY 50 22 LY 51 22 LY 52 22 LY 53 22 LY 54 22
FR LY 56 23 LY 57 23 LY 58 23 LY 59 23 LY 60 23

FI LY(1,1) LY(4,2) LY(7,3)
VA 1.00 LY(1,1) LY(4,2) LY(7,3)

FI LY 10 4 LY 13 5 LY 16 6
VA 1.00 LY 10 4 LY 13 5 LY 16 6

FI LY 19 11 LY 23 12 LY 27 13
VA 1.00 LY 19 11 LY 23 12 LY 27 13

FI LY 31 16 LY 35 17 LY 39 18
VA 1.00 LY 31 16 LY 35 17 LY 39 18

FI LY 43 21 LY 49 22 LY 55 23
VA 1.00 LY 43 21 LY 49 22 LY 55 23

!score items
VA 1.00 LY 61 26 LY 62 27 LY 63 28
VA 1.00 LY 64 31 LY 65 32 LY 66 33

FR TE 1 1 TE 2 2 TE 3 3 TE 4 4 TE 5 5 TE 6 6 TE 7 7
FR TE 8 8 TE 9 9
FR TE 4 1 TE 7 1 TE 5 2 TE 8 2 TE 6 3 TE 9 3
FR TE 7 4 TE 8 5 TE 9 6

FR TE 10 10 TE 11 11 TE 12 12 TE 13 13 TE 14 14 TE 15 15 TE 16 16 TE 17 17
TE 18 18
FR TE 13 10 TE 14 11 TE 15 12 TE 16 13 TE 17 14 TE 18 15
FR TE 16 10 TE 17 11 TE 18 12

!FAITHFULNESS ITEMS
FR TE 19 19 TE 20 20 TE 21 21 TE 22 22 TE 23 23 TE 24 24 TE 25 25 TE 26 26
TE 27 27 TE 28 28 TE 29 29 TE 30 30
FR TE 23 19 TE 24 20 TE 25 21 TE 26 22 TE 27 23 TE 28 24 TE 29 25 TE 30 26
FR TE 27 19 TE 28 20 TE 29 21 TE 30 22

FR TE 31 31 TE 32 32 TE 33 33 TE 34 34 TE 35 35 TE 36 36 TE 37 37 TE 38 38
TE 39 39 TE 40 40 TE 41 41 TE 42 42
FR TE 35 31 TE 36 32 TE 37 33 TE 38 34 TE 39 35 TE 40 36 TE 41 37 TE 42 38
FR TE 39 31 TE 40 32 TE 41 33 TE 42 34

!COLLABORATION ITEMS
FR TE 43 43 TE 44 44 TE 45 45 TE 46 46 TE 47 47 TE 48 48 TE 49 49 TE 50 50
TE 51 51
FR TE 52 52 TE 53 53 TE 54 54 TE 55 55 TE 56 56 TE 57 57 TE 58 58 TE 59 59
TE 60 60
FR TE 49 43 TE 50 44 TE 51 45 TE 52 46 TE 53 47 TE 54 48 TE 55 49 TE 56 50
TE 57 51
FR TE 58 52 TE 59 53 TE 60 54
FR TE 55 43 TE 56 44 TE 57 45 TE 58 46 TE 59 47 TE 60 48

!SCORE ITEMS
VA 0.0 TE 61 61 TE 62 62 TE 63 63
VA 0.0 TE 64 64 TE 65 65 TE 66 66
```

```
EQ LY 2 1 LY 5 2 LY 8 3
EQ LY 3 1 LY 6 2 LY 9 3

EQ LY 11 4 LY 14 5 LY 17 6
EQ LY 12 4 LY 15 5 LY 18 6

!FAITHFULNESS ITEMS
EQ LY 20 11 LY 24 12 LY 28 13
EQ LY 21 11 LY 25 12 LY 29 13
EQ LY 22 11 LY 26 12 LY 30 13

EQ LY 32 16 LY 36 17 LY 40 18
EQ LY 33 16 LY 37 17 LY 41 18
EQ LY 34 16 LY 38 17 LY 42 18

!COLLABORAITON ITEMS
EQ LY 44 21 LY 50 22 LY 56 23
EQ LY 45 21 LY 51 22 LY 57 23
EQ LY 46 21 LY 52 22 LY 58 23
EQ LY 47 21 LY 53 22 LY 59 23
EQ LY 48 21 LY 54 22 LY 60 23

FR PS 1 1 PS 2 2 PS 3 3 PS 4 4 PS 5 5 PS 6 6 PS 7 7 PS 8 8 PS 9 9 PS 10 10
FR PS 8 7 PS 10 9

!FAITHFULNESS ITEMS

FR PS 11 11 PS 12 12 PS 13 13 PS 14 14 PS 15 15
FR PS 15 14

FR PS 16 16 PS 17 17 PS 18 18 PS 19 19 PS 20 20
FR PS 20 19

!COLLABORAITON ITMES
FR PS 21 21 PS 22 22 PS 23 23 PS 24 24 PS 25 25
FR PS 25 24

!SCORE ITEMS
FR PS 26 26 PS 27 27 PS 28 28 PS 29 29 PS 30 30
FR PS 30 29
FR PS 31 31 PS 32 32 PS 33 33 PS 34 34 PS 35 35
PS 35 34

EQ PS 1 1 PS 2 2 PS 3 3
EQ PS 4 4 PS 5 5 PS 6 6
EQ PS 11 11 PS 12 12 PS 13 13
EQ PS 16 16 PS 17 17 PS 18 18
EQ PS 21 21 PS 22 22 PS 23 23
EQ PS 26 26 PS 27 27 PS 28 28
EQ PS 31 31 PS 32 32 PS 33 33

VA 1.0 BE 1 7 BE 2 7 BE 3 7 BE 2 8
VA 0.0 BE 1 8
VA 2.0 BE 3 8

VA 1.0 BE 4 9 BE 5 9 BE 6 9 BE 5 10
```

```
VA 0.0 BE 4 10
VA 2.0 BE 6 10

!FAITHFULNESS ITEMS
VA 1.0 BE 11 14 BE 12 14 BE 13 14 BE 12 15
VA 0.0 BE 11 15
VA 2.0 BE 13 15

VA 1.0 BE 16 19 BE 17 19 BE 18 19 BE 17 20
VA 0.0 BE 16 20
VA 2.0 BE 18 20

!COLLABORATION ITEMS
VA 1.0 BE 21 24 BE 22 24 BE 23 24 BE 22 25
VA 0.0 BE 21 25
VA 2.0 BE 23 25

!SCORE ITEMS
VA 1.0 BE 26 29 BE 27 29 BE 28 29 BE 27 30
VA 0.0 BE 26 30
VA 2.0 BE 28 30
VA 1.0 BE 31 34 BE 32 34 BE 33 34 BE 32 35
VA 0.0 BE 31 35
VA 2.0 BE 33 35

 FR AL 7 AL 8 AL 9 AL 10 AL 14 AL 15 AL 19 AL 20 AL 24 AL 25 AL 29 AL 30 AL
34 AL 35

!SCORE STARTING VALUES
ST 6.07 PS 26 26
ST -1.78 PS 29 29
ST -0.41 PS 30 30
ST 1.92 PS 30 29
ST 9.98 AL 29
ST 1.59 AL 30

!SSE STARTING VALUES
ST 63.30 PS 31 31
ST 103.18 PS 34 34
ST 90.45 PS 35 35
ST 98.34 PS 35 34
ST 24.87 AL 34
ST 20.28 AL 35

!CAUSAL MODEL
FR BE 7 14 BE 8 14 BE 8 15
!FR BE 9 14 BE 10 14 BE 10 15
FR BE 9 14 BE 10 14
FR BE 7 19 BE 8 19 BE 8 20
FR BE 9 19 BE 10 19 BE 10 20
FR BE 7 24 BE 8 24 BE 8 25
FR BE 9 24 BE 10 24 BE 10 25

FR BE 29 14 BE 30 14 BE 30 15
FR BE 29 19 BE 30 19 BE 30 20
FR BE 29 24 BE 30 24 BE 30 25
```

```
!FR BE 34 14 BE 35 14 BE 35 15
FR BE 34 19 BE 35 19 BE 35 20
FR BE 34 24 BE 35 24 BE 35 25

PD
OU AD=OFF SS SC SE TV IT=500


TI Configural Invariance Test GRP 3
DA NI=483 NO=85 MA=CM
CM FI='C:\projects\thesis\may25\group3C.cov'
ME FI='C:\projects\thesis\may25\group3C.me'
!RA FI='C:\projects\thesis\may25\group3C.psf'
SE
1 2 3 4 5 6 7 8 9 10
11 12 13 14 15 16 17 18 19 20
21 22 23 24 25 26 27 28 29 30
31 32 33 34 35 36 37 38 39 40
41 42 43 44 45 46 47 48 49 50
51 52 53 54 55 56 57 58 59 60
61 62 63 64 65 66/
LA
B_SE2_R  B_SE4_R  B_SE5_R  C_SE2_R  C_SE4_R  C_SE5_R  D_SE2_R  D_SE4_R  D_SE5_R
B_SATIS2  B_SATIS4  B_SATI_A  C_SATIS2  C_SATIS4  C_SATI_A  D_SATIS2  D_SATIS4
D_SATI_A  B_FAITH1  B_FAITH2  B_FAITH3  B_FAITH4  C_FAITH1  C_FAITH2  C_FAITH3
C_FAITH4  D_FAITH1  D_FAITH2  D_FAITH3  D_FAITH4  B_RSPT2  B_RSPT3  B_COMF1  B_COMF3
C_RSPT2  C_RSPT3  C_COMF1  C_COMF3  D_RSPT2  D_RSPT3  D_COMF1  D_COMF3  B_COLL_A
B_COLL_B  B_COLL_C  B_COLL_D  B_COLL_E  B_COLL_F  C_COLL_A  C_COLL_B  C_COLL_C
C_COLL_D  C_COLL_E  C_COLL_F  D_COLL_A  D_COLL_B  D_COLL_C  D_COLL_D  D_COLL_E
D_COLL_F  b_A_score  C_A_score  D_A_score  B_A_SSE
C_A_SSE D_A_SSE/

!151 152 153 254 255 256 360 361 362 127 128 129 230 231 232 336 337 338
!90 91 92 93 193 194 195 196 299 300 301 302/

MO NY=66 NE=35 LY=IN BE=IN PS=IN TE=SY,FI AL=FI TY=ZE

LE
B_SE C_SE D_SE B_SATIS C_SATIS D_SATIS IN_SE CH_SE IN_SATIS CH_SATIS
b_FAITH C_FAITH D_FAITH IN_FAITH CH_FAITH
B_ATTI C_ATTI D_ATTI IS_ATTI CH_ATTI
b_collAB C_COLLAB D_COLLAB IN_COLLAB CH_COLLAB
b_score C_score D_score IN_SCORE CH_SCORE
B_sse C_sse D_sse IS_SSE CH_SSE/

!FAITHFULNESS ITEMS

VA 0.0 LY 20 11 LY 21 11 LY 22 11
VA 0.0 LY 24 12 LY 25 12 LY 26 12
VA 0.0 LY 28 13 LY 29 13 LY 30 13

VA 0.0 LY 32 16 LY 33 16 LY 34 16
VA 0.0 LY 36 17 LY 37 17 LY 38 17
VA 0.0 LY 40 18 LY 41 18 LY 42 18

FI LY(1,1) LY(4,2) LY(7,3)
```

240

```
VA 1.00 LY(1,1) LY(4,2) LY(7,3)

FI LY 10 4 LY 13 5 LY 16 6
VA 1.00 LY 10 4 LY 13 5 LY 16 6

FI LY 19 11 LY 23 12 LY 27 13
VA 0.00 LY 19 11 LY 23 12 LY 27 13

FI LY 31 16 LY 35 17 LY 39 18
VA 0.00 LY 31 16 LY 35 17 LY 39 18

FI LY 43 21 LY 49 22 LY 55 23
VA 1.00 LY 43 21 LY 49 22 LY 55 23

!score items
VA 1.00 LY 61 26 LY 62 27 LY 63 28
VA 1.00 LY 64 31 LY 65 32 LY 66 33

FR TE 1 1 TE 2 2 TE 3 3 TE 4 4 TE 5 5 TE 6 6 TE 7 7
FR TE 8 8 TE 9 9
FR TE 4 1 TE 7 1 TE 5 2 TE 8 2 TE 6 3 TE 9 3
FR TE 7 4 TE 8 5 TE 9 6

FR TE 10 10 TE 11 11 TE 12 12 TE 13 13 TE 14 14 TE 15 15 TE 16 16 TE 17 17
TE 18 18
FR TE 13 10 TE 14 11 TE 15 12 TE 16 13 TE 17 14 TE 18 15
FR TE 16 10 TE 17 11 TE 18 12

!FAITHFULNESS ITEMS
VA 1.00 TE 19 19 TE 20 20 TE 21 21 TE 22 22 TE 23 23 TE 24 24 TE 25 25 TE 26
26 TE 27 27 TE 28 28 TE 29 29
VA 1.00 TE 30 30
!FR TE 23 19 TE 24 20 TE 25 21 TE 26 22 TE 27 23 TE 28 24 TE 29 25 TE 30 26
!FR TE 27 19 TE 28 20 TE 29 21 TE 30 22

VA 1.00 TE 31 31 TE 32 32 TE 33 33 TE 34 34 TE 35 35 TE 36 36 TE 37 37 TE 38
38 TE 39 39 TE 40 40 TE 41 41
VA 1.00 TE 42 42
!FR TE 35 31 TE 36 32 TE 37 33 TE 38 34 TE 39 35 TE 40 36 TE 41 37 TE 42 38
!FR TE 39 31 TE 40 32 TE 41 33 TE 42 34

!COLLABORATION ITEMS
FR TE 43 43 TE 44 44 TE 45 45 TE 46 46 TE 47 47 TE 48 48 TE 49 49 TE 50 50
TE 51 51
FR TE 52 52 TE 53 53 TE 54 54 TE 55 55 TE 56 56 TE 57 57 TE 58 58 TE 59 59
TE 60 60
FR TE 49 43 TE 50 44 TE 51 45 TE 52 46 TE 53 47 TE 54 48 TE 55 49 TE 56 50
TE 57 51
FR TE 58 52 TE 59 53 TE 60 54
FR TE 55 43 TE 56 44 TE 57 45 TE 58 46 TE 59 47 TE 60 48

!SCORE ITEMS
VA 0.0 TE 61 61 TE 62 62 TE 63 63
VA 0.0 TE 64 64 TE 65 65 TE 66 66

!FAITHFULNESS ITEMS
VA 1.0 PS 11 11 PS 12 12 PS 13 13 PS 14 14 PS 15 15
```

241

```
!FR PS 15 14
VA 1.0 PS 16 16 PS 17 17 PS 18 18 PS 19 19 PS 20 20

!SCORE ITEMS
FR PS 26 26 PS 27 27 PS 28 28 PS 29 29 PS 30 30
FR PS 30 29
EQ PS 26 26 PS 27 27 PS 28 28
FR PS 31 31 PS 32 32 PS 33 33 PS 34 34 PS 35 35
PS 35 34
EQ PS 31 31 PS 32 32 PS 33 33

FR PS 8 7 PS 10 9 PS 15 14 PS 25 24

VA 1.0 BE 1 7 BE 2 7 BE 3 7 BE 2 8
VA 0.0 BE 1 8
VA 2.0 BE 3 8

VA 1.0 BE 4 9 BE 5 9 BE 6 9 BE 5 10
VA 0.0 BE 4 10
VA 2.0 BE 6 10

FAITHFULNESS ITEMS
VA 1.0 BE 11 14 BE 12 14 BE 13 14 BE 12 15
VA 1.0 BE 11 15
VA 1.0 BE 13 15

VA 1.0 BE 16 19 BE 17 19 BE 18 19 BE 17 20
VA 1.0 BE 16 20
VA 1.0 BE 18 20

!COLLABORATION ITEMS
VA 1.0 BE 21 24 BE 22 24 BE 23 24 BE 22 25
VA 0.0 BE 21 25
VA 2.0 BE 23 25

!SCORE ITEMS
VA 1.0 BE 26 29 BE 27 29 BE 28 29 BE 27 30
VA 0.0 BE 26 30
VA 2.0 BE 28 30
VA 1.0 BE 31 34 BE 32 34 BE 33 34 BE 32 35
VA 0.0 BE 31 35
VA 2.0 BE 33 35

FR AL 7 AL 8 AL 9 AL 10 AL 24 AL 25 AL 29 AL 30 AL 34 AL 35

!SCORE STARTING VALUES
ST 6.07 PS 26 26
ST -1.78 PS 29 29
ST -0.41 PS 30 30
ST 1.92 PS 30 29
ST 8.93 AL 29
ST 1.95 AL 30

!SSE STARTING VALUES
ST 63.30 PS 31 31
ST 103.18 PS 34 34
ST 90.45 PS 35 35
```

242

```
ST 98.34 PS 35 34
ST 24.33 AL 34
ST 18.98 AL 35

!CAUSAL MODEL
FI BE 7 14 BE 8 14 BE 8 15
FI BE 9 14 BE 10 14 BE 10 15
FI BE 7 19 BE 8 19 BE 8 20
FI BE 9 19 BE 10 19 BE 10 20
VA 0.0 BE 7 14 BE 8 14 BE 8 15
VA 0.0 BE 9 14 BE 10 14 BE 10 15
VA 0.0 BE 7 19 BE 8 19 BE 8 20
VA 0.0 BE 9 19 BE 10 19 BE 10 20
!FR BE 7 24 BE 8 24 BE 8 25
!FR BE 9 24 BE 10 24 BE 10 25

FI BE 29 14 BE 30 14 BE 30 15
VA 0.0 BE 29 14 BE 30 14 BE 30 15
FI BE 29 19 BE 30 19 BE 30 20
VA 0.0 BE 29 19 BE 30 19 BE 30 20

!FI BE 34 14 BE 35 14 BE 35 15
!VA 0.0 BE 34 14 BE 35 14 BE 35 15

FI BE 34 19 BE 35 19 BE 35 20
VA 0.0 BE 34 19 BE 35 19 BE 35 20

PD
OU AD=OFF SS SC SE TV IT=500


TI Configural Invariance Test GRP 1
DA NI=483 NO=113 MA=CM
CM FI='C:\projects\thesis\may25\group1C.cov'
ME FI='C:\projects\thesis\may25\group1C.me'
!RA FI='C:\projects\thesis\may25\group3C.psf'
SE
1 2 3 4 5 6 7 8 9 10
11 12 13 14 15 16 17 18 19 20
21 22 23 24 25 26 27 28 29 30
31 32 33 34 35 36 37 38 39 40
41 42 43 44 45 46 47 48 49 50
51 52 53 54 55 56 57 58 59 60
61 62 63 64 65 66/
LA
 B_SE2_R  B_SE4_R  B_SE5_R  C_SE2_R  C_SE4_R  C_SE5_R  D_SE2_R  D_SE4_R  D_SE5_R
B_SATIS2  B_SATIS4  B_SATI_A  C_SATIS2  C_SATIS4  C_SATI_A  D_SATIS2  D_SATIS4
D_SATI_A  B_FAITH1  B_FAITH2  B_FAITH3  B_FAITH4  C_FAITH1  C_FAITH2  C_FAITH3
C_FAITH4  D_FAITH1  D_FAITH2  D_FAITH3  D_FAITH4  B_RSPT2  B_RSPT3  B_COMF1  B_COMF3
C_RSPT2  C_RSPT3  C_COMF1  C_COMF3  D_RSPT2  D_RSPT3  D_COMF1  D_COMF3  B_COLL_A
B_COLL_B  B_COLL_C  B_COLL_D  B_COLL_E  B_COLL_F  C_COLL_A  C_COLL_B  C_COLL_C
C_COLL_D  C_COLL_E  C_COLL_F  D_COLL_A  D_COLL_B  D_COLL_C  D_COLL_D  D_COLL_E
D_COLL_F  b_A_score  C_A_score  D_A_score  B_A_SSE
 C_A_SSE  D_A_SSE/

!151 152 153 254 255 256 360 361 362 127 128 129 230 231 232 336 337 338
!90 91 92 93 193 194 195 196 299 300 301 302/
```
243

```
MO NY=66 NE=35 LY=IN BE=IN PS=IN TE=SY,FI AL=FI TY=ZE

LE
B_SE C_SE D_SE B_SATIS C_SATIS D_SATIS IN_SE CH_SE IN_SATIS CH_SATIS
b_FAITH C_FAITH D_FAITH IN_FAITH CH_FAITH
B_ATTI C_ATTI D_ATTI IS_ATTI CH_ATTI
b_collAB C_COLLAB D_COLLAB IN_COLLAB CH_COLLAB
b_score C_score D_score IN_SCORE CH_SCORE
B_sse C_sse D_sse IS_SSE CH_SSE/

!FAITHFULNESS ITEMS

VA 0.0 LY 20 11 LY 21 11 LY 22 11
VA 0.0 LY 24 12 LY 25 12 LY 26 12
VA 0.0 LY 28 13 LY 29 13 LY 30 13

VA 0.0 LY 32 16 LY 33 16 LY 34 16
VA 0.0 LY 36 17 LY 37 17 LY 38 17
VA 0.0 LY 40 18 LY 41 18 LY 42 18

!COLLABORAITON ITEMS

VA 0.0 LY 44 21 LY 45 21 LY 46 21 LY 47 21 LY 48 21
VA 0.0 LY 50 22 LY 51 22 LY 52 22 LY 53 22 LY 54 22
VA 0.0 LY 56 23 LY 57 23 LY 58 23 LY 59 23 LY 60 23

FI LY(1,1) LY(4,2) LY(7,3)
VA 1.00 LY(1,1) LY(4,2) LY(7,3)

FI LY 10 4 LY 13 5 LY 16 6
VA 1.00 LY 10 4 LY 13 5 LY 16 6

FI LY 19 11 LY 23 12 LY 27 13
VA 0.00 LY 19 11 LY 23 12 LY 27 13

FI LY 31 16 LY 35 17 LY 39 18
VA 0.00 LY 31 16 LY 35 17 LY 39 18

FI LY 43 21 LY 49 22 LY 55 23
VA 0.00 LY 43 21 LY 49 22 LY 55 23

!score items
VA 1.00 LY 61 26 LY 62 27 LY 63 28
VA 1.00 LY 43 21 LY 49 22 LY 55 23

FR TE 1 1 TE 2 2 TE 3 3 TE 4 4 TE 5 5 TE 6 6 TE 7 7
FR TE 8 8 TE 9 9
FR TE 4 1 TE 7 1 TE 5 2 TE 8 2 TE 6 3 TE 9 3
FR TE 7 4 TE 8 5 TE 9 6

FR TE 10 10 TE 11 11 TE 12 12 TE 13 13 TE 14 14 TE 15 15 TE 16 16 TE 17 17
TE 18 18
FR TE 13 10 TE 14 11 TE 15 12 TE 16 13 TE 17 14 TE 18 15
FR TE 16 10 TE 17 11 TE 18 12

!FAITHFULNESS ITEMS
```

```
VA 1.00 TE 19 19 TE 20 20 TE 21 21 TE 22 22 TE 23 23 TE 24 24 TE 25 25 TE 26
26 TE 27 27 TE 28 28 TE 29 29
VA 1.00 TE 30 30
!FR TE 23 19 TE 24 20 TE 25 21 TE 26 22 TE 27 23 TE 28 24 TE 29 25 TE 30 26
!FR TE 27 19 TE 28 20 TE 29 21 TE 30 22

VA 1.00 TE 31 31 TE 32 32 TE 33 33 TE 34 34 TE 35 35 TE 36 36 TE 37 37 TE 38
38 TE 39 39 TE 40 40 TE 41 41
VA 1.00 TE 42 42
!FR TE 35 31 TE 36 32 TE 37 33 TE 38 34 TE 39 35 TE 40 36 TE 41 37 TE 42 38
!FR TE 39 31 TE 40 32 TE 41 33 TE 42 34

!COLLABORATION ITEMS
VA 1.00 TE 43 43 TE 44 44 TE 45 45 TE 46 46 TE 47 47 TE 48 48 TE 49 49 TE 50
50 TE 51 51
VA 1.00 TE 52 52 TE 53 53 TE 54 54 TE 55 55 TE 56 56 TE 57 57 TE 58 58 TE 59
59 TE 60 60
!FR TE 49 43 TE 50 44 TE 51 45 TE 52 46 TE 53 47 TE 54 48 TE 55 49 TE 56 50
TE 57 51
!FR TE 58 52 TE 59 53 TE 60 54
!FR TE 55 43 TE 56 44 TE 57 45 TE 58 46 TE 59 47 TE 60 48

!SCORE ITEMS
VA 0.0 TE 61 61 TE 62 62 TE 63 63
VA 0.0 TE 64 64 TE 65 65 TE 66 66

!FAITHFULNESS ITEMS
VA 1.0 PS 11 11 PS 12 12 PS 13 13 PS 14 14 PS 15 15
!FR PS 15 14
VA 1.0 PS 16 16 PS 17 17 PS 18 18 PS 19 19 PS 20 20

!COLLABORATION ITEMS
VA 1.0 PS 21 21 PS 22 22 PS 23 23 PS 24 24 PS 25 25

FR PS 8 7 PS 10 9 PS 15 14

!SCORE ITEMS
FR PS 26 26 PS 27 27 PS 28 28 PS 29 29 PS 30 30
FR PS 30 29
EQ PS 26 26 PS 27 27 PS 28 28
FR PS 31 31 PS 32 32 PS 33 33 PS 34 34 PS 35 35
PS 35 34
EQ PS 31 31 PS 32 32 PS 33 33

VA 1.0 BE 1 7 BE 2 7 BE 3 7 BE 2 8
VA 0.0 BE 1 8
VA 2.0 BE 3 8

VA 1.0 BE 4 9 BE 5 9 BE 6 9 BE 5 10
VA 0.0 BE 4 10
VA 2.0 BE 6 10

!FAITHFULNESS ITEMS
VA 1.0 BE 11 14 BE 12 14 BE 13 14 BE 12 15
VA 1.0 BE 11 15
VA 1.0 BE 13 15
```

```
VA 1.0 BE 16 19 BE 17 19 BE 18 19 BE 17 20
VA 1.0 BE 16 20
VA 1.0 BE 18 20

!COLLABORATION ITEMS
VA 1.0 BE 21 24 BE 22 24 BE 23 24 BE 22 25
VA 1.0 BE 21 25
VA 1.0 BE 23 25

!SCORE ITEMS
VA 1.0 BE 26 29 BE 27 29 BE 28 29 BE 27 30
VA 0.0 BE 26 30
VA 2.0 BE 28 30
VA 1.0 BE 31 34 BE 32 34 BE 33 34 BE 32 35
VA 0.0 BE 31 35
VA 2.0 BE 33 35

FR AL 7 AL 8 AL 9 AL 10 AL 29 AL 30 AL 34 AL 35

!SCORE STARTING VALUES
ST 6.07 PS 26 26
ST -1.78 PS 29 29
ST -0.41 PS 30 30
ST 1.92 PS 30 29
ST 8.98 AL 29
ST 1.57 AL 30

!SSE STARTING VALUES
ST 63.30 PS 31 31
ST 103.18 PS 34 34
ST 90.45 PS 35 35
ST 98.34 PS 35 34
ST 21.55 AL 34
ST 17.81 AL 35

!CAUSAL MODEL
FI BE 7 14 BE 8 14 BE 8 15
FI BE 9 14 BE 10 14 BE 10 15
FI BE 7 19 BE 8 19 BE 8 20
FI BE 9 19 BE 10 19 BE 10 20
FI BE 7 24 BE 8 24 BE 8 25
FI BE 9 24 BE 10 24 BE 10 25
VA 0.0 BE 7 14 BE 8 14 BE 8 15
VA 0.0 BE 9 14 BE 10 14 BE 10 15
VA 0.0 BE 7 19 BE 8 19 BE 8 20
VA 0.0 BE 9 19 BE 10 19 BE 10 20
VA 0.0 BE 7 24 BE 8 24 BE 8 25
VA 0.0 BE 9 24 BE 10 24 BE 10 25

FI BE 29 14 BE 30 14 BE 30 15
VA 0.0 BE 29 14 BE 30 14 BE 30 15
FI BE 29 19 BE 30 19 BE 30 20
VA 0.0 BE 29 19 BE 30 19 BE 30 20
FI BE 29 24 BE 30 24 BE 30 25
VA 0.0 BE 29 24 BE 30 24 BE 30 25

!FI BE 34 14 BE 35 14 BE 35 15
```

246

```
!VA 0.0 BE 34 14 BE 35 14 BE 35 15

FI BE 34 19 BE 35 19 BE 35 20
VA 0.0 BE 34 19 BE 35 19 BE 35 20

FI BE 34 24 BE 35 24 BE 35 25
VA 0.0 BE 34 24 BE 35 24 BE 35 25

PD
OU AD=OFF SS SC SE TV IT=500


TI Configural Invariance Test GRP 2
DA NI=483 NO=117 MA=CM
CM FI='C:\projects\thesis\may25\group2C.cov'
ME FI='C:\projects\thesis\may25\group2C.me'
!RA FI='C:\projects\thesis\may25\group3C.psf'
SE
1 2 3 4 5 6 7 8 9 10
11 12 13 14 15 16 17 18 19 20
21 22 23 24 25 26 27 28 29 30
31 32 33 34 35 36 37 38 39 40
41 42 43 44 45 46 47 48 49 50
51 52 53 54 55 56 57 58 59 60
61 62 63 64 65 66/
LA
B_SE2_R  B_SE4_R  B_SE5_R  C_SE2_R  C_SE4_R  C_SE5_R  D_SE2_R  D_SE4_R  D_SE5_R
B_SATIS2  B_SATIS4  B_SATI_A  C_SATIS2  C_SATIS4  C_SATI_A  D_SATIS2  D_SATIS4
D_SATI_A  B_FAITH1  B_FAITH2  B_FAITH3  B_FAITH4  C_FAITH1  C_FAITH2  C_FAITH3
C_FAITH4  D_FAITH1  D_FAITH2  D_FAITH3  D_FAITH4  B_RSPT2  B_RSPT3  B_COMF1  B_COMF3
C_RSPT2  C_RSPT3  C_COMF1  C_COMF3  D_RSPT2  D_RSPT3  D_COMF1  D_COMF3  B_COLL_A
B_COLL_B  B_COLL_C  B_COLL_D  B_COLL_E  B_COLL_F  C_COLL_A  C_COLL_B  C_COLL_C
C_COLL_D  C_COLL_E  C_COLL_F  D_COLL_A  D_COLL_B  D_COLL_C  D_COLL_D  D_COLL_E
D_COLL_F  b_A_score  C_A_score  D_A_score  B_A_SSE
C_A_SSE  D_A_SSE/

!151 152 153 254 255 256 360 361 362 127 128 129 230 231 232 336 337 338
!90 91 92 93 193 194 195 196 299 300 301 302/

MO NY=66 NE=35 LY=IN BE=IN PS=IN TE=SY,FI AL=FI TY=ZE

LE
B_SE C_SE D_SE B_SATIS C_SATIS D_SATIS IN_SE CH_SE IN_SATIS CH_SATIS
b_FAITH C_FAITH D_FAITH IN_FAITH CH_FAITH
B_ATTI C_ATTI D_ATTI IS_ATTI CH_ATTI
b_collAB C_COLLAB D_COLLAB IN_COLLAB CH_COLLAB
b_score C_score D_score IN_SCORE CH_SCORE
B_sse C_sse D_sse IS_SSE CH_SSE/

!COLLABORAITON ITEMS

VA 0.0 LY 44 21 LY 45 21 LY 46 21 LY 47 21 LY 48 21
VA 0.0 LY 50 22 LY 51 22 LY 52 22 LY 53 22 LY 54 22
VA 0.0 LY 56 23 LY 57 23 LY 58 23 LY 59 23 LY 60 23

FI LY(1,1) LY(4,2) LY(7,3)
VA 1.00 LY(1,1) LY(4,2) LY(7,3)
```

```
FI LY 10 4 LY 13 5 LY 16 6
VA 1.00 LY 10 4 LY 13 5 LY 16 6

FI LY 19 11 LY 23 12 LY 27 13
VA 1.00 LY 19 11 LY 23 12 LY 27 13

FI LY 31 16 LY 35 17 LY 39 18
VA 1.00 LY 31 16 LY 35 17 LY 39 18

FI LY 43 21 LY 49 22 LY 55 23
VA 0.00 LY 43 21 LY 49 22 LY 55 23

!score items
VA 1.00 LY 61 26 LY 62 27 LY 63 28
VA 1.00 LY 43 21 LY 49 22 LY 55 23

FR TE 1 1 TE 2 2 TE 3 3 TE 4 4 TE 5 5 TE 6 6 TE 7 7
FR TE 8 8 TE 9 9
FR TE 4 1 TE 7 1 TE 5 2 TE 8 2 TE 6 3 TE 9 3
FR TE 7 4 TE 8 5 TE 9 6

FR TE 10 10 TE 11 11 TE 12 12 TE 13 13 TE 14 14 TE 15 15 TE 16 16 TE 17 17
TE 18 18
FR TE 13 10 TE 14 11 TE 15 12 TE 16 13 TE 17 14 TE 18 15
FR TE 16 10 TE 17 11 TE 18 12

!FAITHFULNESS ITEMS
FR TE 19 19 TE 20 20 TE 21 21 TE 22 22 TE 23 23 TE 24 24 TE 25 25 TE 26 26
TE 27 27 TE 28 28 TE 29 29 TE 30 30
FR TE 23 19 TE 24 20 TE 25 21 TE 26 22 TE 27 23 TE 28 24 TE 29 25 TE 30 26
FR TE 27 19 TE 28 20 TE 29 21 TE 30 22

FR TE 31 31 TE 32 32 TE 33 33 TE 34 34 TE 35 35 TE 36 36 TE 37 37 TE 38 38
TE 39 39 TE 40 40 TE 41 41 TE 42 42
FR TE 35 31 TE 36 32 TE 37 33 TE 38 34 TE 39 35 TE 40 36 TE 41 37 TE 42 38
FR TE 39 31 TE 40 32 TE 41 33 TE 42 34

!COLLABORATION ITEMS
VA 1.00 TE 43 43 TE 44 44 TE 45 45 TE 46 46 TE 47 47 TE 48 48 TE 49 49 TE 50
50 TE 51 51
VA 1.00 TE 52 52 TE 53 53 TE 54 54 TE 55 55 TE 56 56 TE 57 57 TE 58 58 TE 59
59 TE 60 60
!FR TE 49 43 TE 50 44 TE 51 45 TE 52 46 TE 53 47 TE 54 48 TE 55 49 TE 56 50
TE 57 51
!FR TE 58 52 TE 59 53 TE 60 54
!FR TE 55 43 TE 56 44 TE 57 45 TE 58 46 TE 59 47 TE 60 48

!SCORE ITEMS
VA 0.0 TE 61 61 TE 62 62 TE 63 63
VA 0.0 TE 64 64 TE 65 65 TE 66 66

!FR PS 1 1 PS 2 2 PS 3 3 PS 4 4 PS 5 5 PS 6 6 PS 7 7 PS 8 8 PS 9 9 PS 10 10
FR PS 8 7 PS 10 9 PS 5 5

!FAITHFULNESS ITEMS
```

```
!FR PS 11 11 PS 12 12 PS 13 13 PS 14 14 PS 15 15
FR PS 15 14

!FR PS 16 16 PS 17 17 PS 18 18 PS 19 19 PS 20 20
FR PS 20 19

!COLLABORATION ITEMS
VA 1.0 PS 21 21 PS 22 22 PS 23 23 PS 24 24 PS 25 25

!SCORE ITEMS
FR PS 26 26 PS 27 27 PS 28 28 PS 29 29 PS 30 30
FR PS 30 29
EQ PS 26 26 PS 27 27 PS 28 28
FR PS 31 31 PS 32 32 PS 33 33 PS 34 34 PS 35 35
PS 35 34
EQ PS 31 31 PS 32 32 PS 33 33

VA 1.0 BE 1 7 BE 2 7 BE 3 7 BE 2 8
VA 0.0 BE 1 8
VA 2.0 BE 3 8

VA 1.0 BE 4 9 BE 5 9 BE 6 9 BE 5 10
VA 0.0 BE 4 10
VA 2.0 BE 6 10

!FAITHFULNESS ITEMS
VA 1.0 BE 11 14 BE 12 14 BE 13 14 BE 12 15
VA 0.0 BE 11 15
VA 2.0 BE 13 15

VA 1.0 BE 16 19 BE 17 19 BE 18 19 BE 17 20
VA 0.0 BE 16 20
VA 2.0 BE 18 20

!COLLABORATION ITEMS
VA 1.0 BE 21 24 BE 22 24 BE 23 24 BE 22 25
VA 1.0 BE 21 25
VA 1.0 BE 23 25

!SCORE ITEMS
VA 1.0 BE 26 29 BE 27 29 BE 28 29 BE 27 30
VA 0.0 BE 26 30
VA 2.0 BE 28 30
VA 1.0 BE 31 34 BE 32 34 BE 33 34 BE 32 35
VA 0.0 BE 31 35
VA 2.0 BE 33 35

FR AL 7 AL 8 AL 9 AL 10 AL 14 AL 15 AL 19 AL 20 AL 29 AL 30 AL 34 AL 35

!SCORE STARTING VALUES
ST 6.07 PS 26 26
ST -1.78 PS 29 29
ST -0.41 PS 30 30
ST 1.92 PS 30 29
ST 10.06 AL 29
ST 1.58 AL 30
```

249

```
!SSE STARTING VALUES
ST 63.30 PS 31 31
ST 103.18 PS 34 34
ST 90.45 PS 35 35
ST 98.34 PS 35 34
ST 22.69 AL 34
ST 19.02 AL 35

!CAUSAL MODEL
!FR BE 7 14 BE 8 14 BE 8 15
!FR BE 9 14 BE 10 14 BE 10 15
!FR BE 7 19 BE 8 19 BE 8 20
!FR BE 9 19 BE 10 19 BE 10 20
FI BE 7 24 BE 8 24 BE 8 25
FI BE 9 24 BE 10 24 BE 10 25
VA 0.0 BE 7 24 BE 8 24 BE 8 25
VA 0.0 BE 9 24 BE 10 24 BE 10 25
!FR BE 10 15

FI BE 29 24 BE 30 24 BE 30 25
VA 0.0 BE 29 24 BE 30 24 BE 30 25

FI BE 34 24 BE 35 24 BE 35 25
VA 0.0 BE 34 24 BE 35 24 BE 35 25

PD
OU AD=OFF SS SC SE TV IT=500
```

Appendix J: A Note on the Development of Collaboration Structure Appropriation Scale

Development of scale to measure appropriation of collaboration structures

As a part of the thesis, we needed to capture the extent of appropriation of the collaboration structures that were outlined in the workbook provided to the participants. In spite of extensive research in IS in the area of GSS and GDSS, no formal instrument or definition was found in IS. Thus, we expanded our search and developed an instrument. Below we describe the approach we took to develop such an instrument. We start with a general overview of collaboration, and then draw from incorporate the learning/training context. We then describe the results of the pilot study conducted to see the convergent validity and reliability of the instrument. Finally, we present the instrument as used in the current study. The approach broadly conforms to the guidance provided in (Boudreau et al. 2001; Straub 1989)

General definition

Definitions and theories are critical to building an instrument. (Wood et al. 1991) presents an extensive review of the theoretical perspectives in behavioral psychology and definitions in this area. This definition, which broadens (Gray 1989) earlier definition, describes collaboration as a verb in a general decision making situation.

Collaboration occurs when a group of autonomous stakeholders of a problem domain engage in an interactive process, using shared rules, norms and structures, to act or decide on issues related to that domain.

In the current study, the stakeholders are students engaged in a learning situation. Their goal is to maximize their learning opportunity.

Expansion on structures

The most important component of the above definition is the focus on shared rule, norms and structures. Drawing on structuration theory, all three can be described as the social structures that participants in a group experience.

Organizational research provides insights into these structures. (Franklin et al. 1976) focuses on support, team building, work facilitation, and goal emphasis as the important structures. Education literature, which has extensive research in the area of collaborative learning, presents five basic elements / structures that are essential (Johnson 1981) i.e. Positive independence, Individual accountability, face-to-face primitive interaction, social skills and group processing. Drawing on both of these literatures, we summarize collaboration structures into five categories i.e. Positive interdependence, individual accountability, supportive interaction, team building efforts and group processing (see Table 7 for description).

Though no instruments existed in education for collaboration, (Franklin et al. 1976) in organizational research provided the initial guidelines for the development of the instrument. An instrument was developed based on that. These items measure the extent of collaboration happening in the groups. These items were piloted to a sample of 65 EMBA students were found to have good internal consistency (inter-item correlation for the items was greater than 0.80 on average). However, two structures i.e. positive interdependence and individual accountability did not converge with the rest of the structures.

Final instrument

An in-depth review of the feedback based on the instrument and literature provided insight into the lack of convergence of the two structures. Both of these, as defined, are structures in the form of artifacts i.e. in a learning context, these are overarching rules imposed on the group by the designer while the other structures are developed by the group themselves. Similarly, in a decision making situation, these structures would be defined by the goals and the mechanism in which appraisal is done. This, it is incorrect to include these in the instrument.

The next step included a further contexturalization of the instrument to fit the experiment. The final instrument has the following questions.

Code	Question	Agreement Scale
Collab1	My partner was friendly and easy to approach *(Support dimension)*	1(Strongly Agree) – 7(Strongly Disagree)
Collab2	My partner paid attention to what I was saying *(support dimension)*	1(Strongly Agree) – 7(Strongly Disagree)
Collab3	My partner encouraged us to work together *(Team development dimension)*	1(Strongly Agree) – 7(Strongly Disagree)
Collab4	My partner emphasized learning *(Goal Emphasis dimension)*	1(Strongly Agree) – 7(Strongly Disagree)
Collab5	My partner helped me enhance my learning *(feedback dimension)*	1(Strongly Agree) – 7(Strongly Disagree)
Collab6	My partner encouraged me to give my best effort *(Goal dimension)*	1(Strongly Agree) – 7(Strongly Disagree)

As described in chapter 4, the showed good convergent and discriminate validity. Discriminant validity was also test with respect to the cohesiveness instrument showing significant divergence. Results of that test are available on request.

Bibliography

Boudreau, M.-C., Gefen, D., and Straub, D.W. "Validation in Information Systems Research: A State of the Art Assessment," *MIS Quarterly* (25:1) 2001, pp 1-16.

Franklin, J.L., Wissler, A.L., and Spencer, G.J. *Survey-guided development: a manual for concepts training* Organizational Development Research Program Center for Research on Utilization of Scientific Knowledge Institute for Social Research University of Michigan, Ann Arbor, 1976, pp. vii, 202.

Gray, B. *Collaborating: finding common ground for multiparty problems*, (1st ed.) Jossey-Bass, San Francisco, 1989, pp. xxv, 329.

Johnson, D.W. "Student-student interaction: The neglected variable in education," *Educational Research* (10:1) 1981, pp 5-10.

Straub, D.W. "Validating Instruments in MIS Research," *MIS Quarterly* (13:2) 1989, pp 147-165.

Wood, D.J., and Gray, B. "Toward a comprehensive theory of collaboration," *Journal of Applied Behavioral Science* (27:2) 1991, pp 139-162.